SACRAMENTO PUBLIC LIBRARY
828 "I" Street
Sacramento, CA 95814
06/12

UNCONTROLLED

UNCONTROLLED

The Surprising Payoff of Trial-and-Error for Business, Politics, and Society

JIM MANZI

BASIC BOOKS

A Member of the Perseus Books Group
New York

Copyright © 2012 by Jim Manzi

Published by Basic Books,
A Member of the Perseus Books Group

All rights reserved. Printed in the United States of America. No part of this book may be reproduced in any manner whatsoever without written permission except in the case of brief quotations embodied in critical articles and reviews. For information, address the Perseus Books Group, 387 Park Avenue South, New York, NY 10016-8810.

Books published by Basic Books are available at special discounts for bulk purchases in the United States by corporations, institutions, and other organizations. For more information, please contact the Special Markets Department at the Perseus Books Group, 2300 Chestnut Street, Suite 200, Philadelphia, PA 19103, or call (800) 810-4145, ext. 5000, or e-mail special.markets@perseusbooks.com.

Designed by Brent Wilcox

Library of Congress Cataloging-in-Publication Data
Manzi, Jim.
    Uncontrolled : the surprising payoff of trial-and-error for business, politics, and society / Jim Manzi.
        p.   cm.
    Includes bibliographical references and index.
    ISBN 978-0-465-02324-0 (hbk. : alk. paper) —
ISBN 978-0-465-02931-0 (e-book)
    1. Social sciences—Experiments.   2. Social sciences—Research.
3. Experimental design—Social aspects.   I. Title.
    H62.M264 2012
    001.4'34—dc23

                                                                2012004409

10 9 8 7 6 5 4 3 2 1

For Margaret Jennings Manzi

CONTENTS

INTRODUCTION

As a young corporate strategy consultant, I once was on a team tasked with analyzing a proposed business program for a major retail chain. This company was considering a very large investment to improve its stores through a combination of a brighter layout, a different mix of merchandise, and more in-store employees to assist shoppers. The company believed consumers would positively receive this program, but the open question was whether it would lead to enough new sales to justify the substantial extra costs it would require. I developed a complicated analytical process to predict the size of the sales gain, including qualitative and quantitative consumer research, competitive benchmarking, and internal capability modeling. With great pride I described this plan to a partner in our consulting firm, who responded by saying, "Okay . . . but why wouldn't you just do it to a few stores and see how it works?"

This seemed so simple that I thought it couldn't be right. But as I began a series of objections to his question, I kept stopping myself mid-sentence. I realized that each of my potential responses was incorrect: an experiment really would provide the most definitive available answer to the question.

Over the next twenty years I became increasingly aware that real experiments were required for adjudicating among competing theories for the effects of business interventions intended to change consumer behavior. Cost changes often could be predicted reliably through engineering studies. But when it came to predicting how people would respond to interventions, I discovered that I could almost always use historical data, surveys, and other information to build competing analyses that would "prove" that almost any realistically proposed business program would succeed or fail, just by making tiny adjustments to analytical assumptions. And the more sophisticated the analysis, the more unavoidable this kind of subterranean model-tuning became. Even after executing some business program, debates about how much it really changed profit often would continue, because so many other things changed at the same time. Only controlled experiments could cut through the complexity and create a reliable foundation for predicting consumer response to proposed interventions.

This fundamental problem, albeit at vastly greater scale and severity, applies whenever we listen to impressive-sounding arguments that predict the society-wide effects of proposed major economic, welfare, educational, and other policy interventions. As an example, consider the deliberations around how to respond to the 2008 economic crisis. The country was facing a terrifying situation, and there was a widespread belief that emergency measures of some kind were called for as a matter of prudence. The incoming Obama administration proposed a large stimulus program, which led to an intense public debate in January and February 2009. Setting aside for a moment ideological predispositions and value judgments, this presented a specific technical issue: What would be the effects of any given stimulus proposal on general economic welfare? This was a practical question worth trillions of dollars that got to the reliability of our predictions about government programs.

The role of government spending and deficits in a major economic downturn has been the subject of extensive academic study for decades, and many leading economists actively participated in the public discussion in early 2009. Paul Krugman and Joseph Stiglitz, both Nobel laureates in economics, argued that stimulus would improve economic performance. In fact, they both argued that it should be bigger. On the other hand, James Buchanan, Edward Prescott, and Vernon Smith—all Nobel laureates in economics—argued that the stimulus would not improve economic performance enough to justify the investment, saying that "notwithstanding reports that all economists are now Keynesians . . . it is a triumph of hope over experience to believe that more government spending will help the US today." This was not an argument about precise quantities, but a disagreement about the policy's basic effects.

Although fierce debates can be found in frontier areas of all sciences, this one would be as if, on the night before the Apollo moon launch, numerous Nobel laureates in physics were asserting that rockets couldn't get as far as the moon, almost as many were saying they could get there in theory but we need much more fuel, and some were arguing that the moon did not exist. The only thing an observer could say with high confidence before the stimulus program launched was that at least several Nobel laureates in economics would be directionally incorrect about its effects.

But the stimulus situation was even worse. It was clear at the time that we would not know which of them were right or wrong even *after the fact*. Suppose Professor Famous Economist X predicted on February 1, 2009, that "unemployment will be about 10 percent in two years without the bill, and about 8 percent with the bill." What do you think would happen when 2011 rolled around and unemployment was 10 percent? It's a very, very safe bet that Professor X would say something like, "Yes, but other conditions deteriorated faster than anticipated, so if we hadn't passed the stimulus bill, unemployment would have been more like 12 percent. So you see, I was right after all; it reduced unemployment by about 2 percentage points."

The key problem is that we have no reliable way to measure the counterfactual—that is, to know what would have happened had we not executed the policy—because so many other factors influence the outcome. This seemingly narrow and technical issue of counterfactuals turns out to be central to our continuing inability to use social sciences to adjudicate most policy debates rationally. This statement is not to make the trivial point that social sciences are not like physics in some ineffable sense, but rather that the social sciences have not produced a substantial body of useful, nonobvious, and reliable rules that would allow us to predict the effect of such proposed government programs.

I believe that recognizing this deep uncertainty should influence how we organize our political and economic institutions. In the most direct terms, it should lead us to value the freedom to experiment and discover workable arrangements through an open-ended process of trial and error. This is not a new insight, but is the central theme of an Anglo-American tradition of liberty that runs from Locke and Milton through Adam Smith and on to the twentieth-century libertarian thinkers, pre-eminently Sir Karl Popper and F. A. Hayek. In this tradition, markets, democracy, and other related institutions are seen as instruments for discovering practical methods for improving our material position in an uncertain environment.

The resulting system of democratic capitalism experiences (and perhaps creates) periodic crises. We are living through one today. And as with all such crises, this has produced a loss of confidence in economic and political liberty. Examining the debates that took place in prior crises of democratic capitalism can help us to navigate this one.

The Great Depression understandably led to an enormous increase in government activity to try to tame markets to work for the common good. But a small group of loosely affiliated thinkers were careful to point out the trade-offs involved. The most important were Popper and Hayek, who argued that this degree of government control—or in Hayek's language, "planning"—would necessarily limit growth because human society is far more complex than the understanding of the planners. Hayek termed this the "knowledge problem." By this line of thinking, we need the trial-and-error process created by the free play of markets, social tolerance, and experiments in living—what Popper called the "open society"—to determine what permits the society to thrive materially, and then to propagate this information. In short, we need freedom because we are ignorant.

It is a subtle but crucial distinction that Popper and Hayek argued not for some kind of absolute freedom, but for social *adaptability*. They were not (nor were Smith and some of their antecedents) arguing against all market regulations, government investments, lifestyle restrictions, and so forth. Rather, they were arguing against an unwarranted assumption of knowledge by those who would attempt to control society's evolution.

In our current crisis, sales of Hayek's 1944 popular classic, *The Road to Serfdom,* have skyrocketed. If we are now living through a more moderated version of the Great Depression, then why isn't the proper response to the current fashion for government control simply to dust off our copies of Hayek and Popper? The short answer is: because of science.

Science and technology have made astounding advances over the past half-century. The most significant relevant developments have been in biology and information technology. The tradition of liberty has always had a strong "evolutionist" bent, in that it has seen order in society as emerging from a process that cannot be predicted or planned, rather than as the product of human design. But as I'll describe in detail, the mechanics of genetic evolution provide a clear and compelling picture of how a system can capture and exploit implicit insight without creating explicit knowledge, and this naturally becomes the model for the mechanism by which trial and error advances society's material interests without conscious knowledge or planning. A further technical development enabled by information technology—the explosion in randomized clinical trials that first achieved scale in clinical biology, and has started to move tentatively into social program evaluation—provides a crucial tool that could be much more widely applied to testing claims for many political and economic policies.

Combining these ideas of evolution and randomized trials led Donald T. Campbell, a twentieth-century social scientist at Northwestern University, to create a theory of knowledge, which he termed "evolutionary epistemology." It has a practical implication that can be summarized as the idea that any complex system, such as our society, evolves beliefs about what practices work by layering one kind of trial-and-error learning upon another. The foundation is unstructured trial and error, in which real people try out almost random practices, and those that work better are more likely to be retained. Layered on top of this is structured trial and error, in which human minds consciously develop ideas for improved practices, and then use rigorous experiments to identify those that work. This is a modernized and practical version of what Popper called "piecemeal social engineering": the idea of testing targeted reforms designed to meet immediate challenges, rather than reforming society by working backward from a vision of the ideal.

"Engineering" is a well-chosen term. This is a much humbler view of social science than what was entertained by the eighteenth-century founders of the discipline, such as Auguste Comte and Henri de Saint-Simon, whose ideology continues to animate large areas of social science. These early pioneers expected that social science eventually would resemble Newtonian physics, with powerful theories expressed as compact mathematical laws describing a vast array of phenomena. Campbell's vision looked a lot more like therapeutic biology: extremely incomplete theory, combined with clinical trials designed to sort out which interventions really worked. His approach is more like searching for a polio vaccine than it is like discovering the laws of motion and putting a man on the moon.

But I will argue that we should be humbler still.

The reason we have increasing trouble building compact and comprehensive predictive theories as we go from physics to biology to social science is the increasing complexity of the phenomena under investigation. But this same increasing complexity has another pernicious effect: it becomes far harder to generalize the results of experiments. We can run a clinical trial in Norfolk, Virginia, and conclude with tolerable reliability that "Vaccine X prevents disease Y." We can't conclude that if literacy program X works in Norfolk, then it will work everywhere. The real predictive rule is usually closer to something like "Literacy program X is effective for children in urban areas, and who have the following range of incomes and prior test scores, when the following alternatives are not available in the school district, and the teachers have the following qualifications, and overall economic conditions in the district are within the following range." And by the way, even this predictive rule stops working ten years from now, when different background conditions obtain in the society.

The problem of generalization would not be news to Campbell—he invented the terminology still used to discuss it. But it is deadly to the practical workability of the idea that we can identify a range of broadly effective policies via experiment. This is because the vast majority of reasonable-sounding interventions will work under at least some conditions, and not under others. For the hypothetical literacy program described above, an experiment to test the program is not really a test of the program; it is a test of how well the program applies to a specific situation.

A brute-force approach to this problem would be to run not one experiment to evaluate whether this program works, but to run hundreds or thousands of experiments to evaluate the conditions under which it works. If it could be tested in a very large number of school districts, we might very well discover some useful approximation to the highly conditional rule that predicts its success. This is the opposite of elegant theory-building, and is even more limited than either Popper's or Campbell's version of social engineering. But it might provide practically useful information.

Of course, this would require that each experiment be cheap enough to make this many tests feasible. Over the past couple of decades, this has been accomplished for certain kinds of tests. The capability has emerged not within formal social science, but in commercial enterprises. The motivation has been the desire to more reliably predict the causal effects of business interventions like the example of the retail-store upgrade program that opened this book. The enabling technological development has been the radical decreases in the costs of storing, processing, and transmitting information created by Moore's Law. The method has been to use information technology to routinize, and ultimately automate, many aspects of testing.

This division of labor should not be surprising. Biological and social science researchers developed the randomized trial, and then the conceptual apparatus for thinking rigorously about the problem of generalization. Commercial enterprises have figured out how, in specific contexts, to convert this kind of experimentation from a customized craft to a high-volume, low-cost, and partially automated process.

I found myself in the middle of this experimental revolution in business when some friends and I started what eventually became a global software company that produces the tools to apply randomized experiments in certain narrowly defined business contexts. In my view, a closer union of formal social science and business experimentation can improve both. Greater rigor can pay enormous dividends for business experiments. And reorienting social science experimentation around using automation and other techniques to run very large numbers of experiments can substantially improve our practical ability to identify better policies in at least some areas.

Perhaps the single most important lesson I learned in commercial experimentation, and that I have since seen reinforced in one social science discipline after another, is that there is no magic. I mean this in a couple of senses. First, we are unlikely to discover some social intervention that is the moral equivalent of polio vaccine. There are probably very few such silver bullets out there to be found. And second, experimental science in these fields creates only marginal improvements. A failing company with a poor strategy cannot blindly experiment its way to success, and a failing society with a dysfunctional political economy cannot blindly experiment its way to health. Therefore, though we should not confuse untested social science theories with reliable predictors of the results of proposed interventions, we will never eliminate the need for strategy and some kind of long-term vision.

Even with all of these qualifications, however, I believe that by more widely applying the commercial techniques of radically scaling up the rate of experimentation, we can do better than we are now: somewhat improve the rate of development of social science; somewhat improve our decisions about what social programs we choose to implement; and somewhat improve our overall political economy. Spread across a very big world, this would justify a large absolute investment of resources and hopefully would help to avoid at least a few extremely costly errors.

The thesis of this book can therefore be summarized in five points:

1. Nonexperimental social science currently is not capable of making useful, reliable, and nonobvious predictions for the effects of most proposed policy interventions.

2. Social science very likely can improve its practical utility by conducting many more experiments, and should do so.
3. Even with such improvement, it will not be able to adjudicate most important policy debates.
4. Recognition of this uncertainty calls for a heavy reliance on unstructured trial-and-error progress.
5. The limits to the use of trial and error are established predominantly by the need for strategy and long-term vision.

The book proceeds in three parts. The first lays out my view of the centrality of experiments to scientific knowledge. The second applies these concepts to describe the limitations of our current social science. And the third draws out what I believe to be practical implications for political action of these findings.

When doing commercial experimentation, I found myself going all the way back to the philosophy of science and the foundations of probability theory when trying to do something as comparatively trivial as figuring out how many Snickers bars ought to be on a convenience store shelf next week. To get beyond mere assertion of belief, it will be necessary to do the same when considering the enormously more complex questions this book addresses. Throughout the book I go into philosophical and technical issues only as far as required to reach practical resolution, but no further.

I hope the payoff will come when a granular appreciation for the nature of the challenges in front of us helps to improve judgments about proposals to meet them, and perhaps to generate a few new proposals.

PART I

Science

Life is a perpetual instruction in cause and effect.
—RALPH WALDO EMERSON

To know that we know what we know, and to know that we do not know what we do not know, that is true knowledge.
—NICOLAUS COPERNICUS

CHAPTER 1

Induction and the Problem of Induction

To make a point to a friend in college, I once walked onto the large platform at the front of an empty physics lecture hall. A metal sphere about the size of a bowling ball hung on a long wire attached to a pivot in the high ceiling. I grabbed the ball, walked to the right side of the lecture platform, held the ball a few inches in front of my nose, and let go of it. The ball picked up speed as it descended toward the middle of the platform, then slowed down as it ascended to its peak on the other side. When it started descending back at an accelerating, deadly pace, I stood as motionless as possible while it gradually slowed to a stop inches in front of my face.

We had both taken a lot of physics, so we both knew rationally that this was a pendulum and the ball would stop before it hit me (as long as I didn't accidentally give it a little shove or lean forward). But it was still deeply counterintuitive not to flinch. I was trying to illustrate that science allows us to overrule our experience and visceral intuition—not just in a book, but at the moment of decision.

How it does this is a fascinating and complicated story.

The Origins of the Scientific Method

Scientific knowledge is defined by a methodology, and to understand this methodology, we must examine its roots and development. Francis Bacon's text *Novum Organum*, written almost four hundred years ago, prophesied the modern scientific method, but it can be understood only in relation to the tradition of Scholastic natural philosophy against which Bacon was reacting.

The Scholastics deployed a combination of Christian theology and classical works—viewing Aristotle as a secular intellectual giant without equal—to try to explain the physical world around them. They viewed any material body as comprising both an inert substratum of primary matter and a quality-bearing essence—its substantial form. The substantial form is what enables the body to interact causally with other bodies. Any material object, for example, possesses weight, color, texture, and all of the other bodily properties, only in virtue of being conjoined with a substantial form of a loaf of bread, bowling ball, chair, or whatever. There is some "essence" of the bowling ball that makes it different from the loaf of bread.

To a modern reader, this sounds like a bunch of gobbledygook, but it resulted from Aristotle's confrontation with a profound mystery. In *Physics,* he asked by way of example why front teeth regularly grow sharp, and back teeth broad, in a fashion that is good for an animal. He claimed that we must go beyond just the interaction of particles, because it cannot simply be coincidence that this arrangement would arise so regularly. Aristotle argued that the formation of the parts of the animal in a manner that is good for the animal requires the existence of what he called a final cause that is "the end, that for the sake of which a thing is done." Some essence of the animal causes interacting particles to organize themselves differently for this animal than for the rock next to it that is also composed of interacting particles. Hence the need for a substantial form that distinguishes the animal from the nearby rock. This was the dominant intellectual method for understanding natural phenomena from the ancient Greeks to Bacon.

Bacon's central argument was not exactly that this was wrong, but rather that it was impractical. He argued that scientists would be more productive if they ruled questions about things like final causes to be out of bounds; if they narrowed the scope of natural philosophy by considering such questions to be metaphysics rather than physics. He was correct. And this turns out to have been one of the most consequential insights in human history.

Bacon was not an ivory-tower philosopher. In addition to his work as a thinker, he was a politician, serving as attorney general and lord chancellor under King James I. It is therefore not surprising that he believed that "the true and lawful goal of the sciences is none other than this: that human life be endowed with new discoveries and powers." Although he did not deny the aesthetic pleasures of scientific discovery and understanding, he viewed science primarily as a tool to "extend more widely the limits of the power and greatness of man."

When Bacon produced *Novum Organum* in 1620, his take on the utility of Scholastic natural philosophy in achieving practical progress was withering:

The sciences which we possess come for the most part from the Greeks. . . .

Now, from all these systems of the Greeks, and their ramifications through particular sciences, there can hardly after the lapse of so many years be adduced a single experiment which tends to relieve and benefit the condition of man, and which can with truth be referred to the speculations and theories of philosophy. And Celsus ingenuously and wisely owns as much when he tells us that the experimental part of medicine was first discovered, and that afterwards men philosophized about it, and hunted for and assigned causes; and not by an inverse process that philosophy and the knowledge of causes led to the discovery and development of the experimental part. . . .

Some little has indeed been produced by the industry of chemists; but it has been produced accidentally and in passing, or else by a kind of variation of experiments, such as mechanics use, and not by any art or theory. For the theory which they have devised rather confuses the experiments than aids them.

He was trying to contrast lack of progress with something we now take for granted but at the time was entirely theoretical: rapidly advancing scientific knowledge. Simply seeing this possibility was a triumph of the imagination, but his greatest intellectual achievement was to lay out a program to achieve it.

To help explain why progress had thus far been limited, Bacon began with a theory that combined two key elements. The first was the observation that nature is extraordinarily complicated as compared to human mental capacities, whether those of individuals ("the subtlety of nature is greater many times over than the subtlety of the senses and understanding") or those of groups ("the subtlety of nature is greater many times over than the subtlety of argument"). The second element of his theory was his belief that humans tend to overinterpret data into unreliable patterns and therefore leap to faulty conclusions, saying that "the human understanding is of its own nature prone to suppose the existence of more order and regularity in the world than it finds." He argued that science should therefore proceed from twin premises of a deep epistemic humility and a concomitant distrust of the human tendency to leap to conclusions.

Bacon believed that this combination of errors had consistently led natural philosophers to enshrine premature theories as comprehensive certainties that discouraged further discovery. Proponents of alternative theories, all of whom had also made faulty extrapolations from limited data to create their theories, would then attempt to apply logic to decide between them through competitive debate. The result was a closed intellectual system whose adherents spent their energies in ceaseless argumentation based on false premises, rather than seeking new information. He describes the method of natural philosophy from the Greeks to his day as follows:

From a few examples and particulars (with the addition of common notions and perhaps of some portion of the received opinions which

have been most popular) they flew at once to the most general conclusions, or first principles of science. Taking the truth of these as fixed
and immovable, they proceeded by means of intermediate proposi-
tions to educe and prove from them the inferior conclusions; and out
of these they framed the art. After that, if any new particulars and examples repugnant to their dogmas were mooted and adduced, either
they subtly molded them into their system by distinctions or expla-
nations of their rules, or else coarsely got rid of them by exceptions;
while to such particulars as were not repugnant they labored to assign causes in conformity with those of their principles.

Bacon hammered at this point to a degree that can seem repetitive to
a modern reader, but that's because we live within the scientific framework that he envisioned. He was arguing against a 2,000-year tradition
of what formal knowledge of the physical world *was*—not in the sense
of a list of facts, but more profoundly, in the way of knowing it.

Building upon the first glimmerings of the scientific revolution in
Europe, Bacon proposed a new method (*novum organum*) that would
start with the meticulous construction of factual knowledge as a foundation for belief and would then rise "by a gradual and unbroken as-
cent, so that it arrives at the most general axioms last of all." He called
this method induction. The practical manifestation of his proposed approach came to be called the scientific method.

He was clear that implementing this approach would not be easy,
and his attempts to foresee what would be required were astoundingly
insightful.

First, and most philosophically momentous, was the shift from the
Scholastic emphasis on inherently different natures of different classes
of objects to an emphasis on how material objects can be observed to interact. In a criticism of the Scholastics, Bacon put this as: "But it is a
far greater evil that they make the quiescent principles, *wherefrom,* and
not the moving principles, *whereby,* things are produced, the object of
their contemplation and inquiry. For the former tend to discourse, the
latter to works." In modern language, he was expressing the viewpoint

that scientists should proceed *as if* they are pure materialist reductionists, *as if* all observable reality can be reduced to particles plus rules for their interaction. Note that he argued that they should do this not because it is more accurate in some philosophical sense, but because it "tends to works." The ultimate goal of Baconian science is not philosophical truth; it is improved engineering.

Second, Bacon understood that science is a human activity that would require a certain mind-set on the part of scientists. Scientists would have to believe that deep knowledge of the physical world was accessible to them through these methods, since "by far the greatest obstacle to the progress of science . . . is found in this—that men despair and think things impossible." Further, he argued that they should not be limited in their subjects of inquiry into the material world, since "whatever deserves to exist deserves also to be known." He described in these passages the person of boundless curiosity who has confidence that he can and should discover the mysteries of the natural world through the scientific method—that is, the modern scientist. He called such people the "true sons of knowledge."

Third, Bacon saw science not only as a human enterprise, but more specifically as a social enterprise, since this endeavor was "one in which the labors and industries of men (especially as regards the collecting of experience) may with the best effect be first distributed and then combined. For then only will men begin to know their strength when instead of great numbers doing all the same things, one shall take charge of one thing and another of another." In a later book, *New Atlantis,* he even described a model for the modern state-supported research university with specialized departments and laboratories, which he called Salomon's House.

Fourth, Bacon had a clear understanding of the roles of what today we call basic and applied research. Although he saw the ultimate goal of science as material benefit, he believed that, paradoxically, focusing on slowly building sufficient experimental knowledge to develop general physical laws ("experiments of Light"), rather than trying to immediately solve specific practical problems ("experiments of Fruit"), would lead to the greatest progress over time. Further, he had the supple understanding that the relationship between basic and applied research would not be one of linear progress from basic research to applied research, but that these would interact and feed off each other in complex and unpredictable ways, saying, "Let no man look for much progress in the sciences—especially in the practical part of them—unless natural philosophy be carried on and applied to particular sciences, and particular sciences be carried back again to natural philosophy."

Fifth, and of the most practical methodological importance, he asserted the primacy of careful experiments as the initial building blocks of scientific knowledge. He contrasted his proposed approach with prior natural philosophy: "Both ways set out from the senses and particulars, and rest in the highest generalities; but the difference between them is infinite. For the one just glances at experiment and particulars in passing, the other dwells duly and orderly among them." He described experimental rigor in the negative, by highlighting those elements of observation in prior natural philosophy that he considered deficient, saying that "nothing duly investigated, nothing verified, nothing counted, weighed, or measured, is to be found in natural history; and what in observation is loose and vague, is in information deceptive and treacherous." He proposed, instead, that experimentation "shall proceed in accordance with a fixed law, in regular order, and without interruption."

Bacon's degree of focus on experimentation at the expense of theorizing can be caricatured. Although he was trying to advance the prominence of careful experiments in creating knowledge, he clearly saw that scientific progress would rely upon an intimate combination of theory and experiment, arguing that "from a closer and purer league between these two faculties, the experimental and the rational (such as has never yet been made), much may be hoped."

But how exactly should experiments be conducted and then combined to create reliable physical laws? It was not until many years later that the concept of the controlled experiment (carefully changing only one potential causal factor and observing the result) was more rigorously distinguished from nonexperimental observation than in Bacon's somewhat impressionistic "verified, weighed, and counted" description.

But the core problem is always how we can generalize reliably from a series of observations, experimental or otherwise, to general principles.

Bacon was, of course, keenly attuned to the centrality of this issue; remember that his fundamental critique of the Scholastics was inappropriate generalization from "a few examples and particulars" to "general conclusions." He recognized that generalization must be done to construct the predictive rules that enable science to create practical benefits, saying that "the induction is amiss which infers the principles of sciences by simple enumeration." But Bacon warned scientists that if his program was implemented, the danger of inappropriate generalization would dog them.

Bacon attempted to define a process of scientific experimentation and inference, but in this he failed; the detailed method he proposed has not been used by scientists in practice. He was never able to explain exactly how the induction of general physical laws from individual observations should work at an algorithmic or logical level. As we'll see, however, the process of scientific discovery turns out to be quite tricky to describe, and resists such algorithmic description. It was only hundreds of years later that philosophers, armed with the enormous advantage of observing science as it was actually conducted, were able to address somewhat more satisfactorily the problem of what Sir Karl Popper would come to call "the logic of scientific discovery."

The Problem of Induction

Writing a little more than a century after Bacon, skeptical British philosopher David Hume focused on the problem of how we can generalize from a finite list of instances to a general rule in *An Enquiry Concerning Human Understanding*. He first established, consistent with Bacon's point that "simple enumeration" is not what we're after, that the development of cause-and-effect rules is central to practical knowledge:

> All reasonings concerning matter of fact seem to be founded on the relation of Cause and Effect. By means of that relation alone we can go beyond the evidence of our memory and senses. . . . This relation is

either near or remote, direct or collateral. Heat and light are collateral effects of fire, and the one effect may justly be inferred from the other.

Hume then proceeded to make a second point: we can never be sure of a cause-and-effect rule developed through induction. In one of the most famous paragraphs in modern philosophy, he provided a nonabstract illustration of why:

> Our senses inform us of the colour, weight, and consistence of bread; but neither sense nor reason can ever inform us of those qualities which fit it for the nourishment and support of a human body. . . . If a body of like colour and consistence with that bread, which we have formerly eat, be presented to us, we make no scruple of repeating the experiment, and foresee, with certainty, like nourishment and support. Now this is a process of the mind or thought, of which I would willingly know the foundation. It is allowed on all hands that there is no known connexion between the sensible qualities and the secret powers; and consequently, that the mind is not led to form such a conclusion concerning their constant and regular conjunction, by anything which it knows of their nature. As to past Experience, it can be allowed to give direct and certain information of those precise objects only, and that precise period of time, which fell under its cognizance: but why this experience should be extended to future times, and to other objects, which for aught we know, may be only in appearance similar; this is the main question on which I would insist.

In modern language, we might say that just because I've been nourished every time I've eaten a thing that is brown, tastes bready, and is shaped like a loaf, how do I know that the next time I eat something of this description it will nourish me?

One could argue that this is outdated because modern biology and chemistry have in fact identified the specific chemical components of the bread that make it nutritious. But how do we know that these chemicals, when supplied in normal quantities and manner, will be nutritious? Well, we have shown in repeated experiments that humans who ingest these chemicals are healthier than those who do not. But how do we know that the connection between these chemicals and health will continue in the future? If we have a further body of theory supported by experiments that explains this relationship at a yet more fundamental level (say, in terms of the demonstrated molecular interactions between the components of the chemicals in bread with various chemicals in the human bloodstream), then how do we know that *this* relationship will continue to hold in future instances? And so on. As we push the frontier of scientific understanding further and further, there is an ever-receding horizon of understanding for which the answer to the question "Why?" must rest either on some a priori belief or on inductive knowledge.

Hume's observation is that to the extent that my belief in a particular cause-and-effect relationship relies on induction, this belief must always remain provisional. I must always remain open to the possibility that although I have never seen an exception to this rule, I might encounter one at some point in the future. An illustrative example is that just because every single time I've let go of a coin in midair it has fallen to the ground, it will not necessarily fall if I let go of it right now. It might, for example, simply sit in midair and not move. Another example is that just because the sun has always come up every day, that doesn't mean it will rise tomorrow. This claim is what I will mean by the Problem of Induction throughout this book.

This might seem like the kind of thing that only a philosopher with too much time on his hands could care about, and in fact, Hume was careful to ridicule the seemingly airy-fairy nature of his concern before his readers could do it for him. The commonsense beliefs that dropped coins fall and that the sun rises are quite valid within the realm of most people's experience—you would not be well advised to make many decisions in daily life that did not assume the existence of gravity or the rotation of the earth.

But consider that if you were in a nonrotating spacecraft far from any large body, and you let go of a coin, it *would* appear to just sit still in the air. Further, someday the sun probably will either implode or disintegrate; then there will be no more sunrises. The Problem of Induction becomes a practical problem when we begin to depart from the arena in which common sense works. Of course, the key value of science is that it provides causal rules that are nonobvious, that is, that extend beyond common sense.

One form of departure from common sense may be to travel to distant reaches of space and time, so that the effects of hidden conditionals (e.g., "Coins drop, *if* I am within a region of significant gravitational influence") become manifest to us when they are violated. But we don't necessarily have to travel into deep space for hidden conditionals to become a practical difficulty. Inductive reasoning applied to the here and now becomes unreliable if the actual causal relationships are sufficiently complex.

Consider a hypothetical example. Gravity is, in a certain way, simple. Coins fall when dropped everywhere on the surface of the earth. Imagine instead that coins fell when dropped in some parts of the United States, but not in others. We could imagine a map of the United States that was colored black in the places where a coin falls when dropped, and white where it does not. Suppose that coins fell when dropped in twenty-five states distributed around the country, but not in the others. The map would have several dozen interspersed black and white regions. Now instead imagine that coins either fell when dropped or not in different counties dispersed around America; you would now see several thousand smaller interspersed black and white regions. We could continue this thought experiment to towns, square miles, square inches, and so on. We would see a salt-and-pepper map of increasingly fine granularity.

Suppose coins either fell or not by square-inch regions but that we did not know which square-inch blocks had gravity, and which did not. If we wanted to figure this out, we might start walking around and letting go of coins, keeping track of the results by coloring tiny blocks on a map of the United States either black or white. After a large number of coin drops, we might look at our map and start to observe patterns (e.g., "All blocks east of the Mississippi have gravity") that are true for all of the coin drops so far. But suppose the true underlying rule (unknown to us) is more like "All blocks east of the Mississippi that are three positions to the left of a non-gravitational block and in a county with above-average rainfall, but not in a state that starts with the letter N, have gravity."

If we went about trying to discover this rule through induction, you can see how difficult it would be. As we continued to drop coins, we might start observing a pattern, but suddenly on the 10,000th test drop find it violated. How would we modify the rule to add a new conditional that would account for this case, given that we have no idea what the hidden conditional might be? Check the average rainfall in the county? Check the population density of the state? Check the proportion of people with red hair who live more than 75 miles but less than 126 miles away? The list of facts that are true for some blocks and not others, and are therefore possible hidden conditionals, is literally infinite. Even if we eventually came up with the right rule, how would we know it was right, and would not be violated by some future drop? The only way to be sure in this thought experiment would be to do a test drop in every square inch—that is, by enumeration rather than a causal rule that permits prediction. And this would solve the problem only in the thought experiment—where we have specified boundaries to the problem as a premise of discussion, such as that we know that gravitational blocks are all one square inch—but not in the real world, where we would never have such an assurance from an omniscient interlocutor. We would have no absolute assurance, for example, that no square-inch blocks had subregions of gravity and nongravity, or that these rules were not time-dependent, and therefore might become completely different one second after we completed our enumeration.

The Problem of Induction can be restated usefully as the observation that there may always be hidden conditionals to any causal rule that is currently believed to be valid. As Hume argued, this problem of hidden conditionals is always present philosophically. Future events will occur at a different time than all of the prior events that inform my rule, and since time-of-event may be a hidden conditional, we can never be sure that the rule will continue to work. As we'll see in the later sections of this book, because of the complexity of the phenomena under study, a more generalized version of the Problem of Induction is the central practical problem in developing useful predictive rules in the social sciences.

CHAPTER 2

Falsification and Paradigms

Experiments and Falsification

Science allows us to make predictions about as yet unseen situations. The most powerful scientific theories make such predictions across a vast array of circumstances. Newton, living in a world of untreated plague, filth, and horse-drawn transport, accurately predicted the motionlessness of a dropped coin on a distant spacecraft centuries in the future. The problem with science is that without rules that generalize from experience, we have nothing more than a catalog of data, but inductive evidence can never tell us with certainty that our generalizations are correct.

Science tries to transcend this problem by testing theories, with a reliance on carefully structured experiments that is the most obvious and consequential methodological difference between modern science and earlier proto-scientific intellectual traditions. We can directly distinguish conceptually between an experiment and a nonexperimental observation. An experiment attempts to demonstrate causality by (1) holding all potential causes of an outcome constant, (2) consciously changing only the potential cause of interest, and then (3) observing whether the outcome changes.

Though in reality no experimenter can be absolutely certain that all other causes have been held constant, the conscious and rigorous attempt to do so is the crucial distinction between an experiment and an observation. Observing a naturally occurring event always leaves open the possibility of confounded causes (or more precisely, it leaves open an intuitively greater possibility than does a well-structured experiment). An experiment expresses the epistemic humility that lies at the root of science. No matter how sure I am of a belief, science demands that I subject it to a test that assumes the possibility of hidden conditionals.

Consider one of the most famous (and probably apocryphal) experiments in the history of science. In about 350 BC, Aristotle argued that heavy objects should fall more rapidly than light objects. Almost 2,000 years later, Galileo supposedly dropped balls of different weights from the Tower of Pisa and observed that they reached the ground at the same time. He concluded that Aristotle's theory was wrong. Now, Aristotle was recognized as one of the greatest geniuses in recorded history. He had put forward seemingly airtight reasoning for why they should drop at different rates. Almost every human intuitively feels, even today, that a 1,000-pound ball of super-dense plutonium should fall faster than a one-ounce marble. And in everyday life, light objects will very often fall more slowly than heavy ones because of differences in air resistance and other practical factors. Aristotle's theory, then, combined authority, logic, intuition, and empirical evidence. But when tested in a reasonably well-controlled experiment, the balls dropped at the same rate. To the modern scientific mind, this is definitive. Aristotle's theory is false—case closed. This is why the experimental method is so powerful. Experiments end debates (though, as we'll see shortly, they usually open up new ones).

What Galileo did not do, however, was prove the validity of the theory that unequally weighted objects in a vacuum would fall at the same rate. His theory passed this test, but of course might fail some future test. This example highlights an important asymmetry: when we carefully consider the results of an experiment in light of the Problem of Induction, experiments can disprove theories by providing counterexamples but cannot prove theories no matter how many times we repeat them, since it is always theoretically possible that in some future experiment we will find a counterexample. Galileo dropped the weights at (very close to) the same place and time, used reasonably dense, smooth balls to minimize wind resistance (which even then was understood to be a complicating factor), and so on, but he couldn't know that there was not some hidden conditional that in different circumstances would have proven his theory incorrect.

In the first half of the twentieth century, Sir Karl Popper developed the foundations of the modern philosophy of science around a formalized version of this idea, which he called falsification. Popper asserted that a scientist typically begins by developing a theory based on whatever data, intuitive insights, conceptual framework, aesthetic views, or other elements he wants. If he's a competent scientist, he then tries hard to find a counterexample that disproves his idea, and if he cannot, he puts forth his theory into the world. Other scientists then try to disprove the theory. As more and more scientists fail to find counterexamples, the theory is accepted as more and more useful as a practical guide to action. Experiments, therefore, can conclusively demonstrate only that a theory is false, but never that a theory is true.

By focusing on this concept, Popper was able to draw out three important implications that are relevant to our discussion.

First, for a statement to be scientific it must be "falsifiable." More specifically, a scientific statement worth investigation must be a nonobvious, falsifiable predictive rule. Nonobviousness means that in practice I don't get any points for predicting that if I let go of a coin in midair, it will usually fall. Falsifiability means that it is possible, at least in principle, to design and execute a test that could prove the theory wrong. For example, "Doubling atmospheric concentration of carbon dioxide will result in a 3°C increase in global temperature within twenty-five years" is by this definition a scientific statement, but "Climate change threatens the planet" is not. Working scientists implicitly apply this criterion in a rough-and-ready way all the time. Famously, the great theoretical physicist Wolfgang Pauli once derided a fuzzy idea presented by a colleague as "not even wrong," meaning that because it couldn't be falsified it wasn't a statement that scientists should spend time debating.

Second, science never provides Truth with a capital T. That is, we must always hold open the possibility that any scientific belief, no matter how well corroborated, might fail some future test. There is no absolute escape from Hume's Problem of Induction. Under this view, when we say that some statement is scientifically proven, this is shorthand for saying something like, "A group of competent scientists believe this theory has passed many rigorous falsification tests, and it can therefore be treated as reliable in practice."

Third, theory precedes experiment. Coming up with a scientific theory is a creative exercise. A scientist may use as inputs the results of prior experiments, observations of the natural world, mysterious intuition, or anything else. At some point she has a new insight, and this is a theory that can then be subjected to falsification testing. Simply putting two chemicals in a test tube to see what happens is not an experiment, but more like an observation that provides some of the raw materials of a theory. If it turns out that this result is nonobvious and these properties are interesting, then there might be a very short route from such an exploratory mixing of chemicals to a very simple theory, such as "Mixing chemical A with chemical B according to the following procedure will produce a compound with the following properties." This theory can be either falsified or corroborated in subsequent experiments. In fact, early chemistry often followed something like this model, as does much modern pharmaceutical development. As a science matures, more and more generalized theories are developed and tested that reduce a wider and wider range of phenomena to a short list of powerful predictive rules.

Theory and experiment are to science what inhalation and exhalation are to breathing. Each is necessary but not sufficient for the whole. And roughly speaking, they alternate: we develop a theory and test it through experiment, leading to further theories that can be tested through new experiments, and so on.

At some conceptual level, of course, falsification is not exactly a new idea—after all, we refer to "trial and error," not "trial and success." And Bacon seems to have understood the basic logic of falsification, saying in *Novum Organum* that "it is the peculiar and perpetual error of the human intellect to be more moved and excited by affirmatives than by negatives; whereas it ought properly to hold itself indifferently disposed toward both alike. Indeed, in the establishment of any true axiom, the negative instance is the more forcible of the two."

But Popper's insight is deep, and so profound that once understood it becomes hard to imagine that it was not always known. It rigorously separates a theory's development from its validation. One can debate endlessly whether humans can really hold an a priori belief independent of experience, whether the physical structure of the human brain leads certain kinds of theories to be developed independent of evidence, and so on. Popper allows science to be operationally indifferent to these arguments. All theories, developed in any fashion, are fair game; their truth, in the scientific meaning of the word, is determined by their ability to withstand rigorous falsification tests. But our acceptance of their truth, therefore, must always remain provisional, since this process is subject to the Problem of Induction.

Falsifiability is a bare-minimum condition—a philosopher's rigorous statement that without falsifiability a statement cannot be scientific. However, some tests of a theory are far more compelling than others. Ideally, as we have seen, a scientific statement can be tested through replicated, controlled experiments.

Corroborating through controlled experiments rather than observing a phenomenon in nature means we can have greater confidence that we have found a true causal relationship, and therefore have a reliable prediction tool. Suppose, for example, I put forward a formula that predicts winners of US presidential elections based on changes in economic growth, and I subsequently predict the winners of three successive elections correctly. It is interesting that my theory passed three successive falsification tests; however, this theory is less reliable than if I could have run multiple elections in parallel versions of the United States in which I changed only the economic growth rate. Given the practical reality that I can't replicate the United States in a laboratory, this means that I will always be less scientifically certain about this kind of theory versus one that I could test using controlled experiments.

Replication—repeating experiments to confirm important and surprising findings—is useful for the obvious reasons of rooting out both deliberate fraud and honest measurement error. But it also has another important function. Because no experimenter can ever be sure she has controlled for all possible causes of an outcome, replication in different labs, in different geographies, under different unarticulated procedural details, and so forth tests the theory in a variety of circumstances and tends to find hidden conditionals. Obviously, it is always possible that the replications will fail to uncover some hidden conditionals because the original experiment and all replications failed to execute the test in a manner that exposed them, but some errors will be discovered this way. Popper refers to any result that cannot be replicated in multiple experiments as an "occult effect" that has no scientific relevance.

This framework allows the definition of the reliability of a predictive rule.

Start with the point that reliability is defined by the correspondence between the predictions of the rule and actual observations within the "prediction class" of outcomes that fall within the scope of the rule. These test observations are not those that were used in any way to create the rule. Any data we used to build the rule is part of the theory-building process, and the theory must be subjected to some kind of falsification test. In practice, this usually means observations that occur after the rule was created, because it is usually impossible to isolate knowledge of preexisting data from the theory-building process.

Next, there are more or less rigorous kinds of observations that can be used to test the predictive rule. Replicated, controlled experiments are more rigorous than uncontrolled observations, though there are shades of gray between these two extremes.

A good example of all this would be defining the reliability of Newton's second law of motion: Force = Mass X Acceleration. In 1800, scientists might have done this by evaluating the mean square error in predicting the acceleration of objects across a variety of experiments that apply a wide variety of amounts of force to objects ranging from very small to very large, plus testing the predictions based on this law for nonexperimental observations of various heavenly bodies. The minimum size and maximum speed of the experimental bodies, and the kinds of observable heavenly bodies, would all be determined by the technical means available in 1800.

This emphasizes an additional powerful feature of experiments. They can allow us, limited only by our technical means, to evaluate the boundaries of the prediction class of observations across which the rule is asserted to be valid. Newton asserted that his laws predict the motion of all bodies. Using modern experiments, we can push this to the edges of the prediction class, and test the rule, for example, with extremely small bodies or at extremely high speeds, and find where it breaks down.

We can therefore define the degree of rigor of tests to be the combination of methodological rigor (ideally replicated, controlled experiments), and rigor in testing the most extreme cases possible that sit within the asserted prediction class.

Combining these considerations, I define the reliability of a predictive rule as its accuracy according to a defined error metric in predicting outcomes of rigorous tests within a defined prediction class. When comparing two predictive rules using a defined error metric and a common list of predictive tests, reliability reduces to accuracy.

There is, however, difficulty in applying such testing to falsify theories, which gave rise to the next major development in the philosophy of science: Thomas Kuhn's idea of paradigms.

Falsification and Paradigms

How do we know that observation X has falsified theory Y? Nothing is ever proven in the abstract; it is *proven to* individuals. Falsification requires that individuals agree first to what has been observed, and second, that they see the contradiction between the observation and the theory. In the simplest case, a scientist with a vested interest in some theory may, like a bought juror in a criminal trial, simply say he doesn't agree that the theory has been falsified. Presumably he would be read out of the scientific community, but what if the community, or a large part of it, has some vested interest or is subjected to coercion? If this were to occur, then progress (or at least progress that can achieve material benefit) presumably would grind to a halt. This has happened in certain instances, such as parts of biological science under Stalin in the Soviet Union.

But even if scientists are acting in good faith, there is a huge problem with falsification. Scientists do not simply propound and test a series of independent theories. They develop networks of interlocking theories and observations, some of which depend on others in extremely complex ways. Often an observation will appear to falsify one theory but in fact falsify a different, related theory, and it's very hard to know this. The formal version of this problem is called the Duhem/Quine Thesis. After the usage of Imre Lakatos, one of Popper's leading students, I'll refer to the general issue as the problem of naive falsificationism.

Consider the textbook example. In the 1840s, scientists observed that the orbit of Uranus did not appear to be following the exact trajectory predicted by Newton's theories, which were based on the gravitational pull of the sun and other known celestial bodies. Did this observation falsify Newton's theory?

Newton's theories had been so successful in predicting such a wide range of phenomena, scientists were reluctant to throw them out based on one observation. They strongly preferred to reconcile the observation with Newtonian mechanics. The French mathematician Urbain Le Verrier used the perturbations in Uranus's orbit to predict the approximate location and mass of what would come to be named Neptune. Subsequent detailed observation of the area where Le Verrier predicted a new planet uncovered an object that corroborated his theory. So the theory falsified by this observation was not that of Newtonian mechanics, but the theory that there was no unobserved planet near what is now known as Neptune.

Faith in Newton's theories was vindicated, and physics proceeded along merrily. As time progressed, however, an increasing number of observations in physics could not be reconciled with Newton's theories, and Einstein developed relativity theory in part to account for these observations. His theory was eventually accepted by the global physics community.

While studying at MIT, I had a very similar experience to Le Verrier's, only with relativity theory playing the role that Newtonian mechanics had for him. Under the direction of a celebrated physics professor I conducted a research project centered on trying to solve a mystery. Measurements taken from an astronomical observatory showing the same patch of nighttime sky in approximately 1910 and approximately 1980 showed objects that were farther apart in the 1980 observations than in the records of the 1910 observations. Based on a set of widely accepted and strongly supported beliefs about how far away these objects were from the earth, scientists estimated their actual rate of movement in space. It appeared that they were moving much faster than the speed of light, contradicting Einstein's Special Theory of Relativity, which held that no physical bodies should be able to travel that fast. The term adopted in the scientific literature for this effect was "apparent superluminal motion." Note the word "apparent."

Faced with this data we could have, in theory, drawn either of the following conclusions: (1) "Einstein's Special Theory of Relativity has been falsified," or (2) "Something else is going on." The second choice meant accepting an observation that contradicted the theory but simultaneously refusing to accept that the theory had been falsified. Was it just willfully ignoring evidence to avoid the first conclusion? Not really, because if we did, we would have had to either develop our own replacement for Einstein's theories that fit all known physical observations, not just this one, better than relativity theory (despite our high opinions of our own abilities, this was not very likely), or fall back on Newtonian mechanics, which had long since exhibited anomalies of its own that led Einstein to develop relativity theory in the first place.

Lots of scientists thought about the problem of apparent superluminal motion and ultimately figured out a clever solution that reconciled the observation with relativity theory. Einstein was vindicated. As a practical matter, until then we all assumed, despite seeming evidence to the contrary, that relativity theory *had* to be right. We were confident that sooner or later somebody would reconcile the observation with the theory. Presumably, if and when Einstein's theories are later displaced by other canonical physical theories, this process will occur again many times.

In 1962, Thomas Kuhn published *The Structure of Scientific Revolutions,* the now-standard account of how sequences of "super-theories" like Newtonian mechanics and relativity come into being and influence the practice of science. Kuhn had completed his PhD in physics at Harvard in 1949, and in describing what he saw practicing physicists do when they showed up for work every day, he put forward the idea of a paradigm, a concept that has been widely misused ever since. Kuhn argued that to make practical progress, a group of scientists accepts an underlying set of assumptions about the physical world, along with accepted experimental procedures, supporting hypotheses, and so on. This paradigm helps to create a coherent discipline. The day-to-day work of scientists is to solve intellectual puzzles that fall within the relevant paradigm. Kuhn calls this normal science, or "worker-bee" science. Anomalies—factual observations that contradict the tenets of the paradigm—are rejected and either they are held aside as problems to be solved later or the paradigm is modified slightly to accommodate them. The former is exactly what happened when we observed apparent superluminal notion.

In Kuhn's description, a successful paradigm works well for a while, until enough anomalies accumulate that either remain unresolved or force the paradigm to be twisted so out of shape that it is clearly unworkable. When a state of crisis is reached, some scientist or group of scientists, often outside the relevant specialty, comes along to provide a new paradigm that works better. Kuhn called this a paradigm shift.

A classic case of all this is the overthrow of the pre-Copernican view that the sun and planets move around Earth. In a somewhat simplified summary, astronomers started by postulating circular orbits for the sun and planets around Earth that fit available data pretty well, but as observational accuracy improved, they had to start adding epicycles (little circles within the circular orbit), then epicycles within epicycles, and so on. What started as an elegant system ended up looking totally crazy and still did not fit the data that well. Eventually Copernicus proposed that the earth moves around the sun. Interestingly, because almost everyone, including Copernicus, assumed circular orbits, this system required even more epicycles than the old Earth-centric Ptolemaic system and was broadly rejected. It required Johannes Kepler to figure out that planets have elliptical orbits, and suddenly there was a much simpler, more elegant and predictive model for the solar system. Then we were off to the races, and Newton ultimately could unify terrestrial and celestial mechanics in three laws of motion, which, importantly, could be tested through direct experiments.

Kuhn made the point that a paradigm is not like a cookbook that lays out a set of agreed-upon theories and procedures in an explicit black-and-white format. It is more like the shared craft knowledge of a group of expert carpenters who have common techniques, methods, tools, and judgments, all of which are passed on through formal classes, apprenticeships, and joint projects A scientific paradigm is a similarly fluid combination of theories that can mutate somewhat in response to evidence; a common, if partially tacit, understanding of the kinds of questions that are interesting; experimental apparatus; methods of analysis that are valid; and so on.

A scientific paradigm's lack of rigorous specification is essential, because it allows scientists within it to respond to evidence that it is wrong by holding aside the evidence and calling it an anomaly, or if the anomaly is considered serious enough, by modifying the paradigm to account for this observation.

Popper's identification of falsifiability as the line between science and nonscience was motivated by his frustration with Freudians, Marxists, and others he believed claimed to be scientific, while consistently either making predictions that were so vague that all evidence could be reconciled to them, or responding to evidence that their theories produced incorrect predictions simply by changing some aspect of the theory and then maintaining that it was "essentially" correct. Bacon described the same frustration with the Scholastics, who, he claimed, when confronted with evidence contrary to a theory reacted so that "the axiom is rescued and preserved by some frivolous distinction; whereas the truer course would be to correct the axiom itself." To the extent that scientists operate as Kuhn described, they seem to act like Popper's non-scientific Freudians or Bacon's prescientific Scholastics. Empirically, when high-level paradigms come into direct competition (e.g., Copernican versus pre-Copernican astronomy, or relativity versus Newtonian mechanics), almost nobody ever switches camps, unless it's very early in his or her career. What happens is that one paradigm stops getting new recruits, and over time the stalwarts of that paradigm retire or die.

This is a pretty depressing picture of science that sounds a lot more like the Modern Language Association than the American Physical Society. Scientific certainty seems to have melted into indeterminacy. If we were to take Kuhn's description as complete, we would have come, inch by inch, pretty close to full circle. What started with Bacon's clarifying call for practically useful knowledge based on experiments was questioned by Hume, retreated into the philosophical-sounding complexity of falsificationism, and finally ended with Kuhn's paradigms, which sound like nothing other than a contemporary form of the Scholastic tradition—endless debates, lack of cumulative progress, inability to adjudicate disputes with facts, etc.—against which Bacon had reacted by developing the scientific method in the first place.

But how could such a process have produced jet aircraft, MRI scans, and mobile phones?

An Integrated View of Inductive Science

Those who study the scientific process often see Popper's and Kuhn's accounts of the scientific process as conflicting. I believe, however, that Popper and Kuhn each described part of the scientific method. Specifically, Kuhn described a process that is a practically workable, if philosophically unsatisfying, resolution of the problem of naive falsificationism.

A paradigm is just a specialized way of being closed-minded, and so on its face seems like a pretty bad idea. And yet paradigms are useful, because making progress requires making some assumptions. If I started my day by demanding that I rigorously prove my own existence before doing anything else, I would never get out of bed. Paradigms are the organizing frameworks that working scientists use to construct theories and interpret the natural world without having to resort to philosophical first principles every weekday morning.

If scientists were unwilling to make assumptions, falsification itself would become impossible, because, as we've seen, they could never know which theory was being falsified by a given observation. Most individual scientists proceed *as if* the paradigm within which they work were unassailable, but this is a mechanism to be able to identify what specific hypothesis they believe has been falsified or corroborated by an individual observation. More precisely, it allows them to act *as if* they know which specific hypothesis has been falsified or corroborated. Because the list of theories that could be falsified or corroborated by any one observation is infinite, it's not enough to rule out some potential theories; one must rule out *all* other potential hidden theories. Of course, ruling out all other competing theories is logically equivalent to assuming that the paradigmatic theory is correct. This is exactly what Le Verrier did when he assumed that Newton was correct, and therefore there must be an undiscovered object of a specific mass and location.

But while individual scientists may consider some paradigms to be literally absolute truth, science as a process always holds a paradigm to be a provisional set of working assumptions, and recognizes that any paradigm is extremely likely, at least based on historical experience, to be undermined and replaced at some point in the future. The title of Kuhn's book, after all, is *The Structure of Scientific **Revolutions***.

A paradigm is too loosely defined to be formally falsified. It is therefore neither scientifically true nor scientifically false, in Popper's sense of a falsifiable theory. Being true, in this strict sense, is not its purpose.

Then by what criterion should we accept or reject a paradigm? As with so much in life, the answer is contained in an ancient Chinese proverb:

Question: Do you want a black cat or a white cat?
Answer: I want a cat that catches mice.

A good paradigm helps scientists generate a network of nontrivial falsifiable predictions along with methods for testing them. Good paradigms catch mice. A paradigm remains dominant as long as it is judged to be better at this task than its alternatives, and is rejected when something more productive comes along. It was never strictly true and never becomes strictly false.

Popper grudgingly accepted this, to some degree, when in the last few pages of *The Logic of Scientific Discovery* he called out a number of what we would now term something like paradigms—atomism, the theory of terrestrial motion, the corpuscular theory of light, and the fluid theory of electricity—and described their role in exactly this light: "All these metaphysical concepts and ideas may have helped, even in their early forms, to bring order into man's picture of the world, and in some cases they may even have led to testable predictions."

But what Kuhn understood was that such "metaphysical concepts and ideas" are not marginal to science, as implied by Popper's tone; they are a necessary and central element of the scientific process as it is actually executed. A paradigm is not a falling-short of humans conducting science that in an ideal world would be purely falsificationist. A flexible paradigm represents a halfway house between naive falsificationism on one extreme and true dogma on the other. Naive falsificationism would bog down into endless debates about first principles. True dogma would prevent any questioning of first principles. A paradigm accelerates progress versus either extreme alternative.

A paradigm is a kludge—slang borrowed from software engineering, for a clumsy, inelegant solution that nonetheless gets the job done—that permits falsification to function in the real world.

Seen this way, the path of the philosophy of science has been not a circle, but a spiral. We have not come back to Scholasticism, but have instead developed an increasingly sophisticated explication of Bacon's call for a "just and orderly" process of generalizing from individual observations to reliable causal rules. In simplified terms, Bacon laid out the scientific program for developing practical knowledge of the material world through careful induction, relying on experiments to isolate causality. Hume made the critical point that there might always be hidden conditionals to any causal rule developed or demonstrated through induction. Next, Popper presented falsification as the practical mechanism through which we could come closest to finding and exposing hidden conditionals, but this solution opened the problem of how we know what has been falsified or corroborated by any observation. Finally, Kuhn showed that for falsification to achieve its purpose of identifying hidden conditionals in practice, scientists make strong, though provisional, assumptions about networks of theories. Paradigms are like sequential, temporary systems of scaffolding used to build the next set of falsifiable predictive rules; they are discarded and replaced when they become less functional than alternatives in moving the scientific project forward.

But move forward in what frame of reference? If the ultimate goal of the scientific project is not the search for absolute truth, but rather that "human life be endowed with new discoveries and powers," then progress must be defined in reference to alternative methods for achieving this outcome.

CHAPTER 3

Implicit and Explicit Knowledge

Evolution and Implicit Knowledge

Evolution through natural selection is a type of trial-and-error process. It is often described as a process that introduces random variations, and then retains those variations that lead to greater odds of survival and reproduction. That is fine as far as it goes, but misses the crucial point that the variations are only partially random.

Imagine a simple game in which I pick a random integer between one and a billion, and you try to guess it. If the only thing I tell you when you make each guess is whether you are right or wrong, then the best you can do is to keep a list of all the failed guesses, and just pick any one of the remainder at random. Call this the "just guess" strategy. Eventually you will get the right answer. On average, it should take you about 500 million guesses.

If, however, I change the rules such that I tell you whether each guess is high or low, there is an automated procedure, called binary search, that will get the exact answer within about thirty guesses. You should always guess 500 million first. For all subsequent guesses, you should always pick the midpoint of the remaining possibilities. If, for example, the response to your opening guess of 500 million is that you are too high, your next guess should be the midpoint of the remaining possibilities, or 250 million. If the response to this second guess is "too low," then your next guess should be the midpoint of 250 million and 500 million, or 375 million, and so on. You can find my number within about a minute.

Both "just guess" and binary search are trial-and-error processes, in that both create cumulative information as they proceed by eliminating failed variations. But binary search is about 15 million times faster. Binary search develops implicit theories, using a simple algorithm without the need for conscious intervention, that improve the odds of success for subsequent guesses. Very roughly speaking, "just guess" is to binary search as "introduce random mutations, and retain successes" is to actual evolution through natural selection.

The challenge faced by evolution is, of course, far more complex—starting with the point that there is no omniscient interlocutor to prove "getting warmer"/"getting colder" feedback. How genetic evolution accomplishes this task of radically accelerating progress versus blind variation plus selective retention, by algorithmically building implicit theories without conscious intervention, is both fascinating and instructive. But understanding it requires that we engage with the evolutionary genetic algorithm itself at a reasonably concrete level.

Start with the generic problem of trying to figure out how to make some complex system achieve improvement against some criterion—for example, applying therapies to the human body to increase longevity, reforming the commercial legal codes that govern a given country to increase total wealth, or operating a large chemical plant to maximize output. One simple approach is to just generate random ideas for improvement, then put them into practice to see whether improvement results. As in the number-guessing game, call this the "just guess" baseline. Science attempts to achieve faster improvement than this baseline by developing explicit theories for improvement, then subjecting them to rigorous experimental tests.

There is, however, an entirely different and potentially competing approach to do better than "just guess": evolution through natural selection. The power of evolution is that it is a system for improvement that develops *implicit* theories for improvement without the need for conscious intervention. In this way it develops and retains *implicit knowledge*. Genetic algorithms (GAs) are computer programs that mirror the biological process of evolution through natural selection. They are used to solve problems such as finding the best schedule for trucks on a delivery route or identifying the best combination of process-control settings to get maximum output from a factory.

Consider the example of a chemical plant with a control panel that has 100 on/off switches used to regulate the manufacturing process. What is the combination of switch settings that will generate the highest total output for the plant? One obvious approach to solving this problem would be to run the plant briefly with each possible combination of switch settings and select the best one. Unfortunately, even in this very simplified example there are 2^{100} possible combinations. This is a surprisingly gigantic number—much larger, for instance, than the number of grains of sand on Earth. We could spend a million lifetimes trying various combinations of switches through blind trial and error, and never get to most of the possible combinations.

The GA is designed to get there faster. It begins with an initial random guess to create a starting point. To establish it, imagine writing a vertical column of one hundred zeroes and ones on a piece of paper. If we agree to let one = "turn the switch on" and zero = "turn the switch off," this could be used as a set of instructions for operating the chemical plant. The first of the hundred would tell us whether switch 1 should be on or off, the second would tell us what to do with switch 2, and so on all the way down to the one hundredth switch.

This is a pretty obvious analogy to what happens with biological organisms and their genetic codes. Therefore, in a GA we refer to this list as a genome. Each individual number in the genome is called a bit. The mapping of genome to physical manifestation is termed the genotype-phenotype map:

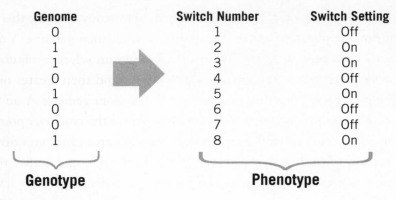

Genome		Switch Number	Switch Setting
0		1	Off
1		2	On
1		3	On
0		4	Off
1		5	On
0		6	Off
0		7	Off
1		8	On

Genotype   **Phenotype**

Genotype-Phenotype Map

In this illustration, the first bit in the genome is zero, which translates to setting switch 1 in the physical factory to the off position. The second bit is an instruction to set switch 2 to on, and so on down to the one hundredth bit.

Our goal is to find the genome that will lead the plant to run at maximum output. The genetic algorithm creates an initial bunch of guesses—genomes—by randomly generating, say, 1,000 genomes. It then follows a simple "recipe"—the genetic algorithm—intended to find genomes that will operate the plant at a very high output. This algorithm repeats the same three steps in an endless cycle: selection, reproduction, and mutation.

Selection comes first. We start by doing 1,000 sequential production runs at the factory (in fact, we typically construct a software-based simulation for this purpose) by setting the switches to the combination each genome indicates and measuring the plant's output for each; this measured output is termed the fitness value. Next, the program eliminates the 500 genomes with the lowest fitness values. This is the feedback measurement in our algorithm—and it is directly analogous to the competition for survival of biological entities.

Next comes reproduction: the algorithmic process for generating new genomes, directly modeled on the biological process of reproduction. First the 500 surviving genomes are randomly assigned into 250 pairs. The GA then proceeds through these pairs one at a time, flipping a coin for each. If the coin comes up heads, then genome A reproduces with genome B by simply creating one additional copy of each; this is called direct replication. If the coin comes up tails, then genome A reproduces with genome B via crossover: the program selects a random crossover point, say, at the 34th of the 100 bits, and then creates one offspring that has the string of zeroes and ones from genome A up to the crossover point and those from genome B after the crossover point, and an additional offspring that has the string of zeroes and ones from genome B up to the crossover point and those from genome A after the crossover point. This is illustrated in the following diagram:

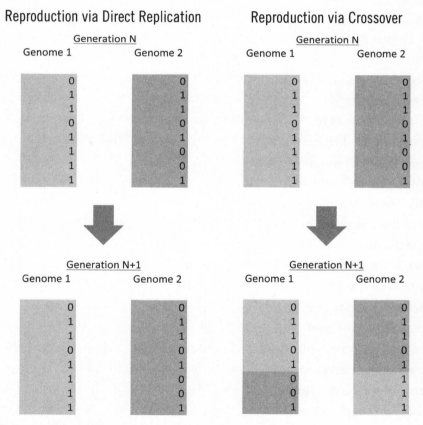

Reproduction via Direct Replication and via Crossover

In this illustration, the two "children" in the case of reproduction via crossover have a mixture of genomes from each parent.

The 500 resulting offspring are then added to the population of 500 surviving parents to create a new population of 1,000 genomes.

In the final step, a soupçon of mutation is added by randomly flipping roughly one bit per 10,000 from zero to one or vice versa.

The new generation is now complete. Fitness is evaluated for each genome; the bottom 500 are eliminated, and the surviving 500 reproduce through the same process of direct replication, crossover, and mutation to create the subsequent generation. This cycle is repeated through many generations. The average fitness value of the population moves upward through these iterations, and in fits and starts the algorithm finds genomes that produce higher output.

This seems like a laborious process, but it works: it usually helps us get the factory to very high output much faster than we could through blind trial and error (i.e., just trying a series of randomly selected combinations of switch settings). Computer scientists were inspired to use this process because they observed the same three fundamental algorithmic operators—selection, crossover, and mutation—accomplish a similar task in the natural world.

Casual discussions of evolution often imply that mutation is the primary method used to search for new genomes, but in fact crossover is the workhorse of the search. Evolution is in this sense conservative—generally trying out new genomes that are very similar to prior successful genomes. Mutations are rare, high-risk bets. Almost all of them fail to improve fitness, but those few that work help the algorithm find new, workable genomes in big leaps.

If we are to use evolution through natural selection as a metaphor, model, or guide to understanding social evolution, I believe that engagement with the implicit algorithmic theory-building that is part of evolution leads naturally to two observations that are different than those that arise from a view of evolution as blind variation plus selective retention.

First, it emphasizes that we need to consider not only the traditional issues of how to design institutions that will allow new ideas to be generated, tried out, and then subjected to some kind of selection mechanism that tends to retain successful new ideas, but also that these institutions should tend to bias the new ideas to have better-than-blind-chance odds of success. This doesn't mean conscious human intervention to develop new ideas, or to focus trial-and-error on some topics, but that wherever possible the rules of the game themselves should be designed to build this positive bias cumulatively. In practical terms, this calls for institutions that don't just generate trials and retain successes, but that encourage cross-pollination and mixing and matching of ideas for improvement.

Second, once we move past a view of evolution as a combination of almost elemental components of blind variation plus selective retention, to an understanding that it incorporates an algorithm for building implicit theories, it becomes obvious that the parameters of the algorithm itself are subject to contention. For one example, why should the mutation rate be 1/10,000 bits rather than 1/1,000 or 1/1,000,000? Or why should 50 percent of reproductions occur via crossover versus 90 percent or 10 percent? The next section evaluates a highly generalized version of these questions, in order to create the foundation for a unified framework that describes the broader competition between implicit knowledge and scientific knowledge.

The Evolution of Evolution

Evolutionary methods can compete with one another. For example, imagine that we have two identical chemical plants, each with a control panel comprising 100 on/off switches. Team A has one hour to figure out the switch settings that will maximize output from the first plant, and team B receives the same task for the second plant. Team A applies exactly the GA described in the prior section. Team B applies the same GA, but the mutation rate is set to 1/1,000 bits rather than 1/10,000 bits. At the end of the hour, one team likely will have found a combination of switch settings that produces higher output than the one the other team has discovered.

We could proceed with such competition more broadly. We could try many settings for mutation rate, for example, to find the one that

worked best over a broad range of cases. In fact, analysts often will execute exactly such computer simulations to optimize parameter settings for a GA. Further, we could imagine an arbitrarily large number
of identical factories and allow ever more profound variations to the
GAs we test in each. Rather than varying mutation rate, for example,
we could try multiple crossover points for mating pairs, then allow mating between more than two genomes, then find entirely different methods than crossover, and so forth. We could continue with ever more
abstract interpretations of what we mean by an evolutionary algorithm,
though ultimately they would all have some mechanism for iterative
implicit learning.

We could extend this competition to allow various nonevolutionary
methods to compete as well. For example, we could also allow an expert chemical engineer to try to optimize one of the plants. She might
constrain the search process using conscious knowledge of physical principles. In the extreme case, she might simply read the label for each
switch, scribble some calculations in her notepad, confidently flip each
switch to a specific setting, and announce that she has the plant operating at maximum output. If her theories are correct, this would be the
fastest possible way to get to the best solution. It seems rational to her
in this case to shortcut the evolutionary process.

In this way, explicit knowledge can compete with implicit knowledge. At this level of abstraction, the internal logic of each approach is
not an arbiter, but rather a theory to be subjected to real-world testing.
The chemical engineer, for example, may assert that she is right, and
may have a very technical and sophisticated argument with extensive
evidence to back this up—but the real test is whether her plant runs at
higher output than the others.

We could extend this to multilevel competition. As an illustration,
imagine 10,000 identical chemical plants lined up in a row. We might
link plants 1–100 as Group 1, plants 101—200 as Group 2, and so on,
and the groups could compete with one another. We could allow the
information from each plant within each group to be combined according to various methods to accelerate progress within that group in

more quickly finding better combinations of switch settings. For example, Group 1 might have the same GA rules as defined in the prior section for each of the 100 plants in its group, but then have some rules for combining results in any given generation to create "champions of champions" (e.g., take the top genome from each plant within the group in that generation, and combine them according to the same selection crossover and mutation rules that apply within each plant). Group 2 might have the same rules at the level of each plant but at the group level might combine outputs using a GA with a higher mutation rate. Group 3 might use various GAs at the plant level but combine these in each generation using a chemical engineer's expert opinion.

I will use the term "vicarious adaptiveness" to refer to an algorithm or other method of making decisions at the plant level that tends to make the group within which that plant sits compete more successfully with other groups. As an illustration, suppose plant 1 sits in Group 1, and the optimization algorithm used in plant 1 is some really stupid method like "always keep every switch off." This will tend to make Group 1 less likely to compete successfully with the other groups. Plant 1 would then be said to have a rule set with low vicarious adaptiveness.

We could extend this concept to a third level, such that Groups 1–10 are part of Super-Group 1, Groups 11–20 are part of Super-Group 2, and so forth. Super-groups can then compete with one another. We could have groups of super-groups and so forth, up to an arbitrarily large number of levels. Vicarious adaptiveness can be defined up through an arbitrary number of levels.

Donald T. Campbell used a mouthful of a term to refer to this kind of multilevel competition in which various kinds of rule sets at one level might or might not help the higher-level groups and super-groups within which they are nested to compete successfully with other groups and super-groups: "nested hierarchies of vicarious selection processes."

As I'll argue later in this chapter, exactly this kind of multilevel nested structure characterizes science, and further, science itself sits within a yet-broader evolutionary hierarchy and therefore can provide no absolute frame of reference for establishing truth. We can answer ultimate questions about a statement's scientific validity only in terms of its vicarious adaptiveness.

Science as Social Tool

To my knowledge, Francis Bacon never used the term "paradigm," but his proposed program can be appropriately thought of as the master paradigm for science. What remains operative from *Novum Organum* is pure method—or rather, a methodological mind-set—denatured from any specific physical theory. This vision defines much of what we mean by modern science, including the key examples described in detail in the first two chapters: the operational premise of materialistic reductionism; an emphasis on structured experimentation; careful measurement and analysis; the belief that what "deserves to exist deserves to be known"; the organization of scientific societies and research institutions; even proto-falsification.

Post-Darwin, the evolutionary metaphor for developing scientific knowledge within this master paradigm is almost irresistible—both Popper and Kuhn used it, for example. But in light of the chemical-factory GA example, the progress of alternative theories within science is not properly analogous to evolution through natural selection. Scientists consciously attempt to isolate causal factors, while one powerful characteristic of evolution is that it proceeds without conscious intervention. It would be more apropos (though still only metaphorical) to say that scientists *breed* theories than to say theories evolve through natural selection.

The "breeding rules" (as it were) for theories are established at a very high level of abstraction by the Baconian master paradigm and then more concretely by the specific paradigm in which a given scientific specialty operates. Of course, the distinction between theories and paradigms is, like so much in science, practically useful but philosophically sloppy. Consider the 1990s race to sequence the human genome. Sequencing new sections became something like a repeatable industrial process. We can imagine a ladder of theories of increasingly fundamental importance and with ever-greater methodological content that ascend from something like our theory about the structure of the next piece of the yet-to-be-sequenced section of the human genome, up through bioinformatics, up through molecular biology, up to the modern synthesis of evolutionary biology. At one end, it is clearly what we would call a very simple theory, and at the other, clearly what we would call a paradigm. In between, it can get murky.

What is a paradigm and what is a theory depends on where you sit. For example, what is strategic to an army lieutenant is a tactic to a colonel; what is strategic to a colonel is a tactic to a general. What is strategic to an individual salesperson at a pharmaceutical company is a tactic to the head of sales; what is strategic to the head of sales is a tactic to the CEO.

The paradigm for some subspecialty within which a group of scientists spend their careers may be an expendable theory from the point of view of some more fundamental paradigm. This is not a simple ladder, either, but instead a complicated network of nested theories and paradigms, many of which depend on others in enormously complex ways. We could envision an upside-down tree, with the trunk labeled as the Baconian master paradigm, and a set of large lower (somewhat intertwined) branches as major scientific disciplines proceeding down through smaller branches as paradigms, subparadigms, and so on, ending with entirely provisional hypotheses as the expendable leaves at the very bottom. We could call this the tree of scientific knowledge. If we peer into some specialty, we see the same kind of network in miniature, and if we zoom out to look at all of science, we see this structure on a grand scale.

For theories within a given paradigm that do not threaten its foundations, methods for evaluating truth are well established (within the relevant specialty), and induction is reasonably straightforward. Sequencing new sections of the genome became a semiautomated process, for example. Workaday astronomy to find new distant bodies has the same flavor. But a theory that challenges the assumptions of a specialty or a paradigm cannot be evaluated according to the rules of that specialty/paradigm, which has become its competitor. It must instead appeal to the higher authority of some superior paradigm. When Copernicus proposed heliocentric astronomy, the various methods, rules, and thinkers collectively representing the discipline of geocentric astronomy could not combine to appropriately judge the worth of his theory. Detailed knowledge of epicycles was irrelevant; adhering to the assumptions of geocentric astronomy was likely an actual hindrance. He appealed the decision to the higher court of the scientifically minded community as a whole.

The only way to adjudicate between two competing theories/paradigms is through competition according to the rules of some superior paradigm. Copernicus challenged specific tenets of geocentric astronomy but still developed his theories in ways that were consistent with specific findings of other scientific disciplines and according to the methodological rules (at that time, still quite primitive) that governed physical science as a whole. At this higher level of abstraction, specialties compete with one another in a framework that operates like evolution from the point of view of the competing specialties but is a competition according to the agreed-upon rules of the superior paradigm to which they both belong. Even this is a simplification; a paradigm is never fully defined, so even these rules for competition are somewhat flexible and subject to at least some change.

But the whole tree of scientific knowledge is really just a section of a much larger conceptual tree of knowledge. Bacon recognized that, as with any paradigm, his method could not be judged in terms of a competing framework, saying of potential Scholastic criticisms of his work, "I cannot be called on to abide by the sentence of a tribunal which is itself on trial."

Science has broadly displaced the Scholastic alternative as a means of developing practical knowledge, but other competitors remain. Common sense, received wisdom, tradition, and so on—basically, various names for implicit knowledge that seems to have mostly evolved without conscious intervention—have not been displaced from most areas of human decision-making. Nonscientific commonsense rules have evolved in various ways analogous to (and perhaps identical to) genetic evolution through natural selection, and are now embedded in our cultural norms. There are theories that some parallel to actual genetic evolution occurs with human ideas, but if any such process exists, we don't yet even begin to understand it. The competitive advantage of science is that it has an effective set of methods that lets us reach reliable, useful insights faster than this alternative for some kinds of problems.

This competition between alternative master paradigms, intellectual traditions, or whatever one chooses to call them is fully evolutionary from the point of view of science. At this extremely high level of abstraction, Baconian science is just another specialty that competes with alternative ways of knowing and doing through a process external to science and its rules.

The decision to accept the scientific method as a whole must therefore lie outside of science. So, the decision criteria for determining to accept any specific scientific finding must ultimately also lie outside of science. In practice, many of the decisions on whether to accept a finding are delegated, as it were, to science as a whole, and then down through various specialties and subspecialties, down to the editorial boards of scientific journals, tenure committees at universities, and so forth. But the broader society can always reserve any of these decisions. It appears not to be vicariously adaptive for a society to demand that science produce specific findings, to forbid that it reach conclusions offensive to established mores, to allocate scientific resources according to bribery or nepotism, and so on. But this is because of the negative effects on the broader society, as judged by the broader society, not because science provides some absolute frame of reference.

In the end, science proves itself not with discourse, but with works. More precisely, we *choose* to demand that the knowledge-finding method that we fund so lavishly—science—focus itself this way, and this appears to be an approach to knowledge-finding that serves our needs.

How we define this demand, however, can be tricky. As Bacon observed, insisting that all scientific activities generate immediate material benefits is not vicariously adaptive at all. Seemingly impractical scientific work seems to pay off in the long run, but we cannot be sure that this is true or that it will continue to be true.

A society that focuses entirely on material benefits might or might not really achieve them very well. One could easily imagine that in certain circumstances a society oriented toward goals other than increasing material power might be far better at accumulating it. For example, the emphasis on reading the Bible for reasons of personal salvation in some European and North American Protestant sects is widely believed to have contributed strongly to the widespread literacy that ultimately was a key ingredient in the economic success of these groups.

And it's unclear whether material benefits are even the right long-term measure of success for a society. Maybe we want a society in which people live frugally but produce great art, literature, and science for ten generations, then are entirely annihilated by a competing society in which people live 1,000 generations in incredible luxury but produce nothing of lasting aesthetic value. To structure our management of the scientific enterprise we must consider what kind of society we want to build. How do we answer that question scientifically?

This realization that science does not provide an absolute frame of reference for truth leads naturally to the conclusion that scientific theories do not correspond to some external reality but are merely predictive tools. This is usually termed "instrumentalism." I do not claim that scientific findings are instrumental, merely that science cannot tell us whether they are. That does not mean that science cannot discover "really" true laws or that science does not make progress toward such truth over time. Science operates *as if* all findings are instrumental and tentative. Life is full of ironies, and this might be the most effective method for finding noninstrumental absolute truth. But science cannot determine that.

I ended the last chapter by raising the question of how we can define a frame of reference for the progress of science—or even whether such a thing is possible—if it has abandoned the quest for absolute truth. The frame of reference is established by the search for practical knowledge. Science clearly is progressive in a very specific sense: it has continued to provide ever-greater capabilities to master our physical environment.

I use an iPhone most days to find my current location on a map. This would be impossible without modern physics. The transistors in the phone rely on effects predicted accurately to several decimal places by quantum mechanics. The Global Positioning Satellites that the phone uses to locate me incorporate in their software the deformation of space-time predicted by relativity theory to achieve accuracy within about fifty feet of my actual position.

We know our physical theories are true in the sense that they enable human capability. Science does not tell us whether theories are true in the classic philosophical sense of accurately corresponding to reality, only that they are true in the sense of allowing us to make reliable, nonobvious predictions.

CHAPTER 4

Science as a Social Enterprise

The Morality and Morale of Scientists

Science does not proceed as a disembodied logical process. It is an activity conducted by human beings. We don't *think* science, we *do* science. While different versions of science exist and compete, as a practical generalization, most scientists as individuals must display both a specific morality and a specific kind of *morale* for science to work.

The bedrock moral requirement for scientists is honesty in acquiring, reporting, and interpreting observations. Scientific fraud will be present as long as it offers potential rewards and human nature remains the same. Scientific institutions enact procedural safeguards against it, but these are at best partial solutions. Science also maintains a culture of honesty about data.

This was brought home to me once when, shortly after graduating from college, I went out to dinner with a group of friends and casual acquaintances. One person told a story about a summer job where she conducted surveys for a market research company. She mentioned that when she was behind on her daily quota of surveys, she would fill in forms herself without conducting the actual interviews. Without hesitation, or even real thought, three of us present who had been trained in science or engineering blurted out some version of "You can't do that!"

Preferring honesty is not unique to science; what was unusual was that the three of us overcame the normal social prohibition against boorishness. It struck me afterward that we had been inculcated with an unself-conscious ethic about never faking data. It was a taboo. We never debated whether it was a good rule, considered nuanced versions of when some kinds of data faking might be valid, or engaged in ironic repartee about it. Our reaction was like that of someone who had touched a hot stove.

Practicing scientists rarely question their professional norms. Rather than being denigrated for this, scientists are held in high regard by the public and are generally seen as contributing to a much higher material quality of life.

Scientists also have a special *morale*. They need it, as they rarely enter the field for primarily financial reasons, but rather tend to derive enormous intrinsic benefits from their work and see themselves as part of a professional guild that benefits humanity. They are generally much less amenable than the general public to restricting, for example, the use of animals in research, federal funding of stem-cell research, or the use of nuclear power. They believe science will create further practical progress in the future. In short, they see themselves as Bacon's "true sons of knowledge."

Both the morality and morale of individual scientists scale up directly to the scientific enterprise. That is, these same values, habits, and beliefs that disproportionately characterize individual scientists can be said fairly to describe science as a whole. The next section will describe other, more paradoxical social aspects of science. Some attitudes that are virtues for individual scientists would be vices for science as a whole, and vice versa.

Scientific Progress as an Emergent Phenomenon

Scientists can be, and often must be, dogmatic. But science as a whole should never be so and, at the highest level of abstraction of physical theories, is not. Kuhn documented many cases in which a new paradigm or theory initially did a worse job explaining many observations than the existing paradigm. We saw an example of exactly this dynamic in the overthrow of Ptolemaic astronomy. At first the heliocentric framework provided a worse fit to astronomical data than the existing paradigm—the new theory predicted the position of observable objects in the sky even less accurately than the old theory. This situation persisted for decades, until Kepler further modified the Copernican framework by asserting that planets have elliptical rather than circular orbits. The proponents of new paradigms often believe they have found keys that will eventually explain so much more, despite the evidence to date. They are scientific entrepreneurs who believe they can see the potential of their ideas.

Each individual scientist has a broad career choice: take the low-risk path of doing worker-bee science within an existing paradigm, or shoot the moon and attempt to upend an existing paradigm. Of course, the choice isn't really binary but rather exists along a risk-reward spectrum. Science needs a portfolio of people to make different decisions along this spectrum, and many aspects of the market for scientific ideas help allocate effort in a manner that will generate maximum benefits.

The vast majority of scientists who believe they have a paradigm-breaking insight turn out to be wrong, just as the vast majority of business entrepreneurs who start companies that they believe will change entire industries turn out to be wrong. Science as a process, however, provides alluring prizes for those who accomplish such feats, and encourages many such entrepreneurs and worker bees to compete. But science is a cruel mistress; as soon as some entrepreneur is proven correct and a new paradigm becomes dominant, the scientific process begins to do three things with this new insight simultaneously: elaborate it, use it, and undermine it. Science exploits individual dogmatism, "as if by an invisible hand," to produce results within a master paradigm that is somewhat dogmatic about method, but nondogmatic about physical theories.

This individual dogmatism is also likely related to an emotional need. Though most scientists may not believe they have individually seen absolute truth, they often believe they are part of a process that brings humanity ever closer to it. To believe otherwise, to see all of science as a mere handmaiden to engineering, would be psychologically debilitating for most people. Bacon identified the belief that truth was impossible to achieve as "the greatest obstacle to the progress of science." Literally zero successful scientists of my acquaintance are, to my knowledge, instrumentalists. Some metaphysical frameworks claim science brings us ever closer to absolute truth, but such beliefs are inherently nonscientific. This belief is the noble lie that many scientists tell themselves; or to be fairer, this is their great leap of faith.

Analogies with Other Emergent Social Phenomena

The parallels between science and markets are striking. This has been noted at least as far back as Michael Polanyi (yet another Austro-Hungarian British émigré) in his 1951 essay "The Republic of Science."

There is, first, what I'll term an evolutionary set of commonalities. Both science and markets abjure absolute authority but encourage competition at multiple levels between nested subauthorities. Both systems deploy trial-and-error learning and ruthlessly eliminate failures. (At least they do so in their pure form; in reality, of course, participants frequently try to corrupt the system and appeal to political authorities to protect their positions.) This creates a hybrid competitive-cooperative structure for each. Over time both of the systems tend toward baroque specialization and complexity.

There is also what I'll term an "open system set" of commonalities.

First, in both science and markets there is a central "invisible hand" phenomenon, in which individual behavior has systematic, unintended, and seemingly contradictory consequences that benefit the system as a whole. In science, dogmatic behavior by individuals with allegiance to some paradigm leads to nondogmatic progress at the system level; in markets, selfish behavior at the individual level leads to growing wealth for the general population at the system level.

Second, as science abandons the intuitively important notion of absolute truth and simply seeks useful, nonobvious, and reliable predictive rules, markets abandon the intuitively important notion of absolute value and simply seek price. But both science and markets have core noble lies/leaps of faith that cut against abandoning exactly these intuitively appealing notions: for scientists, the belief they are approaching absolute truth; for market participants, the belief that economic reward is related to value.

Third, each establishes conflict between participants seeking individual advantage but bounds this conflict with a set of rules. Each system's invisible hand requires both competent regulation and a substrate of morality to work in practice. For science this includes the generally internalized belief in accurately reporting data, along with replication of research, combined with standards bodies to root out inevitable fraud. For markets, this means a general ethic of commercial honesty and "a deal's a deal," combined with an honest court system for resolving disputes and, at a minimum, various kinds of weights and measures, labeling, and other basic regulation. But daily observation by participants that science actually is not seeking absolute truth, nor markets value, tends at least in part to erode this moral foundation and creates an ongoing tendency toward excessively relying on external enforcement. Each conflict has a "game day" in which a theory either performs or does not. For science, this is an experiment; for markets it is the product or program launch.

Fourth, each is properly seen as unnatural by those not fully invested in it, but each requires resources and support from the external population; therefore, each must justify itself to a skeptical public. This justification is ultimately that the field generates material progress. Because each is seen, correctly, as "soulless," each inspires a romantic counterreaction that always bubbles beneath the surface but occasionally boils over into a populist reaction.

These are not the only two systems sharing these characteristics; the common law and representative democracy are examples of roughly analogous systems.

Despite much detail being disputed by modern scholarship, Oliver Wendell Holmes Jr. made similar parallels with common law clear in his major works. The fourth sentence of his book *The Common Law*

(1881) is the famous assertion that "the life of the law has not been logic: it has been experience." The law has proceeded through trial-and-error learning. It avoids comprehensive, top-down definition of legal issues by a unitary authority but instead allows alternative judges and jurisdictions to develop rival interpretations within a common broad framework. The law is structured around rule-bound competition between adversarial parties, who nonetheless all remain "officers of the court." Game day is the trial.

A key theme of *The Common Law* was the law's gradual abandonment of subjective notions of justice in favor of objective measurements of external actions; by the time he wrote *The Path of the Law* (1897), Holmes would go as far as saying that the lack of congruence between actual law and abstract justice was so severe that the law existed purely to allow "the prediction of the incidence of the public force through the instrumentality of the courts."

The common law's noble lie/leap of faith is that practitioners serve some concept of justice; its invisible hand is that a series of disputes in which both sides pursue self-interest under a regime of competent regulation produces, over time, outcomes that tend to support a society capable of creating public order and material abundance.

These deep commonalities across activities such as science, markets, common law, and representative democracy at least indicate the plausibility of a common underlying structure. Each is a noncoercive system for human social organizations to increase material well-being in the face of a complex environment.

They are all methods for obtaining and exploiting practical knowledge through action, and all commingle abstract knowledge and action to various degrees; hence, so-called tacit knowledge. If the environment were simple—if determining the course of action were obvious and relatively static across time—then the complexity and waste of a scientific/market/judicial/democratic process of discovery would not be justified, and central authority would more efficiently impose a common answer. This is the same conflict between explicit and implicit knowledge that we saw in an earlier chapter.

This set of commonalities characterizes any evolutionary system in the face of a complex environment, including natural selection. The distinctive open-systems set of features is enabled by an off-stage (at the hierarchical level of the system in question) authority that holds an effective monopoly on coercion, and mostly restrains the use of force to settle disputes. Those who hold what is ultimately military power refuse to use it to force compliance with one vision of absolute truth, justice, value, or other ultimate ends. This is the practical manifestation of a specific kind of human freedom—what Popper called in a book of the same name "the open society"—that over centuries has disproportionately characterized the West versus the rest of the world.

These systems, though closely related, are not identical. One of the most significant differences is that markets, democratic government, and the common law typically have more legally enforced rules governing means of competition and cooperation than does science. Though the long-run consequences of scientific progress in the physical world obviously can be immense—think of the atomic bomb, jet aircraft, and penicillin—the immediate consequences are usually less obviously so. The broader society can permit more flexibility "within the box" of the scientific process with relatively lower short-term and less-obvious consequences to powerful interests. In markets, courts, and elections, the opposite is true. In this way science is the least immediately "action-entangled" of these systems. Science places many fewer hard constraints on theory development and evaluation, and relies to a much greater extent on mores, prestige, and suasion in regulating behavior than do the other systems.

Science also places the greatest weight on explicit versus tacit knowledge—after all, it does focus on developing formal, testable theories. Superficially, the combination of less reliance on formal rules to control behavior and greater focus on the development of explicit knowledge can make science appear to be one of those intellectual disciplines that are not aimed at material progress—systems that in Bacon's terms "tend to discourse rather than works." Both science and, say, comparative literature or analytical philosophy have paradigms (or at least very paradigm-like "schools of thought"), professional journals, technical jargon, and so forth.

What distinguishes the scientific method from these other disciplines is a specific kind of feedback loop that retains its connection to material reality—that is, experiments. Feedback loops are essential for such a system to create progress. Science entirely without experiments would just be sloppy philosophy.

CHAPTER 5

Science Without Experiments

S tand in a lab when one of the researchers walks in with the first results of a significant experiment. Conversations stop. People put down instruments and look up from keyboards. For one moment, everybody from the principal investigator to the undergraduate intern has only one thought: "Well?"

Some scientific disciplines, however, appear to operate without the benefit of experiments yet still seem to remain firmly within what both the general public and scientists agree is the scientific tradition. These disciplines are of two types: (1) so-called historical sciences, such as geology or parts of evolutionary biology, for which most experiments are impossible in principle because these fields address past events; and (2) fields that make predictions but for which most experiments are infeasible, the principle example being the astronomical sciences.

Historical Science

Historical sciences employ many of the standard techniques of science, such as careful collection and analysis of data, rigorous peer review, attempts to weigh physical evidence for and against various theories, and so on. They are fully scientific in this sense.

But if science's purpose is to develop predictive rules, then historical science is part of the scientific enterprise only to the extent that its product supports building such rules. Historical science is simply another aid to building theories. In this role of inspiring testable hypotheses, it competes with staring at Mount Fuji, contemplating prior bioinformatic studies, and carefully reading *Origin of Species*. The value to science of the overtly scientific-seeming aspects of these activities is not that they are good in and of themselves, but that they enable historical science to perform this function more effectively than alternative methods. It is important to recognize, however, that their role in developing testable predictive rules may be highly indirect, may not be obvious even upon careful observation, and may take a very long time to come to fruition.

Consider the case of the attempt to understand what killed off the non-avian dinosaurs about sixty-five million years ago. In 1980 a team of researchers led by Luis Alvarez, a physics professor at the University of California, Berkeley, discovered a very high concentration of iridium at a geological depth in the earth's crust widely believed to have been formed about sixty-five million years ago. Since iridium is rare on earth but is a significant component of asteroids, Alvarez's team hypothesized that a huge asteroid had struck the earth at this time. They estimated that a meteorite large enough to deposit this much iridium would have been huge, roughly the size of Manhattan. A strike of this size would create a dust cloud that would take about ten years to dissipate, and the resulting temperature reduction likely would kill off many plants, as well as the animals that eat them—such as dinosaurs—but smaller mammals would have a good chance of survival.

The problem for the Alvarez hypothesis was that this impact would have created an enormous crater, and there was no known crater that big. Then, in the 1990s, researchers including NASA's Kevin O. Pope determined that the Chicxulub crater in Mexico matched the size the theory required and was likely formed by an asteroid impact, and the crater was dated to about sixty-five million years ago. Many leading scientists have gone on the record supporting the Alvarez hypothesis. The remaining open issue is that the term "about" from the geological point of view is not precise enough for the biological point of view. There remains some controversy about whether the impact at Chicxulub actually occurred several hundred thousand years after the mass extinction of dinosaurs.

This work clearly used techniques that in normal speech we call scientific. The people who did this work are scientists; Alvarez, in fact, had already won the Nobel Prize in physics by the time he began his investigation. The specific and audacious prediction of the crater, along with its subsequent discovery, is a beautiful example of a successful falsification trial that is not a controlled experiment. How does this example comport, then, with the assertion that science requires controlled experiments?

Remember that whether a statement is "really" true is a nonscientific question. Scientific statements are true in the specific sense that they allow us to make useful, reliable, nonobvious predictions. Their truth is demonstrated in practice. If analyzing past events enables the creation of testable predictive rules, then these rules are what is either scientifically true or not. Everything else is scaffolding.

Astronomical Science

Astrophysics is a trickier case. It routinely makes predictions and develops predictive rules, from ancient predictions of solar eclipses to Einstein's famous prediction about the deflection of light by the sun that his general theory of relativity implies. We can test such predictions against observation, but we cannot conduct controlled experiments.

In one sense, astrophysics can be thought of as scaffolding in the same way as historical science. It builds predictive rules for very distant phenomena, but the same distance that prevents experiments means that these are not predictions about potential human interventions. So, while interesting, these predictive rules become relevant to increasing our control over our physical environment only when they are used to develop yet further predictive rules for potential interventions.

But the phenomena under study in astrophysics have characteristics that allow us to approximate the experimental method, and considering these carefully will help to create the conceptual machinery that will be used in later chapters to understand the weaknesses of nonexperimental social science methods. Astrophysics studies a subject with three characteristics important to approximating the experimental method: (1) vast distances between objects; (2) enormous absolute expanse with reasonable repetition of interactions; and (3) interactions between objects that are dominated by forces that can be modeled as direct extrapolations of forces that can be analyzed at experimental scale.

First, vast distances are crucial because various physical forces attenuate rapidly with distance, and we can therefore use the approximation that almost all the myriad pair-wise gravitational (not to mention quantum and other subatomic, atomic, and molecular) interactions between every particle in the universe and every other particle don't matter. When Le Verrier theorized the existence of a new planet, he could approximate all forces on Uranus by considering only the gravitational influence of the sun plus a few nearby objects; but in theory, its path through space is influenced by gravitational interactions with each individual dust particle in the Crab Nebula. I will describe a situation in which a dense web of interactions either doesn't exist or is mostly immaterial as one of low causal density.

Second, in combination with low causal density, the enormous size of the observable universe means we can come close to replicating many natural experiments. Many predictions can be replicated in many different cosmic regions that are, as a practical matter, independent and not previously observed in relevant detail. As an illustrative example, we wouldn't predict that one crater will be found on one planet, but would build a rule that predicts the presence of craters on each of millions of planets that meet certain specified conditions. We can make such a prediction based on analysis of a small number of planets, and then test the rule repeatedly by examining other previously unobserved planets.

As long as the physical laws themselves do not vary in different parts of the universe, this replication is relevant for testing scientific theories. This is the reverse of a situation I will call holistic integration, in which we had no opportunity for experiments, natural or otherwise, because all parts of the phenomenon under study interacted materially with all others, and hence we could not isolate some subset of the phenomenon as an experimental or observational unit.

Holistic integration and high causal density are similar but not identical. Imagine, for example, that the universe was divided into a million "boxes" by a network of semipermeable membranes, such that within each of these boxes no forces attenuated with distance, creating an environment of immensely high causal density, but that all forces generated within each box remained almost entirely contained and therefore did not operate in any material way on objects in any other box. We would have high causal density for every particle in the universe (and holistic integration within each box), but at the scale of the universe as a whole, we would not have holistic integration. Experiments would be very difficult to control if conducted within any one box, but at the scale of the universe, we could conduct experiments in some boxes and use others as controls. We could, for example, apply external forces to ten of these boxes but not to ten others, and observe whether the test boxes had some change not observed in the control boxes. High causal density makes controlled experimentation hard, as does holistic integration, each for different reasons. I will term the combination of both high causal density and holistic integration as integrated complexity, which would make controlled experimentation all but impossible.

Third, the forces that govern interactions can, at least partly, be analyzed on or near Earth and extrapolated pretty directly to astronomical distances. This is simply an extension of the inevitable inductive problem of generalizing from a finite list of instances to a general rule. Though hazardous, such extrapolation is qualitatively different than hypothesizing unique forces that operate only within the realm of astrophysics and are therefore immune to controlled experimentation, given our current technical capacities. Le Verrier, for example, could rely on experimentally verified Newtonian mechanics, and I could rely on experimentally verified relativity theory, as the central tools for understanding the data we observed about astronomical objects.

In this way, astrophysics is partially underpinned by traditional controlled experiments.

As we've seen, we can never be sure that any experiment actually has controlled for every possible alternative cause of an outcome; there are shades of gray from a purely uncontrolled observation of a natural phenomenon to a tightly controlled lab-bench experiment. In practice, astrophysics achieves some approximation to the ideal of controlled experimentation through natural experiments. It is important to note, however, that without the conditions of low causal density, opportunity for replication, and tight linkage to physical laws corroborated through controlled experiments, certainty presumably would be even worse in these fields than it is in fact.

And as I will discuss later in the book, analysis of social policy usually violates all three of these conditions. First, human social organizations have a causal density that dwarfs anything astrophysics considers. Second, although we can sometimes design experiments for some social programs because we can find "boxes" that are reasonably causally impermeable—for example, testing a literacy program in Atlanta, New York, and Dallas, but not in control areas in Miami, Chicago, and Seattle—many questions of social policy suffer from integrated complexity. Third, despite many promising leads, we do not have the capability to apply experimentally verified findings in chemistry, physics, and biology to explain things like the effect of minimum-wage laws or welfare policy changes.

CHAPTER 6

Some Observations Concerning Probability

Imagine that you run a bank. How should you price the loan to a given prospective borrower who requested a thirty-year fixed-rate mortgage? One big factor would be the odds that the borrower would default. But how should you assess that? One simple approach might be to use the average default rate across all mortgage borrowers for the past thirty years. A better approach might be to use the average default rate of a more targeted "reference class" of borrowers who are more like the person requesting the loan—say, those who had a similar income, down payment, and credit history. Though there might be idiosyncratic unobserved differences between individual borrowers within the reference class, if the bank makes loans to thousands of these borrowers, then, like a casino operator, it should observe a very predictable average default rate. The bank thus can quantify its risk.

But what if ten years after you make such a book of mortgage loans, new technology changes the economy's structure to the extreme disadvantage of this reference class, and the default rates go up higher for these borrowers than they had been historically? The implicit assumption that the next thirty years would be like the past thirty would be exposed as faulty. No matter what statistical analysis we did on the past thirty years of data, it would not expose this hidden conditional, because the technology didn't exist in the prior period.

In highly stylized form, this is basically what happened in the sub-prime mortgage collapse that played a large role in the 2008 financial crisis. The author Nassim Taleb has famously called such unexpected events black swans. Financial analysts call this model risk. After the usage of the great early twentieth-century economist Frank Knight, I'll call this uncertainty.

There is an obvious analogy here to Hume's Problem of Induction. The rule that "making thirty-year fixed-rate mortgages to a large group of people with the following average income, down payment, and credit history will produce a book of business with average default rate X" was reliable in the past but might turn out to be unreliable in the future. This is very much like the observation that just because whenever I've eaten something that looks and smells like a loaf of bread in the past it has nourished me, it does not necessarily follow that if I do so in the future, it will nourish me again. As we'll see later, in social science this issue is not limited to extreme cases but is a pervasive problem.

But before moving on to those topics, I must make some observations regarding probability. This chapter will not be anything like an overview of the entire subject but will simply attempt to clarify some concepts and terminology necessary for the subsequent discussions.

Risk Versus Uncertainty

So far I have discussed mostly deterministic predictive rules—that is, statements that a given set of conditions will *always* produce a given outcome. The search for hidden conditionals is, in effect, the search for adjustments to a deterministic rule in response to a failure of the rule. But almost all asserted predictive rules for human social behavior that claim empirical corroboration include phrases such as "more likely to" or "tend to"—they are probabilistic.

Consider two predictions:

If I throw this coin into the air, it will fall.

If I throw this coin into the air, there is a 50 percent chance that it will land heads-up.

The first prediction is deterministic. The second prediction is probabilistic: it asserts that although we cannot know whether we will get heads or tails, we do at least know the odds of this outcome. Writers often show off by making the point that the contemporary interpretation of quantum mechanics indicates that we can't really be sure of the first prediction, because there is some tiny but finite chance that particles will happen to bunch up under the coin and prevent it from falling. So this apparently deterministic prediction is really probabilistic; we simply believe that the probability of the coin falling is so close to 100 percent that as a practical matter we treat this as a certainty.

Now consider a third prediction:

There is a 10 percent chance of a military coup in Pakistan within the next twelve months.

This prediction asserts that knowledge of the likelihood of a coup is probabilistic, but any reasonable person would question the reliability of the implied probability distribution. That is, how do we know that the odds of a coup really are 10 percent rather than, say, 5 percent or 50 percent? I will refer to predictions for which we can specify a reliable probability distribution (a comprehensive list of the possible outcomes along with odds for each) as "risky" or "probabilistic," and those for which we cannot specify a reliable probability distribution as "uncertain." This will be a crucial distinction for everything that follows.

Of course, this raises the question of how we know we have a reliable probability distribution of outcomes. For example, how do we know that the probability distribution of outcomes for flipping the coin is really 50 percent chance of heads and 50 percent chance of tails? After all, as per the Problem of Induction, we can't be absolutely sure that the coin will fall at all; if it does fall, it might land on an edge and stay there, and so on. That is, we don't even know all the possibilities. The second prediction is really uncertain, but as a practical matter we treat it as probabilistic. Strictly speaking, *all* predictions are uncertain.

How can we know whether such a probability distribution is reliable in practice? As we've seen, the scientific method is designed to determine the practical reliability of predictive rules. But special complications arise when we try to apply the scientific method to a probabilistic statement.

Start with the observation that even if we were to ignore the problems of naive falsificationism, a probability statement is never strictly falsifiable. Consider first the coup prediction. Neither the occurrence of the coup nor its lack of occurrence shows the prediction to be false. The same is true when I flip the coin once: neither heads nor tails on the flip in question falsifies the prediction.

In the case of the coin, it is practical to execute a replicated series of experiments. But even if I flipped the coin a million times and got tails on every flip, the predictive rule still has not been falsified. It is possible that I've simply had an incredible run of luck. There is no number of successive heads that can falsify the prediction with certainty. At some point scientists simply accept that a probabilistic prediction has been falsified.

It's important to note that there is no technical means of resolving how unlikely some outcome must be for a probabilistic prediction to be rationally considered falsified. Nailing down absolute certainty about the truth of any probability distribution through induction is another ever-receding horizon of the scientific method, but one that is unique to probabilistic predictions.

The Reference Class Problem

So, how do we know that a probability distribution, if not absolutely certain to be correct, is reliable enough to be used in practice? More specifically, how would we inductively develop or evaluate this belief, despite any a priori theory we might hold?

As per the prior section, in the case of the coin, we could experimentally flip many coins, or alternatively observe that we have reliable records of millions of coin flips, and note that over any sequence of many flips, we tend to be extremely close to 50 percent heads. Even if we accept that a group of scientists reaches operational agreement about whether this observed fraction of heads is close enough to 50 percent to be accepted, there is yet another problem. If I actually flipped a specific quarter one million times and got 600,000 heads, I would very likely conclude that this specific coin is biased, not that I've falsified the theory that coins in general have a 50 percent chance of coming up heads. I would hold this belief because prior coin flips and many other coins that I could subsequently flip experimentally would all come up heads very close to 50 percent of the time. "Flipped fair coins have even odds of heads and tails" is analogous to a paradigmatic scientific belief that leads me to question the observation when I see it violated—I treat a quarter that doesn't display this result as an anomaly to be resolved through further investigation of the coin, flipping technique, and other elements of the observation itself.

But why would we look at all coins to establish what the "true" probability distribution is for the specific coin I am flipping?

Something is different about this series of flips for this coin that distinguishes it from other sequences of flips. Maybe quarters are different from other coins. Maybe I should look only at coin flips in the past ten years, or only those flipped by this specific person, or only coins flipped in Cleveland, or only those flipped in the dark. In short, what is the universe of events (the reference class) that the next quarter flip for which I want to make a prediction is an example of? This is, of course, simply the search for hidden conditionals to the probability statement.

In the case of coins, we would find that the result is stable to various answers to this question. Across an extremely broad range of intuitively relevant reference classes—all coin flips, only quarters, only quarters flipped at night in France in 1995, etc.—we would see virtually the same result. But the case of the prediction of a Pakistani coup would be very different. First, we would have very few data points. Second, the odds of a coup in a given year would vary a lot between intuitively relevant reference classes, such as all countries; countries with military rulers; countries that have had at least one coup in the past twenty years; majority Muslim countries; former British colonies; and so on. How do we know we've chosen the right subset to develop our probability estimate? We don't.

We could try to get around this problem by alternatively asking about the forecaster's track record. But this raises the entirely analogous question: Track record at predicting *what*? We could consider various reference classes of all predictions made by this forecaster: for coups in former British colonies; any change of any kind to any government; coups in Islamic countries within the past twenty-four months; any kind of event in Pakistan; and so on. How do we know we've chosen the right subset of all prior predictions to develop our probability estimate for the forecaster's accuracy? We don't.

If we could answer these questions—that is, if we already knew of all conditionals in the probability statement—then we would have no uncertainty, merely risk. But we don't ever know this.

Now imagine that every coin in history had always come up heads when flipped. That is, our sample probability for some sequence was 1 under some assumed reference class (i.e., all coin flips). We would still have the exact same reference class problem. We would not know that there was some hidden conditional to the rule "Coins always come up heads" that would be revealed when we tried to apply this rule to some future forecast. After all, this is just the Problem of Induction.

The Problem of Induction, then, is just a special case of the reference class problem where sample probability equals 1 for an assumed reference class. This allows us to unify the concepts of risk and uncertainty. Risk is, in effect, quantified lack of certainty *within an assumed reference class*. Uncertainty is the recognition that we can't ever know that we have chosen an existing reference class that contains, and has correctly exposed, all hidden conditionals that are relevant for any specific prediction. In a complex system, such as people paying off mortgages, this can be a very practical problem. In fact, we will see that this is almost always the source of immense difficulty in scientifically predicting human social behavior.

Ironically, it is often hard for those using probabilistic prediction rules to keep in mind the caveat of uncertainty beyond quantified risk. As a practical matter, the reference class problem tends to be more confusing to most people when the underlying predictive rule is probabilistic than when dealing with the special case of the Problem of Induction, but probabilistic prediction rules themselves often signal that this problem is actually more relevant, since they tend to indicate a less well-understood environment of high causal density in which hidden conditionals tend to be a more significant practical problem for science.

In sum, every purported probability distribution actually floats on a sea of uncertainty. Therefore, the reference class problem never goes away, no matter how sophisticated our statistical methods. It is the phantom menace that haunts all belief that we have quantified our lack of certainty. Just as the Problem of Induction implies that any scientific finding is subject to irreducible doubt, by extension the reference class problem—which, again, is simply the generalized version of the Problem of Induction—means that any probabilistic prediction is subject to irreducible doubt that is never captured by confidence intervals, statistical significance tests, or any other statistical measurement, because such measures of lack of certainty are themselves subject to doubt.

By (unverifiable) tradition, a Roman general who received a triumphant parade upon returning from a conquest had a slave stand just behind his shoulder, whispering over and over again into his ear, "Remember, you are mortal." When using a probabilistic forecast, we should always hear a whisper in our ears reminding us: *The model is never the system.*

CHAPTER 7

The Invention and Application of the Randomized Trial

The Evolution of Randomized Field Trials

Anyone who has ever sought treatment for Lyme disease, depression, or even the flu knows that evaluating the effectiveness of therapeutic treatments is an excellent example of detecting causality in a poorly understood environment of high causal density. For all their progress finding cures and treatments for major ailments, even our best medical researchers are still a long way from comprehending the human body. As an illustration, research published in the *Journal of the American Medical Association* in 1998 estimated that more than 100,000 people per year die in US hospitals because of adverse reactions to drugs that had been *correctly* administered.

There are several reasons for this. Any effort to treat one ailment or injury can produce extended chains of physical reactions, many of which may take a long time to come to fruition, and any of which can be of comparable or greater health impact than the initial problem. The effects for the same intervention can vary dramatically for different individuals, or for the same individual at different times. Small variations in the intervention may create large differences in the outcome. These are classic signs of an extremely complex system.

The obvious scientific approach would be to undertake a painstaking series of replicated controlled experiments to measure the effects of various interventions under various conditions. This is, in fact, a reasonable description of what the medical research community does. The major challenge is how to control for potential causes of health outcomes other than the intervention of interest. In practical illustrative terms, if we give a human subject a pill we think might reduce blood pressure, and simply measure blood pressure before and after taking the pill, we don't know that the intervention caused any measured change in blood pressure, because blood pressure naturally fluctuates over time. We need to answer the counterfactual question: "But for this intervention, what would blood pressure have been?"

Attempts to understand the causal relationships between medical interventions and health outcomes extend back to the beginnings of recorded history. Throughout most of this history, there was a conflict between theory-based and experience-based medicine (or roughly, between deductive and inductive medicine). The sources for the theory varied from religious superstition in societies such as ancient Egypt, Babylon, and Assyria to more rationalistic ideas in the classical Greek, Roman, and medieval Islamic cultures. But as per Bacon's indictment, no matter the source of the theory, it was generally useless. As an example, the practice of bloodletting, based on the medical theory of "draining away one of the four bodily humours," began about 3,000 years ago and was widespread until the nineteenth century.

In the premodern period, experience-based medicine made real progress in some areas, especially surgery. For example, an Egyptian papyrus dated to about 1500 BC documents a procedure approximating modern jaw surgery. Because many successful surgical procedures are so immediately and dramatically effective, abstract debates about causality are not necessary (the answer to the "but for" question is obvious), enabling useful, conscious, trial-and-error progress.

Progress for therapeutics was more problematic, however, because the change in outcomes usually was not so immediate or dramatic, and often manifested as a reduction in the probability of a disease or an increase in the probability of recovery. In information-processing slang, we would say that the "signal-to-noise" ratio (the size of the effect compared with the size of the natural variation in the measurement of interest) is much lower for therapeutics than for surgery.

Nevertheless, experience-based medicine did make at least limited progress with therapeutics throughout history. Examples of crude but conscious comparisons between alternative treatments appear sporadically throughout the ancient, medieval, and early modern worlds. The biblical book of Daniel includes the story of the empirical comparison between two dietary regimens in the sixth century BC. Later, Islamic scholars developed a tradition of testing proposed therapies, in which they specifically distinguished between the concepts of observation (*tarassud*) and testing (*tagriba*). In the tenth century AD, al-Razi reported a purposeful trial of bloodletting in Persia, and by the eleventh century, his successor Ibn Hindu used purposeful comparative tests to find that specific plants and herbs could be used to treat various illnesses. In 1025, Ibn Hindu's contemporary Avicenna (Ibn Sina) laid down a structured set of principles for experimental testing of therapeutics in the epochal *Canon of Medicine*. At about the same time in China, Ben Cao Tu Jing gave ginseng to one runner and withheld it from another to test its effects on breathlessness. Surely a large number of similar purposeful comparisons were made throughout history without being formally recorded.

Some combination of conscious testing and an evolution-like process, in which those who followed certain health practices tended to survive, has over thousands of years created some useful traditional remedies. Well-known examples include use of horse chestnut (contains the active ingredient in the modern drug Aescin) as an anti-inflammatory, cinchona bark (quinine) as an antimalarial, and opium poppy (codeine) as an analgesic. A nontrivial portion of the modern pharmacopeia was derived from these traditional therapeutics. Modern research has identified dozens of widely used pharmaceuticals that are derived from higher plants that, in turn, were used in traditional medicine to treat the same ailments.

Although much of this knowledge was useful, it should not be romanticized. Lists of traditional medicines from the dawn of recorded history through the early modern period are rife with treatments that we now know to be useless or counterproductive, such as bloodletting, eating feces, and ingesting ground powdered mummy. Much of this has always been rain dances. But even for those premoderns who were trying to create therapeutic improvement, it was difficult to identify and eliminate the worthless remedies, and therefore progress was glacial.

Evaluation was the crucial missing ingredient for more rapid progress; an effective feedback loop was absent. As the scientific revolution progressed, doctors/scientists in Europe and North America attempted to more carefully evaluate claims of efficacy. The huge problem remained how to answer the "but for" question without the capacity to physically control all other possible causes of an outcome change to isolate causality, as scientists would in a lab experiment.

This problem was not solved all at once, but a workable methodology evolved from the mid-eighteenth century to the mid-twentieth century. James Lind is conventionally credited with executing the first crude but recognizable clinical trial. In 1747 he divided twelve scurvy-stricken crew members on the British ship *Salisbury* into six treatment groups of two sailors each. Each pair had cases "as similar as [Lind] could have them," though this was very approximate; Lind later described one treatment pair as "two of the worst patients." He tried to hold all other potential causes of change to their condition as constant as possible: "They lay together in one place, being a proper apartment for the sick in the fore-hold; and had one diet common to all." He observed that the two patients treated with citrus juice showed by far the greatest improvement.

In the more than two hundred years since, the fundamental concept of the clinical trial has not changed. Scientists attempt to find two groups of people alike in all possible respects, apply a treatment to one group (the test group) but not to the other (the control group), and ascribe the difference in outcome to the treatment. This avoids the requirement for a detailed understanding of the physical mechanism by which the treatment operates—for example, Lind did not have to know anything about vitamin C or the details of human biochemistry to conclude that citrus juice somehow alleviated the symptoms of scurvy— but places an enormous burden on the assumption that the two groups are identical other than the treatment of interest. The term "control group" was not chosen arbitrarily. This is a method for moving from observation to controlled experimentation to test therapeutic hypotheses. It is a direct application of Baconian science to applied human biology.

In the nineteenth century, intellectual leadership in the experimental evaluation of diseases and their cures was seized by the Continental European physiologists, most famously Claude Bernard. The physiologists emphasized controlled experiments. What they meant by "controlled" was quite intuitive, and consistent with Lind's basic idea: to identify all the known causes of variation in outcome for the clinical condition being studied, and then carefully hold constant each of these other than the treatment of interest between the test and control groups. This is more or less what Galileo did when he dropped two dense, smooth balls, so as to control for the known effects of friction.

Further, when the effect of the treatment was dramatic enough, scientists of that era could deploy clinical trials without worrying much about any other factors. A classic case is the 1882 anthrax vaccine experiment that made Louis Pasteur an international celebrity. In response to a challenge from a competing scientist, and in the face of intense public interest, Pasteur gave his anthrax vaccine to twenty-five head of cattle and no vaccine to another twenty-five, and then gave all fifty animals a lethal dose of the disease. All twenty-five vaccinated cattle survived, and all twenty-five untreated cattle died. Health outcomes for these fifty animals over that time period became, in practical terms, monocausal; therefore, any imprecision in matching test and controls was overpowered by the combination of the almost immediate deadliness of anthrax and the essentially perfect effectiveness of the vaccine. It was as if it were a test of whether it makes sense to use a parachute when jumping out of an airplane. Developing the vaccine required scientific brilliance; tests of its effectiveness could withstand almost any

methodological imprecision. Unfortunately for humanity, very few proposed new remedies have such dramatic results.

Although they made real scientific progress—Claude Bernard famously discovered some functions of the pancreas and liver, for example—
the physiologists confronted in the human-body-plus-environment a
system so complex that creating reliable controls for therapeutic experiments typically exceeded their capabilities. Like us, they just did not
know all the causes of the state of health of any given person, and so
could not reliably hold them constant.

This wasn't for lack of diligent and intelligent effort. Nineteenth-
century researchers were highly focused on the problem of control and
were well aware of the role of experimental "noise" (or more properly,
not-as-yet-understood causes of the outcome) in obscuring the causal
relationship between treatment and effect. They used blinding—keeping physicians who performed various steps in a trial blind to which
participants were in the test group—to reduce observer bias. Such observer bias could be caused, for example, by a doctor who believed that
the proposed treatment was life-saving, and therefore consciously or unconsciously recorded symptoms as less severe for the treatment group
than for the control group. These researchers also relied on the best
available clinical judgment to match like cases, and tried to exploit institutional settings in which treatments and environmental variables
could be as consistently managed as possible.

But they continued to run into the same seemingly insurmountable
problem of the inability to control experiments properly. Given their
limited knowledge about the body-plus-environment system, their efforts to design and interpret experiments would devolve to the question
of who got to judge the similarity of cases, a decision that in turn required knowledge of the disease's causes, which were contested claims.

To my knowledge, the brilliant but erratic American polymath C. S.
Peirce was the first person to discover the solution to this problem when
he executed a randomized, blinded experiment in 1884 to test percep-
tions of small differences in weights (though the concept of assigning
test treatments by drawing lots had been discussed hypothetically as

early as the late 1600s by Flemish physician Van Helmont). Peirce did not stumble into this research design. He had developed a deep, interlocking set of theories on pragmatic philosophy, logic, inference, and probability that specifically linked induction to explicit randomization.

There appear to have been sporadic attempts at randomization in psychology and social science over the next several decades, but the first definitive execution of a social science experiment with randomized assignment of a large number of subjects to test and control groups was a 1928 experiment at Purdue University that tested the effect of exemption from examinations. The dominant methodology for establishing test and control groups continued to be matching of like cases, as it was in medicine.

In the 1920s and 1930s, Polish statistician Jerzy Neyman, who established the Biometric Laboratory in Warsaw, and the great British statistician and geneticist R. A. Fisher, who was working at the agricultural Rothamsted Experimental Station in Hertfordshire, rediscovered, extended, and applied many of these same principles. Fisher formalized this work into the field now known as design of experiments (DOE), after the title of his enormously influential 1935 book. He based his analysis on a series of experiments designed to evaluate the effectiveness of various fertilizers on potato crop yields, and this work directly inspired medical researchers. One of his central insights was that randomly assigning treatments (or in clinical trial terms, randomly assigning patients to the test versus control groups) permitted researchers to conclude reliably that differences in outcome were caused by differences in treatment. More precisely, as long as researchers understood the distribution of outcomes in the population from which the test and control groups were randomly chosen, then they could apply statistical tests to obtain reliable estimates of the probability that these differences in outcome were caused by differences in treatment.

It is not surprising that Peirce, Neyman, and Fisher all worked out their theories in response to experiments with biological organisms. In an environment of high causal density, such as is normally present in biology, the number of causes of variation in outcome is enormous, and each has significant potential effects compared with those of the potential cause of interest. We don't know enough to list each of them and hold them constant, but if we randomly assign patients to the test and control groups, then these hidden conditionals won't confound our estimate of treatment causality. Random assignment in experiments is another statement of epistemic humility.

As a hypothetical example, suppose researchers in 1950 wanted to test the efficacy of a pill designed to reduce blood pressure but did not know that about 10 percent of the human species has a specific gene variant that predisposes them to adult-onset hypertension. If the researchers selected 3,000 people, and randomly assigned 1,500 to a test group who are given the pill and 1,500 to a control group who received a placebo, then about 150 patients in each group should have the gene variant of interest (though the researchers would have no explicit information about this and wouldn't even have thought to investigate it). Therefore, when these researchers compared the change in blood pressure before and after taking the pill for the test group versus the control group, their estimate would not be biased by a much higher proportion of patients with the gene variant of interest in one group or the other. The purposes of randomization, therefore, are: (1) to help prevent experimenter bias from assigning systematically different patients to the test versus control groups, consciously or unconsciously, and (2) more subtly, yet more profoundly, to hold approximately equal even those potential sources of bias between the test and control groups of which we are ignorant. It is a method designed to create controlled experiments in the presence of rampant, material hidden conditionals.

Obviously this balancing between the test and control groups usually is not exact because of sampling error; therefore, all else being equal, larger group sizes will enable us to get closer to even distributions of all such factors across the test versus control populations. The relevant statistical science is designed to assess our degree of certainty in drawing causal inferences given (1) the size of the groups, and (2) the difference in outcome between the test and control population samples (the "signal") as compared to (3) the general level of variation in outcomes in the overall population (the "noise").

Credit for formally integrating this technique into clinical trials to create the modern randomized field trial (RFT), in which patients are assigned randomly to the test and control groups, is usually given to Sir Austin Bradford Hill, the statistician for a set of British clinical trials on the use of streptomycin to treat pulmonary tuberculosis in the 1940s. (Such trials for therapeutics are more typically termed randomized control trials, but I'll use the social science nomenclature of RFT throughout the book for clarity, rather than specific name variants unique to various subject areas.) Recently, however, Sir Iain Chalmers has brought to light an earlier carefully randomized trial: a 1938 US Public Health Service trial of pertussis vaccine in Norfolk, Virginia. The lead investigator in this trial, Joseph Bell, the assistant chief of the Foreign Quarantine and Immigration Division and an instructor in epidemiology at Johns Hopkins School of Hygiene and Public Health, employed a table of random-sampling numbers to assign patients to the test and control groups.

Bell seems to me to have been an insufficiently recognized methodologist. In this trial he also deployed the "intent-to-treat" principle: considering all of those selected for the vaccination group as the test group, regardless of whether they were actually vaccinated. This is because those who are selected for treatment but refuse or do not get the vaccine for some other reason could vary in some way from those who are selected and do receive it. For example, they might be more irresponsible, and therefore less likely to comply with treatment regimens for other unrelated conditions and also have worse diets. This might seem picayune, but there have been cases of very large modern RFTs, such as the Coronary Drug Project (a large experiment launched in 1965 to determine the effectiveness of certain drugs in improving cardiovascular health), in which just this compliance effect dominated the causal impact, and failure to account for this would have validated an ineffective drug. In essence, compliance can act as a marker for all kinds of other behaviors and characteristics that can have a large effect on health outcomes.

Further, Bell recognized that in the case of patient or environmental characteristics reasonably believed to influence a trial's outcome, we can make sure that the test and control groups have nearly identical proportions of these characteristics without sacrificing randomization. We can do this by first classifying patients into subgroups defined by those characteristics, and then randomly assigning members of each subgroup to the test or control group in the same proportion as for all other subgroups. In Bell's case, this meant dividing metropolitan Norfolk into fourteen geographic sections and randomly assigning patients into the test and control groups for each section, then combining the section-level test and control groups into a total test group and a total control group.

In a modern RFT, this technique of explicitly preventing imbalance between the test and control groups for certain known potential confounding factors is termed stratification. If done properly, it helps to reduce the bias created by imperfections in matching test and control patients due to sampling error, and is often done for a short list of obvious characteristics such as age, sex, race, and relevant baseline disease characteristics. One key observation, therefore, is that therapeutic RFTs represent a hybridization of pure randomization and analytical matching of the test and control groups—researchers seek the benefits of randomization, supplemented by matching on plausible causal drivers of the outcome of interest on a "belt and suspenders" basis.

The RFT had been developed in its modern form by the 1940s. In a contemporary clinical trial, an RFT for a therapy is normally the third in a sequence of trial phases. This sequence begins with smaller, non-randomized experiments to establish a lack of large practical problems in executing the therapy (Phase I); proceeds to a second test for some evidence of efficacy with no obviously terrible effects (Phase II); then goes to the formal RFT (the Phase III clinical trial); and finally concludes with Phase IV postmarketing surveillance of actual performance after the therapy is released for general application by clinicians.

The RFT is a relatively new piece of technology—newer than the automobile or the airplane, and about the same age as color television or the electronic computer. Over the past sixty years, it has driven out alternative means of determining therapeutic efficacy wherever it can be applied practically. It is now all but universally accepted as the so-called scientific gold standard for evidence of a causal relationship between treatment and outcome in medical science. There have been more than 350,000 documented therapeutic RFTs, and their use is accelerating: about 10,000 are now performed per year. In fact, therapeutic RFTs are one of the most important components of modern experimental science as a whole. The United States alone spends about $30 billion annually on them, which is far larger, for example, than NASA's annual budget, and dwarfs the cost of such contemporary iconic Big Science projects as the Large Hadron Collider.

Controversy and Resistance

Like many innovations, the RFT faced fierce resistance from incumbents. Though the motives of some resisters weren't always pure or their arguments purely rational, the most rigorous resistance identified real limitations of the RFT.

One source of resistance was discomfort among some scientific investigators with randomized controls as opposed to other methods of experimental control, such as those Lind and the physiologists practiced. This was mostly a technical debate, and it was over by the early 1970s, resolved fully in favor of randomization because of the advantages described in the prior section. It's not surprising that the forty-year period from the 1930s to the 1970s is approximately the duration of a professional lifetime. This was a standard paradigm shift within a specialist technical community. If you're going to do clinical trials at all, the intellectual case for randomization is so strong that pretty much any researcher beginning a career would employ it; only those whose prior research findings, public commitments in scientific controversies, and so on were threatened would oppose the innovation. Of course, if a specific researcher simply refused to accept randomization, there is no absolute philosophical argument that could compel acceptance. This is a case of pure paradigm competition.

A much broader and more sustained resistance to RFTs and indeed any clinical trials came from physicians, who, like all humans, resist external direction, particularly when it affects their authority and prestige. Randomization was one element of a package of research reforms, including blinding, performing experiments, and legally proscribing therapies that failed experimental tests, that dramatically reduced physicians' autonomy, prestige, and scope of judgment. As is the case with some current-day doctors who resist "evidence-based medicine," they feared that this would make them more like production workers executing a rote script than independent professionals, and this provides ample reason for them not to like RFTs.

One such objection some physicians made was that although many clinical outcomes, such as quality of life and comfort, were important parts of the clinician's criteria in determining treatment, the Baconian attitude of careful measurement led researchers to focus on quantitative outcomes rather than the most important ones. This is a valid point, at least for some clinical conditions, for example, in the case of a chronic mental illness that creates unpleasant but not life-threatening feelings. On the other hand, it is not very relevant for an acute disease that causes death within weeks.

A second such objection was that the human body is holistically integrated and that the Baconian attitude of isolating a specific disease state and testing a discrete treatment missed the forest for the trees: the whole point of medical care should be overall quality of life. This viewpoint has wide contemporary popularity and is often termed, appropriately enough, holistic medicine. In the RFT framework, this could be stated as the idea that the appropriate measurement period for any clinical trial is always the entire lifetime of all patients and controls, and that the measured outcomes must include all significant health indicators. Once again, this objection carries much more practical weight for chronic diseases than for acute, life-threatening illnesses. That is, a reasonable person might very well claim that treating sinus infections with antibiotics could, over years and through complicated behavioral pathways, lead to both changes in the development of the body's immune system and patient lifestyle choices that result in his being worse off than if he had been treated by nothing more than hot tea and rest. On the other hand, no reasonable person at risk for smallpox would use this logic to refuse vaccination for the disease.

A third and more fundamental objection was that even if one were to accept that, all else being equal, treatment A was more likely to produce a better result than treatment B, all else is never equal. Patients have varying co-morbidity, are at different stages of life, have different lifestyles, needs, and home situations, and so on ad infinitum; therefore, in practice, clinical judgment is required to determine the best course of action for a specific patient. A practicing physician, under the view this objection implies, should take the results of clinical trials as one factor in an inherently subjective decision process. In addition to its intellectual content, it is obvious that this argument can be used as a politically expedient way for clinicians to retain power and to refuse to act on findings.

Even considered independent of interest, however, this intellectual criticism carries great weight. Medical treatments operate in an environment of high causal density, which is why the RFT was developed in the first place. Said differently, there are usually many hidden conditionals to any predictive rule, such as "Treatment X is the best method for alleviating condition Y." If this were not the case, then simple observation would usually suffice to determine efficacy, as it has for thousands of years of trial-and-error learning about some kinds of surgery, or as it did for Pasteur in testing his anthrax vaccine. By example, this concern that all else is never really equal would be highly relevant for a treatment that demonstrated better results than the best available alternative for 52 percent of sufferers of a complex, chronic lifestyle-related disease with extensive and varying co-morbidity, but a worse outcome than the alternative treatment in 48 percent of cases. The wide variation of treatment effectiveness versus the best alternative indicates significant hidden conditionals, and numerous realistic treatment alternatives exist. This objection can be applied to quite serious medical conditions as long as the believed effect of the complexities contextual issues create are of comparable magnitude to the improvement the tested treatment creates, so that although on average the "best" treatment performs best, in a large proportion of instances within the test and control populations, alternative treatments appear to do as well or better.

A single RFT as a guide to therapeutic practice, then, is most appropriate for treatments in an intermediate zone of signal-to-noise: On the one hand, these treatments are not effective in more or less every case, or else the conclusion would be obvious without the need for sophisticated controls. On the other hand, they do not show improvement in a small enough majority of cases that even if a trial shows both statistical and practical significance, it cannot provide a practical guide to action because too many other factors would have to be considered to make a rational decision.

This raises the Achilles' heel of any randomized experiment: generalization. What we really know from a given RFT is that this specified list of patients who received this exact treatment delivered in these specific clinics on these specific dates by these specific doctors and nurses had these differences in outcomes as compared to control patients. When we want to use this result to guide action, we must ask: "How can we reliably generalize this observation to a reliable, nonobvious predictive rule?"

CHAPTER 8

Limitations of Randomized Trials

The Problem of Generalization

If biology is an environment of greater causal density than physics or chemistry, then psychology and social science, which evaluate human mind and behavior, study environments of even higher causal density. The working assumption among medical researchers is that there is a reasonably uniform biological response to a given chemical, much as physicists assume that physical laws are uniform across space and time in order to generalize experimental results to universal physical laws. This is a tolerable engineering approximation for something like a biological agent injected into the bloodstream for an acute condition. It is much less so when the effect of some tested program, say, changing the recommended medical practice for a specific hospital, has an extremely long chain of causation between action and outcome, and is highly dependent for its effects on the social context in which it is executed. As we move from even such attenuated medical interventions to social science interventions, this issue becomes far more severe: there is no (currently scientifically understood) biological basis for the causal effect of a social program like a change in school curriculum, so the "complications" *are* the causal mechanism.

In certain respects, the so-called soft social sciences deal with the hardest problems. Therefore, it is not entirely surprising that the most rigorous thought about generalizing experimental results did not arise in physics, or even biology, but in psychology and sociology.

In 1957 Donald T. Campbell developed the idea of distinguishing between what he termed internal and external validity to describe this problem:

> Validity can be evaluated in terms of two major criteria. First, and as a basic minimum, is what can be called internal validity: Did in fact the experimental stimulus make some significant difference in this specific instance? The second criterion is that of external validity, representativeness or generalizability: To what populations, settings or variables can this effect be generalized?

Campbell described internal validity as "a basic minimum" for a trial. It was an immense intellectual achievement to develop the techniques of the randomized trial, but Campbell's point emphasizes the degree to which the RFT represents only one of the steps toward a scientific approach to clinical medicine. If we consider a single RFT to be, in Baconian terms, a "duly and orderly" executed experiment, the problem of external validity is really just a special, and especially challenging, case of the standard scientific problem of generalizing a reliable predictive rule from a finite list of instances.

The machinery of scientific inference can be applied to this specific problem of generalization from individual RFT experimental results to useful predictive rules.

First, as we've seen in the earlier chapters, the most direct technique that science has developed to start reliably generalizing experiments is replication. Some clinical trials, especially those addressing lifestyle changes over many years with large test groups, are difficult to replicate for economic reasons, but across hundreds of thousands of cumulative RFTs, there has certainly been some replication. In 1992 the Cochrane Collaboration was established by the British National Health Service to create a library of RFT results in a format allowing standardized comparisons across tests. Researchers have developed methodologies to enable meta-analysis of multiple related RFTs to more reliably estimate treatment effects and understand the generalizability of results. These same methods can be used to plan prospective replications of existing RFT results, where desirable and practical. Increasingly, replication and near-replication are used to validate and refine findings.

Second, though a classical RFT tests efficacy, or treatment impact under ideal conditions, in recent decades the research community has increasingly emphasized pragmatic RFTs, which are designed to test effectiveness, or treatment impact under typical clinical conditions. As we move from classical biological treatments with relatively short causal pathways to interventions that materially depend on context, efficacy becomes somewhat theoretical, and pragmatic tests become more relevant. To the extent that these contexts will vary in implementation, running near-replications—variations of pragmatic RFTs under a variety of such conditions—becomes important to establishing generalizability.

The third technique involves enmeshing the findings of a specific RFT within a broader biological theory. Medical RFTs are rarely falsification tests in any meaningful sense. Candidates for pharmaceutical treatments, for example, usually are identified through a process of trying substance after substance in a lab. Although so-called rational drug design, which develops drugs deductively from theory, has made significant strides in the past couple of decades, there is not a comprehensive body of pharmaceutical theory that, as in something like Newtonian physics, permits a wide range of theory-derived predictions that can then be tested. It is more like very early lab-bench chemistry. An RFT often represents the falsification test of a theory only in that we typically are testing the clinical impact of a substance that we theorize should generate improvement in human patients because, after trying many near-randomly chosen compounds, it has already shown laboratory promise and then performed well in subsequent animal tests. This obviously makes generalization much more hazardous.

The horrifying thing, from the perspective of someone who wants to act rationally based on an RFT result, is that even if we did only a single RFT without replication, never mind a sophisticated sequence of trials to try to determine the causes of variance across these replications, we must assume that if we did such replications, we would see some variance in results. Conceptually, all of these possible replications are out there; we just happened to do one of them.

A single RFT does nothing to expose hidden conditionals related to implementation effectiveness. A series of RFTs can help to expose them, but we never know with certainty that we have found all of them, no matter how many tests we have run. There is *never* an absolutely reliable probability distribution for external validity developed through replication. The guidance that RFTs provide is always subject to uncertainty, rather than mere risk, because this guidance is always subject to the reference class problem. Typically the practical question for us is whether we face a situation that is more like flipping a coin, where we see great stability in estimates across almost all intuitively relevant reference classes, or more like predicting a coup in Pakistan, where we see wild variance across reference classes.

We can never eliminate uncertainty in predicting future events based on RFT results by running a series of replication attempts, but what if we placed the results of these trials in the context of a broader body of scientific knowledge that establishes more reliable rules for generalization? In the extreme, this broader base of knowledge will still be subject to the same lack of philosophical certainty as any other scientific belief, but like doing replications, at a practical level, this can improve reliability of generalization in many cases.

Like our example of the reference class problem when applied to flipping coins, all of this is hypertechnical when applied to many of the historical, heroic triumphs of RFT testing. When researchers observed the results of the polio vaccine trials of 1954, they were confident the results could be generalized directly and reliably to successful implementation, because this RFT sat in the context of prior successful vaccine rollouts and was supported by a commonsense physical theory that the effects of the chemical placed in the bloodstream should, within a wide range of clinical conditions that could be reasonably specified and executed, protect against polio. The result was clear enough, the disease horrible enough, and the alternative treatments so poor that any reasonable person would have prescribed it to someone in the target population, with very rare exceptions.

Scientists were justified in seeing this test as asking simply, "Does the vaccine work or not?" because they could assume this background knowledge that would allow them to generalize the result reliably. But this type of background assumption is not usually valid when interventions, even health care interventions, become more behavioral, because our corroborated body of scientific knowledge that explains normal human behavior sufficiently well to permit such reliable generalization is so limited. By this point, we have moved in shades of gray to an intervention that is fundamentally behavioral, and therefore all but indistinguishable from the kind we normally would see as the subject of social science, such as a change in classroom size, criminal sentencing guidelines, or welfare eligibility rules.

Consider, as a practical illustration of this problem, a widely discussed RFT reported in 2009 that tested the effect of free primary medical care on a specific childhood disease for a sample of 1,300 test patients in Ghana versus a randomized control group of the same size. The study found that adult guardians of test-group participants reported through diaries that they brought their children to more annual visits to formal care, but fewer annual visits to the kind informal care offered by traditional healers, than did the adult guardians of the control group. The study reported no statistically significant improvement in health for the test group versus the control group.

What conclusion can we draw from this RFT that will allow us to allocate medical resources more effectively in the future? In developed economies, many informed commentators believe that the marginal value of incremental health care spending is very close to zero. Some of these commentators believe this study helps prove that, even in less-developed countries, the marginal value of medical spending is very low. Other commentators may believe that traditional medical practices are grossly undervalued by a technology-focused Western medical establishment and that this study is further evidence that traditional healers are just as effective in treating many conditions as are degreed professionals. Others may believe that standards of formal care in many developing countries are very low, and that this is evidence that the clinics in this study delivered poor care. Yet another theory is that there are many examples of people overreporting in diaries behavior they believe to be socially desirable, and that parents who did not take much advantage of free health care for their children likely lied about this in their diaries, so there was probably very little difference in actual delivery of care.

So this study proved anything from marginal health care spending is not valuable, to traditional remedies are just as valuable as Western medicine, to standards of care are very poor in Ghanaian clinics, to people tend to lie when filling out activity diaries, to people won't bring their kids to the doctor without a better incentive than free care. Obviously one could come up with other theories; further, real theories of each type would be more circumscribed and nuanced than these somewhat stylized examples. In each case, however, our background assumptions determine what theory has been falsified or confirmed. We operate, as all experimental verification must, within some paradigm of beliefs that are not tested in the experiment. What does this study therefore indicate we should do? Anything from avoid generic health care spending increases in Ghana, to spend more on formal care in Ghana, to improve its standards, to provide publicity and support for traditional healers, to design studies that don't rely on diaries, to pay parents' transportation costs in developing countries for additional doctor visits.

Even though this is a simplified example, it illustrates the point that we often cannot reason from a single RFT to a predictive rule that is sufficient to guide future action. Because the causal pathways tend to be long and poorly understood for behavioral interventions, and our theories for human social behavior used to support generalization from them are not yet soundly scientific, this generalization process is far more hazardous than for tests of, say, a pharmaceutical intervention for an acute disease. In a later chapter, we will see that the acute critiques the leading economist James Heckman leveled against RFTs in social science will center on precisely this issue.

Recognizing the difficulty in generalizing an RFT should not blind us to its importance and power. In an environment of sufficiently high causal density, if we don't have randomized control for our experiments, we never face the problem of generalization because we don't even have valid experimental results at the foundation of the inferential edifice. Without internal validity, in other words, there is no point in worrying about external validity. Further, *no* scientific experiment, or series of experiments, self-generalizes. Dealing with this problem was the central issue in the philosophy of science before the RFT was invented, and remains so today. The randomized field trial is an enormous accomplishment, developed through centuries of effort. It has pushed into new areas the frontier of questions that can be addressed through the scientific method. But as with all aspects of science, there are practical limits to its usefulness.

Does Smoking Cause Lung Cancer?

A second important limitation of RFTs is that some important questions cannot be subjected to structured experiments, yet still require us to make decisions.

As we have seen in a prior chapter, entire scientific fields, such as astronomy, must rely on observational data. This can produce reliable scientific knowledge because several conditions obtain: relatively low effective causal density; opportunity for extensive independent replication of natural experiments; and hypothesized causal rules that can be developed as direct extrapolation of physical forces proved through controlled experiments.

Clinical medicine sometimes faces analogous conditions, the classic case being the causal relationship between smoking and lung cancer. This linkage was the subject of an intense methodological debate in the middle of the twentieth century that established many of the analytical canons of chronic-disease epidemiology. The arguments that raged around this question echoed various key methodological disputes in the social sciences that will appear in later chapters.

The smoking–lung cancer debate can only be understood in the context of the times. In contemporary America, lung cancer is the single most deadly form of cancer, and is second only to heart disease as a cause of death. But this is not an immutable fact of nature. Up until about 1900, lung cancer appears to have been extremely rare. It exploded in much of the developed world in the twentieth century. The increase in lung cancer incidence immediately after WWII, in particular, was staggering—just between 1948 and 1952, rates increased by 21 percent in America, 30 percent in France, 31 percent in England and Wales, 45 percent in Italy, and 68 percent in Japan. Nobody knew when, or if, these rates would plateau. In the 1950s, this understandably created a crisis atmosphere, and lung cancer was widely described as an epidemic.

The combination of several factors around 1900—the adoption of automatic rolling machines in the 1880s that made cigarettes much cheaper, the widespread distribution of cigarettes to soldiers in WWI, and generally increasing wealth—resulted in a massive increase in smoking, which continued to build for decades, in the advanced countries. Many researchers hypothesized that this was a major cause of the rising tide of lung cancer, after a twenty- to thirty-year lag (reflecting the typical time between the onset of smoking and the development of the disease).

Of course, many other things also changed throughout the developed world over this same time period. There were competing plausible hypotheses for causes of the epidemic that included increased air pollution by the gases and dusts industry created; the use of asphalt on roads; the increase in automobile traffic; exposure to gas in World War I; the influenza pandemic of 1918; and working with benzene or gasoline.

Many of the key intellectual architects of therapeutic RFTs were leading participants in the public debates over the causes of the epidemic. Famously, R. A. Fisher, author of *Design of Experiments,* continued to argue through the end of his professional life around 1960 that the causal link to smoking had not been proved, because without randomization we could not rule out various plausible confounders. On the other side, Sir Austin Bradford Hill, of randomized streptomycin trials fame, argued that this link had been established with sufficient certainty to justify various public health actions against smoking.

We now know that Hill was correct. Enormous evidence of the effect of smoking on lung cancer has accumulated over the past half-century, including at least one true RFT. Though it would be impossible in a nontotalitarian society to force a random group of people to smoke regularly, a long-term randomized trial reported in 2005 that a program that successfully reduced smoking had, after about fifteen years, produced a statistically significant decline in mortality and lung cancer.

But the relevant methodological question is not whether Fisher or Hill was correct about this linkage in the 1950s and 1960s, but which of the decision logics that each employed is a more reliable guide to making decisions across some reference class. Just because somebody who thinks he can beat roulette by always betting on red happens to win on his first spin, it does not mean we would be wise to rely on this method for making money in a casino. We would like to know over what scope of decision-making, if any, a method for establishing causality that does not require strict randomization will lead to better decisions than one that does.

In the current era, nonexperimental therapeutic findings remain dramatically less reliable than proper experimental findings. In a well-known 2005 paper, Dr. John Ioannidis, a professor at the Stanford School of Medicine, evaluated the reliability of forty-nine influential studies (each cited more than 1,000 times) published in major journals between 1990 and 2003 that reported effective interventions based on either experimental or nonexperimental methods. More than 80 percent of nonrandomized studies that had subsequent replications using stronger research designs were contradicted or had found stronger effects than the replication, whereas this was true for only 10 percent of findings shown initially in large RFTs. To repeat: 90 percent of large randomized experiments produced results that stood up to replication, as compared to only 20 percent of nonrandomized studies.

Nonetheless, methodologists often claim that no one nonexperimental study should be considered definitive, but that an accumulation of evidence must be considered. Hill, in one of the most cited papers in the history of epidemiology, provided a working definition of that field's method for establishing causality. He created a list of nine "viewpoints" that could be used to consider an inference of causality: strength, consistency, specificity, temporality (i.e., cause must occur before effect), biological gradient (i.e., a dosage-response relationship), plausibility, coherence with other scientific findings, experiment (which Hill agrees can create the "strongest support" for causality), or analogy with other scientific findings. These were an extension of a shorter list of five arguments presented in the US surgeon general's 1964 report on the health effects of smoking, which in turn built upon the canons of induction presented by John Stuart Mill in the prior century.

Although these are often still taught as the "Bradford Hill criteria," Hill specifically denied that nonexperimental causal inference could proceed according to a set of rules. He believed the process to be inherently judgmental. This seems to be correct, at least for epidemiology. Even today, after decades of efforts to refine, extend, or replace this list of viewpoints, no widely deployed algorithmic method exists to establish causality using observational data.

In practice, these complexities were less relevant for smoking and lung cancer, for several reasons.

First, the association data was unusually strong. As the surgeon general's report emphasized, there had been dozens of retrospective and prospective analyses, almost all of which pointed in one direction. And the apparent strength of the effect was enormous: regular smokers were consistently shown to be about *ten times* as likely to have lung cancer as nonsmokers.

Second, the strongest alternative hypothesis—Fisher's argument that there might be some unobserved genetic variant that predisposed some people both to smoking and lung cancer—was extremely implausible. The surgeon general's report argued persuasively that the gigantic increase in lung cancer over a few decades showed that *something* had changed between 1900 and 1950. If it's not realistic that the human genome changed that rapidly all around the world, then even if there is some gene-environment interaction (which subsequent research has shown to be the case), by definition, an environmental change was implicated.

Third, the asserted causal mechanism—sucking hot, chemical-laden smoke into your lungs many times per day for decades—was viscerally obvious, even if there were large interaction effects with other environmental and genetic factors. It is generally agreed by sophisticated epidemiological methodologists, including those who disagree fundamentally on many points, that "lists of causal considerations are pretty good rules of thumb when the system being assessed is simple, but in cases where an assessment of causation demands more than common sense, these lists are not going to be terribly useful."

Fourth and finally, Hill emphasized that causality should not be considered in the abstract, but in the context of the plausible costs and benefits of action versus inaction. Society suddenly faced an exploding epidemic that was a leading cause of death, with rapidly rising incidence that nobody knew would stop increasing. To the extent that the practical proposals for interventions were low-cost and relatively non-coercive (e.g., public health advertising campaigns and labeling requirements), then, as Hill put it, the "standards before we convict" ought to be much lower.

This emphasizes that ultimately we care about interventions. Knowing that smoking causes lung cancer is interesting and useful, but we need to be able to predict the effect of potential anti-smoking programs on lung cancer rates and other negative outcomes. Many of the initial attempts to improve health based on the linkage between smoking and lung cancer were unsuccessful, and this continues to be the case for many contemporary interventions. In general, when subjected to randomized trials, it is difficult to find good evidence for successfully applying public health announcements, in-school interventions, and the like to reduce smoking. Although common sense indicates that the general air of social opprobrium that has descended on smoking over the past half century has likely led to a decline in the proportion of the population that smokes, it is hard to prove that some discrete public communications interventions accomplished much. What has been shown to be effective in many RFTs is nicotine replacement therapy: a chemical intervention combined with detailed health counseling.

In summary, then, the debate about the causal link between smoking and lung cancer was characterized even in 1964 by an enormously powerful "signal" of causal influence that is obvious in the simplest correlation analysis, and that was consistently demonstrated in dozens of independent analyses; an implausible mechanism for selection bias; a short, biological causal pathway; a rapidly escalating problem that was one of the leading causes of death in the society; and a proposed set of comparatively low-cost and minimally coercive interventions. Over the succeeding decades, testable chemical interventions, notably nicotine replacement therapies, were developed that could be shown in RFTs to reduce smoking rates, and a resulting reduction in mortality rates.

Many public health problems share some of these characteristics. But almost no social policy debates do. The underlying difference is the centrality of many human minds and wills in the causal pathway.

PART II

Social Science

If your experiment needs statistics, you ought to have done a better experiment.

—ERNEST RUTHERFORD

It is the mark of an educated man to look for precision in each class of things just so far as the nature of the subject admits.

—ARISTOTLE

CHAPTER 9

Nonexperimental Social Science

A Physicist, a Historian, and an Economist

Imagine that a hypothetical US president is considering his options vis-à-vis Iran's rapidly developing nuclear weapons program. First a science adviser enters the room and predicts that if the Iranians take a certain quantity of fissile material and compress it into a sphere of a particular size under specific conditions, then it will cause an explosion large enough to destroy a major city. Next a historian enters the room and predicts that if external attempts are made to thwart Iranian nuclear ambitions, then a popular uprising will ensue sooner or later, and force changes in governments until Iran has achieved nuclear capability.

The president would be incredibly irresponsible to begin debating nuclear physics with his science adviser, even if the president happened to have trained as a physicist. Conversely, the president would be incredibly irresponsible *not* to begin a debate with the historian. This likely would include having several historians present different perspectives, querying them on their logic and evidence, combining this with introspection about human motivations, considering prior life experience, consulting with non-historians who might have useful perspectives, and so on.

Next an economist walks into the room. She predicts a certain amount of change in Iranian employment if the CIA were to successfully execute a proposed Iranian currency-counterfeiting scheme designed to create additional inflation in Iran for the next five years. Is this more like the historian's prediction or the physicist's prediction?

Superficially she might sound a lot more like the physicist. She would use lots of empirical data, equations, and technical language. Some parts of the prediction would have some firm foundation, for example, a buildup of alternative production capacity at all known manufacturing plants based on measurement of physical capacity. But lots of things would arguably remain outside the grasp of formal models. How would consumer psychology in Iran respond to this change, and how would this then translate to overall demand changes? How would the economy respond to this problem over time by shifting resources to new sectors, and what innovations would this create? How would political reactions to inflation in Iran lead to foreign policy changes, provoking other countries to war and other decisions, which would in turn lead to economic changes within Iran? And so on, ad infinitum.

How would the economist respond if challenged with respect to the reliability of her prediction with such questions? As far as I can see, with recourse to three kinds of evidence: (1) a priori beliefs about human nature, and conclusions that are believed to be logically derivable from them, (2) analysis of historical data, which is to say, data-driven theory-building, and (3) a review of the track record of prior predictions made using the predictive rule in question.

The physicist's answer to challenges to the reliability of his prediction is simple: *Please view the following film taken from a long series of huge explosions that result when independent evaluators combine the materials I described in the manner I described.* Note that this prediction is not absolutely certain. It is *possible,* as per Hume, that the laws of physics will change one second from now, or that there is some unique, undiscovered physical anomaly in Iran such that these physical laws do not apply. But for all practical purposes, the president can take this predictive rule as a known fact.

The reason the physicist need concentrate only on controlled experiments is that these are accepted as the scientific gold standard for testing theories. Note that the first president faced with this kind of a briefing actually had an enormously expensive experiment conducted in Trinity, New Mexico, before using nuclear weapons.

The problem with the economist's reference to her version of (3) is that, in practice, so many things change in a macroeconomic event that it is not realistic to isolate the causal impact of any one factor. It is really more observational data, and to call some of these macro-events natural experiments is almost always to dress up rhetoric in analytical language. Even the definition of the event within the continuous flow of history embeds all kinds of assumptions.

In the end, sciences produce a body of engineering knowledge that lets us make practical predictions with tolerable reliability: an airplane of this design will fly; this vaccine will prevent smallpox; and so on. On the key issues about which we seek predictive guidance from economists it is possible to find highly credentialed economists who answer with great certainty, but it is just as easy to find equally credentialed economists who give the opposite answer with equal certainty. For example, if we proceed on roughly our current path of projected deficits, will we severely damage the economy? But if we spend a trillion dollars on stimulus in the face of the current economic slowdown, will that improve economic performance and grow employment significantly? Alternatively, if we cut the minimum wage, would that grow employment? And so on.

I've purposely picked three example questions that are asserted to be among the practical policy areas for which the economics profession has reached greatest consensus. N. Gregory Mankiw, a well-known professor of economics at Harvard and former chair of President George W. Bush's Council of Economic Advisors, has written some of the most influential economics textbooks in use today. In the fifth edition of *Essentials of Economics* (2008), Mankiw summarized fourteen findings that have achieved widespread acceptance among economists. Among them are:

Fiscal policy (e.g., tax cut and/or government expenditure increase) has a significant stimulative impact on a less than fully employed economy.

A large federal budget deficit has an adverse effect on the economy.
A minimum wage increases unemployment among young and un-
    skilled workers.

In fact, 10 to 20 percent of practicing economists disagree with each
of these assertions; but more fundamentally, even if we assume them to
be correct, they are too vague to really help settle policy arguments. In
the Introduction, I listed several Nobel Prize–winning economists who
in early 2009 presented opposing predictions for the net effects of the
proposed stimulus program, in part because they disagreed about the
magnitude of the stimulative effect of deficit spending. In the same year,
another very public debate occurred between James Buchanan (1986
Nobel Prize in economics), who endorsed the view that large projected
federal deficits would have an adverse effect on the economy, and Joseph
Stiglitz (2001 Nobel Prize in economics), who argued that the dangers
were overblown and that many of the likely effects would be salutary.
Also in 2009 a third debate arose, this time between Gary Becker (1992
Nobel Prize in economics), who argued that cutting the minimum wage
would increase employment, and Paul Krugman (2008 Nobel Prize in
economics), who argued it would not.

When it comes to deciding what policy actions to take, we should
listen carefully to economists and other social scientists, but we
should treat their assertions differently than we do scientific predictions. Their predictions should be subjected to useful cross-examina-
tion by laymen, weighing of technical and nontechnical opinions,
introspection concerning human motivation, and all the rest. Beyond
this, we should always keep in mind the unreliability of such predictions and treat the fog of uncertainty about the potential effects of
our actions as fundamental when considering what to do. I'm not arguing that social science is valueless—I would no more advise a president to make a major economic decision without professional
economic advice than I would suggest that he make a decision about
war and peace without consulting relevant historians—but I am arguing that we should be extremely humble about our ability to make

reliable, useful, and nonobvious predictions about the results of our policy interventions.

These limitations are inherent to the methodology of nonexperimental social science. Later I will discuss two examples of famous nonexperimental social science findings developed by excellent methodologists, to demonstrate how these limitations manifest themselves, and why analytical techniques that purport to address them typically are inadequate.

For this purpose, my use of the term "social science" will refer to the fields that primarily focus on interventions in human social organization—economics, political science, sociology, criminology, and the like—rather than individual psychology. Obviously, psychological theories and experiments often inform social interventions, but I will consider these as they do so, rather than attempting to venture into the vast field of psychology as a whole.

The subsequent chapters in this part of the book evaluate these problems in a wider range of relevant settings and try to show that they can be very partially ameliorated through increasing use of controlled experimentation. But although experiments can help and should be aggressively pursued, our scientific knowledge of any human social organization will remain extremely limited even when these experiments are deployed extensively.

Chapter 10 shows that businesses have experienced the same problems in developing nonexperimental knowledge as have more formal social sciences, because they face the same complexities. Chapter 11 reviews the extensive application of randomized trials in certain parts of the business world to build rules that predict human response to interventions. This shows both the material advantage created by experimentation, and also the limitations of this method for guiding action. Chapter 12 describes the experimental revolution currently burgeoning across numerous social science disciplines: criminology, social welfare, education, economics, and political science. These experimental methods and approaches will demonstrate striking parallels to those reviewed for therapeutic medicine and business. This common structure emerges from addressing common underlying problems, and allows certain process and structure recommendations for how to drive greater experimentation into social science. These experiences will also encourage humility about what social science is likely to accomplish.

The Development of Nonexperimental Quantitative Social Science

We have seen that as we shade from physics to biology to behavior, causal density rises, making the Problem of Induction ever more central to the challenge of developing scientific knowledge. This requires greater sophistication in designing and interpreting internally valid experiments that test, refine, and advance our understanding. Further, as interventions shade from those that can affect an isolated unit of analysis to those that operate in a social context—by example, from a polio vaccine shot to subsidized health care in Ghana—holistic integration becomes an ever more central issue, making both tactical and strategic generalization more difficult to achieve, even when they are based on internally valid experiments. These problems become exponentially more severe when we move to the kind of broad-based social and economic interventions social sciences tend to focus on—for example, whether the United States should spend a trillion dollars on a stimulus program, whether we should convert our system of public education to one in which parents can choose schools, or whether we should decriminalize certain drugs. The maze of causation is now far beyond anything that physicists or biologists typically have had to address.

Prior to the creation of modern social science, we simply had history, with its tradition of recording facts and making assertions based on these facts plus narrative appeals to commonly held understandings of human motivations and experiences. This was nonscientific, in that it did not make claims for the kinds of reliable, nonobvious, and useful predictive rules that characterize science. In the terms of this book, history is informed common sense. As science's prestige became pervasive among the educated populations of Europe and its satellites in the eighteenth century, numerous thinkers attempted to apply scientific methods to the study of human social behavior.

The French Enlightenment, in particular, was central to the creation of the modern social science ideology. Auguste Comte and Henri de Saint-Simon were explicit in arguing that the methods of natural science provided the model for developing predictive laws for human society. Comte argued that human understanding in various fields proceeded in three stages: theological, metaphysical, and finally, positive. Positive understanding is achieved when we can grasp valid causal relationships between phenomena. In modern language, we would say that knowledge proceeds from mythology to philosophy to science. Comte believed that humanity had achieved "positive" (i.e., scientific) understanding in various fields in the order of their complexity: mathematics, astronomy, physics, chemistry, biology, and finally sociology.

It was clear to the earliest social scientists that the natural sciences of their era (astronomy, chemistry, and physics) achieved spectacular success by discovering and stating physical laws as equations (e.g., Kepler's laws of planetary motion in astronomy, Boyle's Law in chemistry, and by far the most significant, Newton's laws of motion in physics). Even though the early social scientists could not achieve this level of success, they strove toward it as an ideal and believed that this is what social science would ultimately look like when it matured.

John Stuart Mill, who popularized this positivist idea in English translation, put forward a description of economic reasoning that remains an excellent description of the methods of economics (and more broadly, nonexperimental quantitative social science). He argued that despite the inability to conduct controlled experiments in social sciences, thinkers could reason from introspection to general predictive rules—saying that "observation of what passes in our own minds, warrants us in inferring" general rules.

In an argument somewhat akin to Sir Karl Popper's doctrine of falsification, Mill argued that one role of empirical observation is to "verify" a given causal rule by "by comparing, in the particular cases to which we have access, the results which it would have led us to predict, with the most trustworthy accounts we can obtain of those which have been actually realized." He believed that careful observers could identify the "disturbing causes" that created a discrepancy between the prediction of a rule and the actual event. For example, a social scientist might promulgate a predictive rule that a US president will fail to win reelection if the unemployment rate exceeds 10 percent. If, in a specific future election, a president were to win reelection with 11 percent unemployment, the social scientist might observe that there was a disturbing cause created by the fact that the nation was at war and the president was viewed as an indispensable leader.

But what if there are myriad "disturbing causes," many of which are as important as the cause of interest in determining the outcome of the situation? At a practical level, in an environment with high causal density, those invested in some theory will always be able to find a reason why it has failed. Conversely, we frequently will find that our predictive rules are consistent with some events for some period, but then find that the rules suddenly fail to work. This may be merely a philosophical problem for the rule that dropped coins fall, but is a very practical problem for predictive rules about human society. Controlled experiments are severe tests that can give us rational confidence about the reliability of predictive rules. As per an earlier hypothetical, if we have a rule that predicts U.S. presidential election winners as a function of a set of economic factors, seeing this rule pass three tests of predicting presidential elections doesn't provide the same confidence that we have identified a reliable relationship as if we had been able to construct parallel earths in which we varied only these economic factors, and observed this rule worked under that test.

The problem of how we can develop nonobvious, reliable predictive rules without controlled experiments has so far been deadly to Comte and Mill's dream of rational social science. To illustrate why, we must dive into the mechanics of nonexperimental social scientific analysis by reviewing in detail a couple of case studies that show the failure of the standard methods of quantitative social science to sufficiently account for the causal density and holistic integration of human society. I have purposely selected examples that should show nonexperimental methods in a positive light.

First, both asserted findings are nonobvious, but plausible. The first is that Republican presidents have tended to cause increases in income inequality, and the second is that legalized abortion in the 1970s reduced crime in the 1990s. My argument will not be that these claims are wrong—in fact, I believe quite strongly that at least post-1980 Republican policies likely have increased inequality, and am completely agnostic on the potential causal relationship between abortion and crime—but rather that the methods used to claim analytical demonstration of each causal relationship are not reliable.

Second, each of these should be a very high-quality analysis, and is accessible to evaluation at various levels of technical detail. Each is a recent finding that has been widely discussed in the public square; is supported by a critically acclaimed book written for nonspecialists; is backed by formal research by the author; and was produced by a social scientist widely considered to be among the best methodologists in his field.

In neither case do I argue that the analysis is not useful or interesting, just that it does not establish a causal relationship with sufficient certainty to be the basis for a rational prediction of the effect of a change in policy. Further, the criticism in each case is not of the social scientists, but of the tools that they employ.

Have Republican Presidents Caused Income Inequality?

The first example is a regression model presented by Princeton public policy professor Larry M. Bartels in his 2008 book, *Unequal Democracy*. The book received the Kammerer Award from the American Political Science Association (APSA) as the year's best political science publication in the field of US national policy. The citation for the award specifically calls out "the care taken in the analysis" and "the rigorous application of controls." Professor Bartels served as president of the APSA Political Methodology Section from 1993 to 1995.

The most widely discussed finding in the book was a regression analysis, based in part on an updated version of analysis from his 2004 academic paper, "Partisan Politics and the US Income Distribution," which reviews the changes in incomes for the rich versus the poor under Democratic versus Republican presidents from 1948 to 2005. Bartels asserts that the differences in the behavior of Republican versus Democratic presidents have been a leading cause of the rich gaining relative income versus the poor, saying these presidential differences were "the most important single influence on the changing US income distribution over the past half-century."

If true, this would be an amazing finding. Common sense tells us that lots of things should affect income inequality in the United States over decades: to name a few, decisions by the Congress, Supreme Court, and Federal Reserve; changes in international economic competition; technological developments that enhance some people over others; changes in immigration rates and sources; changes in social mores and beliefs; and being at war or peace.

Bartels obviously understands that the causal environment in this situation is complex, and he calls out two specific examples of causal density: "The price of oil and the increasing participation of women in the labor force are just two of a great many economic and social forces beyond the control of presidents that might be expected to affect the American economy and, perhaps patterns of income equality." And a few sentences later he makes the point that interaction effects are material: "However, because these long-term trends have been so glacial, and so intertwined, it is very difficult to discern their distinct effects on the shape of the income distribution." He then immediately follows this with an assertion that this isn't really such a big problem after all: "Fortunately, from the standpoint of *political* analysis, the very fact that these social and economic trends have been gradual and fairly steady implies that their effects are unlikely to be confounded with the effects of alterations in control of the White House." The obvious question is how we know the net causal effect of a great many intertwined social and economic forces has been gradual, fairly steady, and not confounded. This assumption is crucial, and we will see it reflected directly in his model.

Based on these assertions, Bartels builds a set of regression models that attempts to explain changes in income inequality in any given year as a function of six variables. One of these variables is last year's party of the president. The other five are meant to "hold all other factors equal," so as to be able to isolate the causal effect of presidential party on income inequality. Two of these five other variables are potential causal factors that Bartels has called out in the prior paragraph: last year's change in the price of oil, and last year's change in female labor force participation.

The remaining three variables in the model are not underlying causes. The fourth variable is last year's income growth at the 95th percentile (i.e., growth "trickles down"). But in his model, last year's income growth at the 95th percentile was driven by the causal factors, so this is in effect a "year 2 impact" of these causal factors. Finally, he understands that this short list of four factors cannot conceivably describe all of the "great many economic and social forces" that affect income distribution, so he says that "rather than attempting to pinpoint how these and other long-term trends have affected patterns of income growth, I simply allow for the possibility that the expected income growth rates have changed over time by including linear and quadratic trend terms in my analysis." In plain English, he adds two variables to his equations to fit his curves to the historical trend of the data, rather than to explain this historical trend as a function of underlying causes. One of these trend variables is the number of years since 1948 for each year, and the final variable in the model is the square of the number of years since 1948 for each year. And that's it. Bartels is claiming he has isolated the effect of presidential party on inequality with those six variables.

Consider a couple of the most important simplifying assumptions Bartels makes here.

First is the assumption that presidential actions affect income distributions for only one year (other than the simple trickle-down effect of growth in incomes at the 95th percentile on lower percentiles in subsequent years). There are plausible long-term causal mechanisms that could have almost no effect for years, but then have large effects only in much later periods—most obviously including appointments to the Supreme Court and Federal Reserve, but also including everything from negotiating hard-to-reverse treaties to subtle changes in attitudes created by the bully pulpit. Did Reagan's effects on the change in distribution of incomes in America really end in 1989?

Second is the assumption that out of all the potential confounding causes for inequality, only oil prices and female labor participation should be included in the model as specific causes, and that the model has captured *all* of the other possible causal factors through his "linear and quadratic trend terms." In effect, this implicitly assumes that there is some inherent underlying propensity for growth in inequality to accelerate over this period. But there is no "trend generator" out in the real world; there is just an extraordinarily complex set of causes that have combined in extraordinarily complex ways to create the factual pattern of change in income dispersion observable over the past sixty years.

Bartels argues that all of this is quibbling, because "the apparent effects of presidential partisanship are insensitive to a variety of alternative strategies for taking account of secular changes in the structure of the American economy and society."

But in fact, the relationship between presidential partisanship and income inequality is incredibly sensitive to plausible changes in assumptions. Consider the example of the one-year lag between a president's actions and effects on income inequality.

Using the raw Census data tables, I observed that income inequality does tend to rise under Republican presidents (lagged one year—e.g., Jimmy Carter gets credit for 1981) and fall under Democratic presidents (lagged one year). But when I did the simple test of changing the lag to two years, the entire apparent effect disappears: inequality moves about the same amount in an average year under a president of either party lagged by two years.

Bartels points out in footnote 7 of his research paper that "almost no partisan pattern was evident in the analysis using presidential partisanship lagged by two years." Given the commonsense observation that a president often has influence that extends more than eleven months beyond his last day in office, this is a central analytical issue that he needs to resolve; to do so, he cites two academic papers that he believes show his assumption is "consistent with macroeconomic evidence regarding the timing of economic responses to monetary and fiscal policy changes."

But first note that a president can affect a far broader range of policies than monetary and fiscal policy—for example, regulatory decisions, Supreme Court and Federal Reserve appointments, negotiating trade treaties, antitrust enforcement, seeking out or settling wars, etc.—that could have large long-run impacts on income dispersion that might become fully manifest only years after he leaves office. And also note that any given policy action may take far longer to affect income dispersion than it does to affect macroeconomic aggregates.

And these papers don't appear to claim a one-year rather than a two-year window for the impacts they do analyze. One paper estimates that (1) the peak impact of a tax shock on GDP should be reached by one *to two* years after the taxes change, and thereafter continue indefinitely; and (2) the peak impact of a spending shock should not be reached until *two to four* years after the spending change, and then continue indefinitely. The other paper estimates that numerous effects of monetary shocks extend for *two years or more*. And remember, these monetary shocks typically are the result of Federal Reserve actions, so this two-years-or-more window itself might not start until years after a president has left office and the Federal Reserve chairman he appointed takes some action.

Bartels goes on in footnote 7 to say of the zero-year and two-year lagged regressions that "the resulting regression models fit the data less well." But if the regression purports to isolate the causal impact of presidential partisanship, then its assumptions must be justified independently of fitting the data. To justify them because they fit the data is to assume the conclusion.

For this kind of a social reality, such model-tuning (for example, the one-year lag versus a two-year lag; including oil prices and female labor force participation versus the myriad other potential control variables;

using a linear plus quadratic trend terms versus searching for additional explicit control variables, etc.) is inevitable, because the complexity of the real world overwhelms the tool of regression analysis. If we could run an actual controlled experiment, we could test his theory, but in practice, we cannot; therefore, we have no scientific resolution to the question of the causal effects of Republican versus Democratic presidents on income inequality.

Did Legalized Abortion Cause a Reduction in Crime?

For the second example, consider *Freakonomics*, the massive 2005 best seller, and one of the most widely read economics books of modern times. The author (along with *New York Times* reporter Stephen Dubner) is Steven Levitt, a distinguished economics professor at the University of Chicago. Levitt was awarded the John Bates Clark Medal as the best American economist under forty.

Among the most widely discussed passages in *Freakonomics* was Levitt's assertion that a significant fraction of US crime reduction in the 1990s can be linked to changes set in motion by *Roe v. Wade* in 1973. The basic asserted causal mechanism is that the increase in abortions disproportionately eliminated potential future criminals. Note the striking parallel between this argument and the argument that increases in smoking began to cause the huge and sustained increase in lung cancer rates after a similar delay.

The intuitive notion that increasing the availability of abortion should reduce the proportion of unwanted children, and in turn create social benefits, was a controversial but widespread discussion point in the original public legalization debates of the 1960s and '70s. But the idea that one could trace this effect analytically, and that it accounted for as much as a *majority* of the early 1990s decline in crime, was extremely novel in the context of contemporary criminology debates. If accepted, it would revolutionize our understanding of a large swath of public policy.

A project to tease out the effect of abortion on crime suffers from the problems typical to such social science analysis. In this case, several fertility control technologies—most importantly the birth control pill—plus a huge variety of social trends that plausibly affect abortion rates and/or crime emerged in the same era as legalized abortion. The argument Levitt makes in his professional publications is that we can control for these other effects. But this is extremely difficult if these other effects became evident at the times, in the places, and for the population subgroups where abortion legalization had its first effects.

In the face of this complexity, the first argument offered for a causal link between abortion and crime in the relevant chapter of *Freakonomics* presents the results of a natural experiment: the five states that liberalized abortion laws prior to *Roe* (Levitt terms these "early legalizers") experienced a crime reduction prior to the nonrepeal states. The authors then buttress this conclusion by referencing other analyses that are simplified and popularized representations of pattern-finding techniques: one showing that the states with the highest abortion rates in the 1970s experienced the greatest crime drops in the 1990s, and a second showing that for states with high abortion rates, the entire decline in crime was among the post-*Roe* cohort. Finally, they note that Australia and Canada have seen similar results. The whole argument in the book is about four hundred words long.

The more serious justification for the causal linkage, naturally, is in the 2001 academic paper, "The Impact of Legalized Abortion on Crime" (hereafter, DL 2001), which provided the original basis for this claim. In this paper, we find Levitt and coauthor John Donohue III putting forward five separate arguments to support their thesis: the same natural experiment, three regression models, and the observation that the decline in crime at the national level started to take place just about fifteen to twenty years after *Roe*. The logic of the various regression analyses in the paper was (as with the Bartels analysis) to "hold all other factors equal" and isolate the causal change created by the change in the abortion rate. Most of the academic debate about this paper has revolved around the details of the regression analyses. I'll highlight a few of the most important points in what became a fairly standard battle of dueling regressions.

In response to the claimed linkage between abortion and crime, other academics published alternative versions of the same analysis, using slightly different assumptions, that did not show any such effect. Levitt and Donohue, of course, quickly replied by arguing that one should use their preferred specifications. Then two Federal Reserve economists published a crucial criticism in which they showed that the software implementation of the equations presented in DL 2001 had an important error and that once this was corrected and some other technical changes were made, the asserted effect of abortion on crime was no longer evident. Levitt and Donohue responded by agreeing that the error was made but that they could once again measure a smaller but significant impact of abortion on crime by correcting this error; doing the analysis with some further technical adjustments; and, most important, using a different data set massaged differently to reflect better how people moved among various states after having abortions—in their words, to replace "the crude abortion proxy used in our first paper" with a "a more thoughtful proxy."

The revealing observation is not that there was an analytical error in the paper (which almost certainly happens far more often than we like to think), but that once it was found and corrected, it was feasible to rejigger the regression analysis to get back to the original directional result through various defensible tweaks to assumptions. If one could rule out either the original assumptions or these new assumptions as unreasonable, that would be better news for the technique. Instead we have a recipe for irresolvable debate.

Other academics then attempted to replicate the same analysis for the effect of legalization of abortion in the United Kingdom. They also discovered that depending on the exact specification of data sets and assumptions made in the regression model, the effect on crime would sometimes appear, and sometimes not. The researchers were clear about this:

> Lastly, it must be noted that few of our results are robust to different specifications and samples. . . . The fragility of the results in this paper serve to emphasize the difficulty researchers have in identifying causal effects of social change such as abortion legalization on crime rates

some years hence, particularly given the myriad of other social changes occurring over the same time and which may dilute any effect.

Once again, regression analysis cannot tell us the effects of abortion on crime, because different reasonable assumptions for the analysis lead to completely different answers. In the next chapter, I'll dig deeper into the details of a regression analysis that I did to show why this problem is inherent to the method (and to the broader class of non-regression pattern-finding methods), when applied to comprehend human social behavior. There is no way out through cleverer analysis of this kind.

One way to get around all of this confusion would be to run an experiment. A purposeful experiment to force a random sample of states to implement abortion legalization has never happened in American history, and almost certainly never will. However, as mentioned earlier, both *Freakonomics* and DL 2001 evaluate the "natural experiment" that some states legalized abortion earlier than others (though it should be noted that DL 2001 was clear that this natural experiment was not dispositive).

The essence of this analysis was to show that crime rates tended to change at pretty close to the same rate in the early legalization states as a group as in the rest of the country when the purported causal effects of abortion on crime could not yet have appeared (1976–1985) but that starting around 1990, crime rates began to fall much more rapidly in the early legalization states than in the rest of the country.

Using national crime reports, I constructed a simple chart of the ratio of population-weighted violent crime rate in the early legalizers versus all other states through 1997, the last year analyzed in DL 2001. In years when this ratio is above 1, the early legalizers have a higher violent crime rate than the control group; when it is below 1, the reverse is true. See the first chart on p. 114.

Superficially, this appears fairly compelling: the early legalizers have a reasonably consistent violent crime rate relative to the rest of the country for more than twenty years, but then in about 1990, this rate begins to drop—just when the DL 2001 theory says it should. But the reason it is helpful in this natural experiment to have five states subjected to the

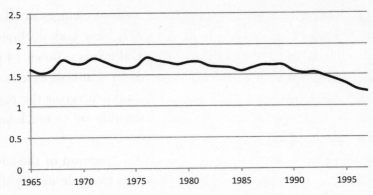

Relative Violent Crime Rates: Early Legalizers Versus Non–Early
Legalizers (1965–1997)

treatment, rather than one big state with the total population of all five,
is that we can see change in relative crime that came after abortion legalization in five settings (different laws, social settings, economic conditions, and so on), and that makes it less likely that we are seeing a
simple coincidence that crime happened to start to drop about twenty
years after abortion legalization for totally unrelated reasons.

If we plot the relative crime trend for each of the five states individually, then the picture becomes far less persuasive:

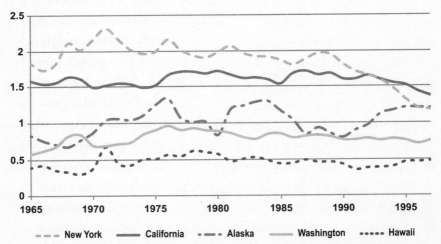

Relative Violent Crime Rates: Early Legalizers Versus Non–Early Legalizers (by
state) (1965–1997)

There appears to be almost a random scatter of changes in relative rates of violent crime between 1990 and 1997: New York declines 35 percent, while Alaska increases 50 percent; California is down 14 percent, and Hawaii is up 11 percent; Washington is almost exactly flat. The total rate across the early legalizers goes down versus the rest of the country only because New York and California are so much larger than the other three states.

The natural experiment cannot resolve the question of the causal impact of abortion on crime, either. What this example mostly illustrates are the problems with most natural experiments in the social sciences. These are several and severe.

First, causal density is very high, so sample size is critical, but many natural experiments have far too few data points. In fact, many of the most important questions (e.g., Should we execute a stimulus program?) can be executed only at the national level, so we have no control group at all unless we want to conduct cross-country analysis in which the differences between societies become so profound that control becomes impractical. Many other questions occur at the state level, or are done by a very small number of more local jurisdictions, so sample sizes are still very small, as in the abortion-crime example.

Second, a national society is holistically integrated; therefore, it is hard to get causal impermeability between the test and control groups. In the abortion-crime debate, for example, I indicated that a significant technical issue was how to account for the reality that people move between states. By illustration, the causal effects of abortion legalization in California in the early 1970s partially propagated to Washington, Arizona, and other states by the early 1990s as people moved. Approximate data exist on how many people of what ages moved between what states in what years, but we know neither whether within these groups people who moved had a greater or lesser inherent propensity to crime than those who did not, nor whether they were more or less influential in shaping attitudes and behaviors that affected the behavior of those who lived around them in their new state of residence. This problem of "causal pollution" becomes especially severe for evaluating long-term

effects, which of course is often what is most important to us in evaluating social interventions.

Third is the possibility of systematic, unobserved bias between the
individuals or places that are subject to the treatment in the natural experiment as compared to those that are not. Consider the abortion-
crime example. All kinds of plausible differences in political culture,
social evolution, rational expectation for future challenges, and so on
could vary between the early legalization states and the rest of the country. As one hypothetical illustration, it might be that those states that legalized abortion early did so because the structure of the relationship
between their state legislators and political interest groups tended to be
systematically different than those states that did not, and this difference
also caused criminal-justice behavior to change differently in these states
than in other states over the ensuing decades, thereby resulting in different crime rates. Even now, we have no idea to what degree such differences are the true causal drivers of any difference in outcome we see
for the early legalizers versus the rest of the country. This is the irreducible problem for any such social natural experiment that does not
use strict randomization for assignment to the test population, no matter how large the same size.

In short, the abortion-crime natural experiment combines all three
problems: small sample size, integrated complexity, and potential selection bias. It is an extremely unreliable guide to causality.

In *Freakonomics,* Levitt and Dubner write that *Roe* is "like the
proverbial butterfly that flaps its wings on one continent and eventually
creates a hurricane on another." But this simile cuts both ways. It is presumably meant to evoke the "butterfly effect": meteorologist Edward
Lorenz's famous description of a global climate system with such a
dense web of interconnected pathways of causation that long-term
weather forecasting is a fool's errand. The actual event that inspired this
observation was that, one day in 1961, Lorenz entered .506 instead of
.506127 for one parameter in a climate-forecasting model and discovered that it produced a wildly different long-term weather forecast. This
is, of course, directly analogous to what we see in the abortion-crime

debate and Bartels's model for income inequality: tiny changes in assumptions yield vastly different results. It is a telltale sign that human society is far too complicated to yield to the analytical tools that nonexperimental social science brings to bear. The questions addressed by social science typically have none of the characteristics that made causal attribution in the smoking–lung cancer case practical.

This shortcoming arises not because nonexperimental social science is somehow insufficiently tough-minded, but because the phenomenon of human social behavior is so complex. Businesses are notoriously practical and results-oriented, and have sunk vast resources into trying to develop useful, reliable predictions for behavior in the absence of experiments. In doing so, they have run into the same problems and hit the same dead ends. I know, because I spent years doing it.

CHAPTER 10

Business Strategy as Applied Social Science

Strategic Competition Versus Natural Competition

It is hard to exaggerate the strength of America's competitive position in the world economy in September 1945. The United States accounted for about one-half of all global manufacturing output, had the most technologically advanced economy in the world with ample supplies of natural resources, and could protect this state of affairs with an invincible military backed by a nuclear monopoly. Most of the rest of the world was either in ruins, preindustrial, or under the control of Communist regimes that smothered economic energies. The primary business challenge was to ramp up production rapidly and efficiently to meet demand. In the 1950s, the popular culture thought of American big business as so dominant that the primary public policy challenge was to restrict its power. But beneath the surface, the world was changing in ways that became obvious only later.

By the 1960s, global production capacity largely had been restored; by the 1970s, Europe and Japan had started to compete effectively again, and oil shocks battered the economies of the developed world. Large business saw cozy oligopolies under threat, and by the late 1970s, the dominant executive psychology moved from complacency to fear of new competitive challenges. Major companies were losing market share, facing pricing pressure from new lower-cost competitors, and being forced to confront new entrants with the ability to compete on product features and technological sophistication. From the perspective of these companies, it was as if a protected ecological niche suddenly had been invaded by all kinds of competitor species.

In 1963 Bruce Henderson, a farsighted purchasing executive who had recently lost his job at Westinghouse, convinced the Boston Safe Deposit & Trust Company to give him one room and a salary to form a consulting firm that within a couple of years was known as the Boston Consulting Group (BCG). He turned out to be one of the most original and influential business thinkers of the twentieth century.

The first major insight that put BCG on the map was the "experience curve": a quantified prediction rule that costs per unit tend to decline at a fixed rate as a company makes more and more of an item. By illustrative example, an auto manufacturer that had built 10,000 units of a specific type might observe that the 1,000th of these cars had cost $10,000 to manufacture, the 2,000th had cost $8,000, the 4,000th had cost $6,500, and the 8,000th had cost $5,100. Each cumulative doubling of production in this example reduces cost per unit by about 20 percent. (For some other company making toasters at a different factory, this unit cost reduction per doubling might be 10 percent or 30 percent or some other number, but the percentage is constant for any given process.) An experience curve of this type could allow the auto company to predict what cost per unit would be in the future, as a result of subsequent doublings. The company could know *today* what it would cost to produce the 100,000th car.

This would be a powerful scientific finding, in the sense of being a useful, reliable, and nonobvious predictive rule. In theory, the company could use this model to price cars at, say, $4,000 per unit now and lose money on the next few thousand, but seize market share from competitors who priced their cars with the aim of making money at current production costs. This would allow the company to race down the experience curve ahead of rivals, and therefore build an insurmountable cost advantage. It would be able to make money for a very long time by pricing above its own cost, but below the costs of competitors who got behind.

Does it work? Yes and no. The effect is real, and can be measured. It has been used to make correct, nonobvious predictions in many cases. One of the most famous is Texas Instruments, which used predictions of future cost reductions—which turned out to be accurate—to very aggressively price early electronic calculators in the 1970s, and rapidly grow sales and market share. On the other hand, as a basis for making strategic decisions, the experience curve is radically incomplete. For example, what if a competitor develops a new production technology that is vastly more efficient? Or what if a new kind of product is introduced that is superior in cost or functionality? Or what if other competitors have access to lower-cost capital? These and many other complexities make a linear application of the experience curve concept, in isolation from a more holistic understanding of a strategic situation, extremely hazardous. The Texas Instruments calculator business, in fact, imploded after several years of amazing growth when other competitors refused to play along.

Awareness of these kinds of complexities led BCG to try to incorporate more and more factors into various strategic frameworks. The most famous of these is the growth-share matrix, which attempts to allow a large, multidivisional corporation to use capital more effectively by categorizing its business units. For example, the framework argues that those units that generate more free cash flow than they can profitably invest back into their line of business ("cash cows") should provide cash to other parts of the business, and those that have opportunities to invest more cash than they can generate internally at returns above their cost of capital and into high potential market share positions that can exploit experience curve advantages ("stars") should use the excess cash the cash cows generate. Behind kindergarten-like imagery of cows and stars, this framework incorporates a sophisticated consideration of profits, capital structure, and market share. Yet even this is a gross simplification of real-world business competition.

How should such tools fit into business decision-making? Near the end of his professional life, Henderson wrote *The Logic of Business Strategy* (1984), a slim but profound book that summed up his deepest thoughts about this topic.

Henderson held a decidedly Darwinian view of business. He argued that for many generations humans have competed with one another as other biological organisms always have, a phenomenon he termed natural competition. In his view, businesses are simply vehicles for human competition in the form of extended networks of partial cooperation.

However, once humans evolved the specific capabilities of our species—imagination, logic, forethought, and the will to consciously commit resources today in return for future advantage—we could move beyond mere biological competition. Strategic competition, in which some competitors think through the chain of competitive responses and counterresponses that would result if they were to take various potential actions, allows them to choose actions to maximize their competitive success. Henderson argued that strategic competition offers immense time compression versus natural competition. In effect, by figuring out where natural competition is headed over many future trial-and-error steps, and jumping there in one big step, the strategic competitor compresses many evolutionary steps into one premeditated leap. The experience curve was, under this view, an early first step, and the growth-share matrix a second step, on the road to an ever more comprehensive model to predict the evolution of natural competition, and take advantage of it.

Henderson characterized natural competition as "evolutionary" and strategic competition as "revolutionary." His distinction between natural and strategic competition is, of course, an example of exploiting precisely the distinction between implicit and explicit knowledge, as defined earlier.

Careful premeditation is the key to making sure this isn't a potentially disastrous leap in the dark. As with all scientific knowledge, the key is to understand causal relationships well enough to create useful, nonobvious, and reliable predictive rules. Henderson was clear about this: "To accomplish this revolution, the preparation must be conservative, careful, precise, and all inclusive. . . . Meticulous staff work must be continued until cause and effect become sufficiently predictable to justify the massive commitment of non-recoverable resources."

His vision of what must be known to compete strategically was incredibly demanding. We don't just need to have partial or fragmentary predictive rules, but we need to understand the entire system in which we are competing, including the ability "to understand competitive interaction as a complete dynamic system that includes interaction of competitors, customers, money, people, and resources," and "to use this understanding to predict the consequences of a given intervention in that system and how that intervention will result in new patterns of stable dynamic equilibrium."

This is far beyond anything comprehended by experience curves and growth-share matrices. It would be extremely useful, but is anything like it possible in the real world? (It also raises the obvious question of why a society that had access to all of this would allow the messy and expensive process of market competition in the first place.) Henderson claimed we were getting close to this capability. Although strategy development was still embryonic, we had the promise of "precision, elegance, and power within a reasonable time period." He didn't define this time period, but he implied that this was something on the order of a generation or so.

We are more than twenty-five years on from this judgment, and I see no danger of our developing the kind of comprehensive knowledge that Henderson said true strategic competition required. In retrospect, his prediction seems hubristic to the point of outlandishness. Why has it proved so difficult?

Macro-Strategy Versus Micro-Strategy

I graduated from college the year Henderson published *The Logic of Business Strategy*, though I knew nothing about it and probably wouldn't have cared if someone had handed me a copy. I had studied science with the intention of becoming an academic in math and physics. As college progressed, however, I had become increasingly fascinated by applying mathematics to predict human behavior. After a year in a PhD program devoted to this topic, I decided that the academic life wasn't for me. Needing to pay the rent, I took a job at AT&T's research laboratories, and despite being in a technical organization, found myself drawn into business debates. I was shocked to discover that I found them fascinating, and so sought out a job in strategy consulting, which I understood in some vague way to specialize in analyzing these kinds of issues.

This was the late 1980s, and strategy consulting had already become an established industry dominated by BCG, Bain (a BCG spin-off), and McKinsey. There was also a well-worn career path: Ivy League degree, followed by two years as an analyst at a strategy consulting firm, followed by an MBA at Harvard, Stanford, or Wharton, and then a return to consulting as an associate, followed by about seven years of long hours to make partner. I fit almost none of that profile.

But a number of years earlier a young consultant at BCG, W. Walker Lewis, had left to create another spin-off strategy consulting firm, Strategic Planning Associates (SPA). The firm was founded with the specific purpose of using more analytically sophisticated and data-intensive computerized analysis than was then typical in the strategy consulting industry. Therefore, one of the senior partners was open to the idea of a person with a somewhat nontraditional, technical background like mine as an experiment.

I started work at SPA in 1987, at age twenty-three, and immediately loved it. It was as if someone had designed the perfect environment for me to pursue what had become my interests. It was far less theoretical than I thought academia to be, but focused on rigorously applying data and analysis to develop strategies to outsmart the accumulated intuitions and experience of huge companies. It played directly to all of my youthful ambitions and vanities.

My first assignment was as the junior member of a team charged with developing a strategy for the leading competitor in a mature industry that made commoditized glass-based products. I was tasked with modeling the economics for every production line in every factory in the United States for the whole industry. In effect, I built an actual, empirical version of the economist's famous supply curve for each product by combining physical principles of chemical engineering with painstakingly collected data about our client's and its competitors' facilities. This meant that we could determine, by product, the level at which each production line in the industry would maximize profits, and could predict the multiple-year effects on prices, and therefore profits, of potential investments in production capacity. Like a card counter in a casino, the client could use proprietary knowledge to take rational actions, while seeming to make the kind of risky bets that everybody else at the table had to make.

This specific situation was almost ideal for deploying Hendersonian strategy: our models were underwritten by physical science; there were only four relevant competitors; these competitors behaved according to similar rationales; technology change was slow; there were few relevant substitute products; and so forth. Therefore, we could use this knowledge to predict competitive response to our client's prospective actions. For a time it appeared that this client could turn dials in its own business and drive industry behavior so as to make an enormous amount of money. It was a heady experience.

But two problems subsequently emerged.

First, not everyone at the client agreed that the actions this strategy dictated were responsible for driving profit improvements. Evaluating competing claims for program effectiveness in a business usually is not simple, because we have no rigorous answer to the fundamental counterfactual question in all program evaluation: But for this action, what would performance have been? Suppose that over the three years after this client began implementing this strategy, annual profits went from $1 billion to $1.5 billion, but over that same period, the economy as a whole started to grow faster, one competitor exited a key market, a new technology from an adjacent industry began making significant inroads into this industry, and the client also replaced the head of sales and instituted a process improvement program in its factories. Which of these potential factors deserve how much, if any, of the credit for the profit improvement? Executives use experience, observation, and data to form intuitive judgments about this, and everybody has an obvious incentive to inflate his own contribution and to denigrate that of others.

As with evaluations of surgery versus evaluations of therapeutics, as a practical matter some programs have effects that are so obvious that this question becomes academic; in such instances, the informed judgment of an experienced professional can be reliable. A classic case is a cost reduction created by increased productivity in a factory with no reasonable prospect of a change in consumer perception. On the other hand, most business changes that affect consumer behavior, and therefore revenue, tend to be far more ambiguous. In the longer run, and from the perspective of the economy as a whole, some companies survive and grow, while others go bankrupt or are acquired. In this way, packages of such judgments, as embodied by entire firms, receive some form of feedback. But of course, this is just natural competition, or evolution, and as such does not allow us to know which specific decisions contributed to success or failure. It is pure implicit knowledge.

The second problem with our strategic plan was that after several years, changes in the competitive environment made the modeling clearly obsolete—much like what happened to Texas Instruments after executing an analogous strategy for its calculator product line based on the experience curve. Innovative technologies came on the market, and figuring out the best strategy in that new environment required forming judgments about how this technology might change over time, how consumer preferences would evolve, and so on. Further, a new competitor entered the market that was part of a larger, integrated enterprise, and was making decisions that violated the economic assumptions of our framework, because they apparently were less concerned with making money in this market than in serving some larger corporate objectives. They refused to play by the rules assumed in our model. But since even profitable investments in new-factory capacity take years to pay out, this meant that the early capacity investments might create less economic profits than we had originally expected.

These two problems—the inability to rigorously evaluate the effectiveness of strategies, and growing deviation between reality and the assumptions of the strategy within the time frame the strategy required to create economic profits—kept cropping up as I did more projects, even in the most successful strategy work. They were really manifestations of one underlying problem: the analytical model of the business was always incomplete. *The model is never the system.*

One reaction to this observation in the wider business community was strategic nihilism: the rejection of the idea that strategy was useful, and the belief that the whole strategy exercise was more or less a scam. In Henderson's terms, this is the argument that analytically derived strategic competition was impractical and that the route to success lay in superior execution of natural competition. This appeared in several guises. Interestingly, the theme that united all of them was that strategy ignored the "human element."

One major strand was that what really mattered was motivating and empowering the people who made up the organization. In other words, strategy is make-believe, and only execution is real. Tom Peters and Robert Waterman's epochal business best seller, *In Search of Excellence* (1982), was the founding text of what became a huge movement to empower employees. The emotional energy behind this movement was a cri de coeur of the middle manager: *I matter! I'm not just some piece on your chessboard.* Though it eventually descended into a kind of snake oil that verged on promising to undo the inexorable grinding away of stable, high-wage middle management jobs caused by globalization and the ceaseless advance of information technology, this critique was premised on a very real insight: one of the most severe blind spots of strategy as it was actually practiced was insufficient recognition of the importance of human agency and motivation.

The other major strand was less an organized movement than daily resistance by executives. Picture a been-there-done-that senior executive who refused to accept an analytically derived strategy because of some plausible objection that resisted quantification and analysis. This kind of objection was a practical version of the observation that the analytical models the strategists used were incomplete, and importantly, that there was no way to even scope the relative impact of many outside-of-the-model effects versus those the model considered. Typically the most compelling of these objections would be linked to arguments about human behavior: potential customer reactions to proposed strategies, potential competitive reactions that violate the assumptions of our economic framework, and potential creative technological or business process innovations.

A classic example for American consumer products companies was what we came to call "the Walmart bomb." A senior sales executive often would react to some strategy he didn't support—say, eliminating some products or changing prices—by saying something like, "Sure, that might make us an extra $20 million, but it will put the whole Walmart account at risk, and if we lose them, we go out of business." It's plausible, terrifying, and usually not analyzable. It makes business strategy inherently judgmental. Not coincidentally, like physicians arguing for control of treatment regimens, it retains power in the hands of the relevant executive. But also like those objections, it carries great intellectual weight.

Two alternatives to strategic nihilism were attempted by those who saw that the strategy models were incomplete but wanted to find a way to make strategy work. They went in basically opposite directions.

The first was to build ever more general frameworks that could incorporate things like technological change, human motivation, more complex analyses of competitive intent, and so on. Call this approach "going macro."

Though it continues to the present time, the macro approach probably reached its intellectual apogee with the publication of the massive tomes *Competitive Strategy* (1980) and *Competitive Advantage* (1985) by Harvard Business School professor Michael Porter. In them Porter lays out the most famous and influential of the strategic frameworks in his "five forces" model, which purports to identify the characteristics that make some industries more profitable than others. He combines this with his taxonomy of "generic strategies" to provide a framework to assist corporate executives in creating shareholder value through strategic decision-making.

Here is a standard graphical representation of the five forces model:

The Five Forces Model

This is obviously simplified; for example, each of these forces is further subdivided, and book chapters have been written about how to approach and analyze each. Nonetheless, this framework is really just a very detailed and intelligent list of issues, and words about how to think about them, logically grouped into categories, and then visually arranged into a semicircle. It is not a model in the sense of a definitive set of rules that makes falsifiable predictions in the way that the experience curve predicts the cost of the 100,000th car after we have produced only 10,000 of them.

Empirically, as such models or frameworks or whatever we want to call them become more general, they have always become nonfalsifiable methods for organizing our thoughts. This reflects our ignorance. In practice general frameworks like the five forces model serve as (1) a checklist to make sure we don't forget to consider various issues that experience has shown to be potentially important, and (2) narrative description of how to think about them, sometimes incorporating analytical tools such as the experience curve or growth-share matrix for subproblems, as a starting point for the real analytical and intuitive thought process we use to make judgments in an environment of high uncertainty. This is far from useless but is also pretty far from Henderson's vision of analytically derived strategy.

The second approach to reflecting the incompleteness of existing strategy models was to "go micro" by tackling somewhat more bounded problems. That is, rather than asking what tools would be required to do analytical strategy development, we instead ask what we could do with the analytical tools we could actually build.

This was mostly the route we took at SPA. We believed that *our* competitive advantage was skill in inventing and applying creative analytical approaches, so we looked for instances where this could create a lot of economic value. We attacked problems such as establishing where to invest in telecommunications networks, redesigning production processes for manufacturing companies, and matching financial assets and liabilities to increase shareholder value. The whole game was to operate at a more strategic level than either operational businesspeople or analytical technical specialists, but to not become so strategic that non-analyzable factors would overwhelm the benefits achieved through careful analysis and modeling.

A simplified example was an attempt to improve the economic performance of the glass-based products manufacturer that I referenced earlier. A mathematical method called a linear program (LP) was conventionally used to figure out what combination of products a factory should produce to make the most money. The reason a complex algorithm was useful was that the decision to make any one product on a given line at a given time would affect the economics of all the others (in the language of this book, a factory is holistically integrated). Technical specialists did this work, and it was difficult to create value here, as anybody could learn the math in school, buy commercial software, and apply the technique. It was already commoditized.

But we hypothesized that by adding specific kinds of warehouse space, we could permit new production possibilities in the factory that produced greater profitability. We next hypothesized that by going upstream from the factory, we could integrate decisions about raw materials purchasing that would drive further profit improvements in the factory by changing the trade-offs the LP faced. We iteratively conducted quick analysis to evaluate our hypotheses, improved our understanding, and ultimately built a sufficiently complete analytical model to change decisions for the whole chain from raw materials through manufacturing and on to the warehouses to increase total corporate profit. Like the earlier efforts to model and exploit the industry supply curve for the same company, this made them a lot of money for some period of time.

Guessing about these opportunities, understanding their economic leverage, and developing integrated decision models based on them was not yet standard practice; therefore, it could produce abnormal profits for our client and high wages for us. But because we insisted on creating analytical knowledge, it was not the inherently intuitive guru-like insight of macro-strategy. That meant that eventually it would become commoditized, which is precisely what happened in this case. Across the industrial economy, what were originally manufacturing optimization tools gradually were also used to routinize optimization of functions such as warehouses, raw materials purchasing, and so on. What was innovative yesterday becomes routine tomorrow. So, a successful career in micro-strategy meant constantly inventing new methods. As I'll review in the last part of this book, this is a good example of the overall process by which high-wage jobs are created and then destroyed in the information economy.

Just as we saw with nonexperimental scientific fields, such as parts of evolutionary biology or astrophysics, many of the most successful applications of micro-strategy were tightly linked to experimentally validated physical engineering principles. For example, a key step in improving the economics of the glass products manufacturer was the ability to find relationships between changes in raw materials and changes in yield (some of which previously had been tested in chemical engineering experiments). The manufacturing environment was simple enough that we could find robust, stable statistical relationships that would hold under any reasonable analytical assumptions. This is a simpler problem than smoking-lung cancer, and therefore not nearly as complex as abortion-crime.

I did a lot of this kind of work, but because of my background in predicting human behavior, I ended up trying to build models for pricing, product introductions, and other consumer-oriented decisions. I discovered that I could build analytically sophisticated theories all day long, but it was very difficult to know whether they were correct, because by making slightly different assumptions in the analysis, I could get very different answers for the best predicted course of action. Micro-scaling down from macro-strategy development didn't bound the problem enough to eliminate the same issues that had plagued the original strategists operating at a grander level, because the same root problem was still present: as long as we were trying to predict human behavior, the problem was too complicated for the analytical tools at hand.

I used detailed case studies to illustrate this for social science analyses, and I'll present a similar one that shows these problems for a kind of business analysis I did many times. Unlike the grand themes of politics and morality, this is a down-home example: trying to predict the effect of changing the name of a convenience store.

Will QwikMart Sell More If We Rename It FastMart?

I was once asked a seemingly simple question by a senior executive of a company that operated 10,000 convenience stores, of which 8,000 were named QwikMart, and 2,000 were named FastMart. (I will mostly use retailer examples to describe business analysis of human behavior, because they are so familiar to most readers; and, as in this case, I will anonymize all brands, data, and names to preserve confidentiality.) The executive observed that average annual revenue per store was $1 million in the QwikMart stores and $1.1 million in FastMart stores. She wanted to know whether the company would increase sales by changing the names of all the QwikMart stores to FastMart.

Her question was not easy to answer reliably. We quickly determined that a difference this large was extremely unlikely to have occurred randomly, but we obviously couldn't just assume that the name on the front of the store caused sales to be higher. So, the first logical question to ask was whether there were systematic differences between the QwikMart and FastMart stores other than brand name that might account for the difference in sales. The list of plausible candidate causal sales drivers that could vary on average between the QwikMart and Fast-Mart groups was very long, typically including, as a few practical examples: physical size of the store, how long the store had been open, number of people who lived near the store, average income of people who lived near the store, average number of children per family living near the store, number of nearby competitor locations by brand, relative quality of merchandise at each competitor store, number of parking places, traffic count on the road in front of the store, ease of access from the road, distance to nearest highway, visibility of store and signage, number and quality of other complementary nearby retailers, exact interior store layout, number of open hours per week, number of in-store employees, tenure and background of store manager and employees, mix of employees by skill level, match of employee demographics to customer demographics, amount of shelf space allocated to each department, number of individual products by department, exact position of each product on each shelf, total inventory on hand and inventory mix by department, number of stock-outs by department by day of week and time of day, number of checkout positions or cash registers, deployment of anti-theft technology, cleanliness of the store, quality and maintenance of interior lighting, presence of an ATM in the store, level of TV, radio, print, and other channel of advertising we had done for the market in which the store operated, level of competitive advertising in the same market by channel, relative quality of advertising copy we and competitors had executed for each market, and so on, in practical terms, ad infinitum. It is manifestly an environment of high causal density.

We could do our best, however, to hypothesize as many potential causal factors as we could bring to mind, and then, where practical, collect data on each of these factors for every store. The analytical task in front of us was to determine whether there was a residual difference in sales between the QwikMart and FastMart groups after "holding all other factors equal," then to assert that brand difference must have caused the residual sales difference. Note the parallel between this and the social science models from the last chapter. We would argue a single causal effect could be isolated if all other potential causes are held constant, by analyzing historical data, rather than actually running a field experiment. Henderson's dream of comprehending the entire causal system with sufficient precision to make the decision rationally would be achieved in this one little corner of the world.

As a starting point, one might collect data on, say, 1,000 factors thought to influence sales, then observe that larger stores tend to sell more than smaller stores—in fact, on average, each additional 1,000 square feet of store size is associated with an additional $40,000 in annual sales. (Note the careful and important hedging in the term "associated with," as opposed to "caused by.") We could use this to normalize the sales for each store to reflect its sales versus what would be expected based on its size, and then continue this kind of procedure for each of the factors on our list. We could declare that whatever difference in sales remains after we have adjusted for all factors other than brand is the difference in sales caused by brand. The standard method for doing these adjustments is to create a regression equation of the form:

$$\begin{aligned} \text{Annual Sales of a Store} = \ &\$40,000 \times \text{Store Size} \\ &+ \$20,000 \times \text{ATM in Store} \\ &\quad (1 \text{ if store has ATM, 0 if no ATM}) \\ \\ &+ \ldots \\ &+ \$50,000 \times \text{Store Brand} \\ &\quad (1 \text{ if store is FastMart, 0 if store is QwikMart}) \end{aligned}$$

This is the kind of equation you will see in countless business (and economics, political science, sociology, and other quantitative social science) journals. The conclusion is typically couched as "$50,000 is the estimated impact of store brand after controlling for other factors."

But if I apply the same critical lens to my own work that I applied to the Bartels and Levitt social science regressions, the problems with this assertion can be seen clearly.

First, remember that we can never know we have identified and collected data on all the potential causal drivers of sales. Therefore, we cannot eliminate error that arises because brand is a statistical proxy for a variable either we never considered or for which we could not get data. Adjusting for some but not all of the other potential control variables often does more harm than good in estimating the effect of one particular potential cause of interest, and there is no way to know which without knowing the true list of *all* variables that actually cause sales. This problem goes by many names. I'll refer to it as omitted variable bias.

Second, even among the variables for which we have collected valid data, causal density is higher than it might appear from even a very long list of potential causes of sales, because the various causes typically interact. For example, let's say that having an ATM in the store drives sales in large stores both because it draws incremental customers into the store and puts more money in the pocket of all customers who use it; but in small stores, on balance it reduces sales, because in addition to these effects it also creates so much crowding near the cash register that it discourages customers to an extent that more than outweighs its positive benefits. In other words, sometimes an ATM helps sales, and other times it hurts them. The jargon term for this is an interaction effect.

But in our regression equation, we can have only one coefficient for the variable "ATM in store," which must be either positive or negative. The standard remedy for this problem is to add interaction terms into the equation. We could replace the variable "ATM in store" with two variables: "ATM in store AND store is large" and "ATM in store AND store is small," and therefore create a separate estimate for each variable. Unfortunately, not only are there many such interactions, but also higher-order interaction effects in which interactions themselves interact. For example, an ATM may increase net sales in most large stores, but not in highway rest stops, which tend to be very crowded due to high traffic, and at which speed is more crucial than usual to the customers. So we would need to replace the interaction term "ATM in store AND store is large" with two terms: "ATM in store AND store is large AND store is in highway rest stop" and "ATM in store AND store is large AND store is not in highway rest stop." These interactions-with-interactions can expand indefinitely. In a complex system driven by human behavior, interaction effects are not peripheral issues, but usually are central to the phenomenon under consideration. One thousand potential causal variables could become 10,000 potential causal variables, and entirely overwhelm our dataset of 10,000 stores.

Third, the direction of causality between control variables and the outcome of interest is often unclear. For example, do increases in store size cause increases in sales? There are many intuitive reasons why making a store physically larger could do this: there is more space to display items better; more inventory can be kept in front of consumers; it allows for a more spacious and pleasant shopping experience; it might create more visibility from the street and entice more customers to stop; and so on. On the other hand, higher sales might have led management to expand stores incrementally over time as sales grew faster in them. A third possibility is that there are also lots of ways in which store size could simply be a proxy for other real causes of higher sales: markets in which we do more advertising and so have higher sales may tend to have cheaper land and thus have larger stores; highway rest stop locations are the highest sales stores, and the authority that manages these rest stops might mandate large stores, etc. That is, more size might cause more sales, more sales might cause more size, or some other factor may cause both. Most likely, of course, is that all three are going on at once. But when we "control for" any factor, we implicitly assume that it is a causal agent in a specific direction—that this variable causes the outcome (or at least that it proxies very well for causal agents).

In sum, in real business problems in which we attempt to construct a regression model from historical data to predict some aspect of human behavior, the combination of the three problems I've just described— omitted variable bias, prevalent high-order interaction effects, and variable intercorrelation—presents enormous practical obstacles. Many attempts have been made to circumvent these difficulties.

One is to force structure on the model based on beliefs about causality that are external to the model. As a simple practical example of this, unconstrained application of regression methods might result in a positive coefficient for average price; that is, an indication that higher prices cause higher sales. The model-builder might "know" that higher prices should, all else equal, cause lower sales, and therefore decide not to include this variable. (You might be surprised at how often this kind of thing happens.) But of course such approaches beg the question of how we know our beliefs about causality are correct.

Alternatively, numerous non-regression pattern finding methods have been developed to attempt to build models using different mathematical approaches to the same problem: how to predict the effect of changes in various potential causal factors of an outcome without making structural assumptions. I'll refer to regression and these other non-regression techniques collectively as pattern finding. There is always some hot new pattern-finding algorithm that promises to do this. Most of these approaches have arisen in the new computational environment of large datasets and cheap processing power, and are therefore termed machine learning or data mining techniques. Well-known examples include decision trees, case-based reasoning engines, neural networks, modern implementations of Bayesian statistics, clustering, and support vector machines, as well as various hybrids and extensions of these methods.

I have used such algorithms many times to analyze real business problems. Each tends to have specific application niches in which it demonstrates performance that is better than alternative methods (e.g., neural networks for rapid credit card fraud detection). But none of these can resolve the three core problems of omitted variable bias, interaction effects, and intercorrelation indicated in the example above, because these problems are not at root a result of some unique shortcoming of regression as a method, but are inherent to the phenomenon under study. In fact, though these problems are exacerbated by small samples of, say, thousands of data points, they still apply to the largest datasets. We could have 10 million individual customer records for a very large bank, rather than 10,000 stores, in our database, and though this might (or might not) partially ameliorate the problem of having enough data to specify a large number of interaction effects, it would do nothing about omitted variable bias, and often will not help much at all with the problem of intercorrelation.

A third approach is to add another kind of data: the dimension of time. We could look at data on some stores that have been rebranded from QwikMart to FastMart and see what happened.

The company had previously rebranded one hundred QwikMart stores FastMart, and we could treat this as a natural experiment. If we compared the change in sales in these stores after being rebranded versus before being rebranded, we would entirely eliminate the problem of how to control for differences other than brand between stores, because we would be comparing the same stores at different points in time. The trade-off would be the introduction of a new source of bias: that the rebranded stores might have experienced a change in sales even if we had not rebranded them. If annual sales are down $22,000 (or 2.2 percent) per store on average for these rebranded stores, it might be because the economy entered a major recession. As always, the analyst must answer the question of the counterfactual: But for the rebranding, what would sales have been?

Of course we have the balance of the 9,900 stores in the chain as a potential control group. If the rebranded stores had dropped 2.2 percent in sales, but the rest of the chain was down 3.2 percent, we might attribute the 1 percent difference to the rebranding. But what if all one hundred of the rebranded stores were in Chicago? Then it might seem more sensible to compare them only to other stores in Chicago, since the recession may have been more or less severe in Chicago than nationally. There may be all kinds of other causal changes over this period with disproportionate effects in Chicago versus the rest of the country. But all of the rebranded stores were QwikMart—so shouldn't we compare the change in performance of the rebranded stores to change in performance of only the other QwikMart stores, since various non-brand causal changes may have disproportionately affected QwikMart stores? Or should we compare them only to QwikMart stores in Chicago? Suppose the rebranded stores were larger, on average, than other stores. Should we compare the rebranded stores only to a similar size mix of QwikMart stores in Chicago? And so on. What, in other words, is the appropriate reference class for analysis of this list of one hundred rebranded stores?

The standard methods for addressing this question are to either (1) try to identify a specific subset of stores that are most like the rebranded stores, normally termed matching, or (2) use some pattern-finding method to predict the outcome of *change* in sales after purportedly controlling for all other factors (the typical regression version of such a pattern-finding model on changes is normally termed pooled regression). The first is much like the abortion-crime natural experiment, and the second is much like what Bartels and Levitt did with their regression models. Matching is the more conceptually straightforward, though both methods will have the same underlying weakness: we don't know what factors other than rebranding affected the rebranded store group differently than whatever control group we choose.

Suppose management selected these stores for rebranding because they knew a new competitor was entering this market, or because these stores looked the worst and were therefore believed to be likely to have rapidly deteriorating sales. An infinite number of possible reasons based on future expectations might have introduced significant bias in selecting the stores for rebranding versus the control group. Suppose each store manager had the right to decide whether his or her store was rebranded. All kinds of considerations might have played into, for example, the decision to repaint or the manager's performance in operating the store afterward. With any pattern-finding method, the number of unconsidered or incompletely considered potential sources of bias may be infinitely long.

This bias may be so large that rebranding cannot be considered the primary cause of the effect. In any natural experiment, the first step is to ascertain the bias in selecting the case group versus the control group. But this analysis can be misleading. To take an obvious example, what if an analyst wanted to study the effect of holding higher levels of inventory on later sales, and therefore looked at the natural experiment of the change in sales for stores that did major inventory buildups as compared to the other stores that did not do these buildups over the same time period? The problem, of course, is that inventory buildups or draw-downs are sometimes based on a manager's foreknowledge of local demand changes. Unfortunately, most bias issues inherent in studies of existing data aren't nearly so obvious.

Pooled regression (and similar methods) simply builds a regression equation in which the predicted outcome is "change in store sales" rather than store sales. The terms of the equation attempt to control for all possible causes of change other than rebranding. This is generally superior to building such a model simply on store sales, because the causes of variance *between stores* (e.g., the list of reasons a specific store in downtown Chicago has different sales than a specific store in rural Oregon) are generally far more significant than the causes of variance *within stores over time* (e.g., the list of reasons the change in sales from June to November in the downtown Chicago store is different than the change in sales from June to November in the rural Oregon store). But, as per the discussion of matching, unobserved reasons for exactly such biases in comparing changes within stores over time to changes within other stores over the same time period do exist are often subtle, and typically have larger causal impacts than the causal impact of the program of interest. The same classes of problems observed with straight regression are present with pooled regression, usually less severely, though unfortunately they are still plausibly severe enough to make the method unreliable.

How can we know that even the best of these methods is correct? Various measurements of statistical significance, confidence, and so on cannot tell us, because the open question is whether we have violated the assumptions that go into such models. Having many analysts look at the problem, and seeing whether we reach a consensus can't tell us, because if they are all missing relevant data—which in this kind of situation is always a realistic possibility—they will all reach the same faulty conclusion. For the same reasons, hiring new, smarter analysts, collecting more data, or applying new algorithmic methods cannot tell us whether we're right.

The only generally reliable way to test our theory is the approach that C. S. Peirce, Jerzy Neyman, and R. A. Fisher discovered many decades ago: roughly speaking, pick a random sample of QwikMart stores, rebrand them as FastMart, and compare what happens in them to a control group of stores that we do not rebrand. But of course, if we are going to rely on the experiment as the definitive measurement of the causal effect anyway, then why not just skip all of the analysis and run the experiment?

Well, for one thing, rebranding a test group of, say, fifty stores likely would cost on the order of $1 million. Although it's not free to do research and analysis, it's a lot cheaper than that, and I might find that such models improve my guesses about which theorized programs end up succeeding in experiments. For another, once I've completed the experiment, I will face the problem of how to generalize the results from the specific test stores to predict the effects of rebranding the other 7,950 QwikMarts. In other words, just as we saw with therapeutic RFTs, theory prioritizes some potential experiments over others as users of scarce resources, and also generalizes results from experiments to other untested entities.

A company can earn a lot of money by making experiments a central element of how it makes decisions—specifically as the preferred method for program evaluation. All else equal, an organization in a consumer-focused industry that does this will have a material competitive advantage over those that do not. But experiments must be integrated with other nonexperimental methods of analysis, as well as fully nonanalytical judgments, just as we saw for various scientific fields. I described the manner in which this is done in science as "philosophically unsatisfying," but as we'll see in the next chapter, the way it is accomplished in a real for-profit business makes that look like a discussion on the porch of Plato's Academy.

CHAPTER 11

The Experimental Revolution in Business

The Rise of the Experimentalists

As in medicine, people with business problems to solve have always experimented informally to try to understand what works and what doesn't. The first grain merchant in ancient Mesopotamia who sold in more than one location probably tried a new idea out in one shop before bringing it to another. The value a more rigorous approach creates is greater reliability and more precise results.

While medical scientists were applying R. A. Fisher's ideas from *Design of Experiments* to invent the modern RFT, businesses started deploying the same ideas to experiment formally with production. Fisher was trying to determine the effect of fertilizers on crop yields. This is much like determining the inputs, temperature settings, and so on that would maximize yield for a manufacturing process. From the 1940s onward, process engineers developed a sophisticated body of knowledge for using a series of experiments to do this.

Since Fisher, there have also been pockets of successful randomized experimentation in consumer-oriented business environments—for example, consumer goods companies running test markets for new products, or catalog companies running randomized tests of alternative catalog covers. The information technology revolution has allowed this same type of experimentation to be applied much more broadly, a movement that began about twenty years ago and continues to gather force today.

In retrospect, SPA turns out to have been a fertile environment for an assault from within on the reigning ideology of strategy. Because of the company's analytics-intensive approach, those of us who were addressing consumer-focused issues directly confronted the problem of the indeterminacy of pattern-finding methods in environments of very high causal density. We weren't snowed by the claims of those building the mathematical models, because we were doing the math ourselves. A few guys in the generation ahead of me at the firm figured out that experiments offered the opportunity for a revolutionary advance well before I did. One built an extremely successful consulting practice around the idea within the firm. But others left consulting and applied the concept more broadly.

I opened this book with the story of an SPA partner who asked me a version of the question that ended the last chapter: Why not just run an experiment? His name was Rich Fairbank. In 1988 he and another SPA consultant named Nigel Morris went on to start the credit card company Capital One. Fairbank and Morris believed that applying the experimental method to business could go way beyond the factory, and set out to prove it, breaking down the process of operating a credit card company into discrete steps, and using constant controlled experimentation to improve performance. Suppose, for example, marketers wanted to know whether a credit card solicitation would meet with greater success if it was mailed in a blue envelope or in a white one. Rather than debate the question, the company would simply mail, say, 50,000 randomly selected households the solicitation in a blue envelope and 50,000 randomly selected households the same solicitation in a white envelope, then measure the relative profitability of the resulting customer relationships from each group. Fairbank was clear about this in an interview years later. "When we started this company," he said, "we saw two revolutionary opportunities: We could use scientific methodology to help us make decisions, and we could use information technology to help us provide mass customization."

In 1988 this was a radical idea. Fairbank and Morris approached dozens of financial services institutions before they found a small regional bank that would back them. Credit card companies had done test launches for a long time, but the key insight was making relentless experimentation the core methodology for understanding consumer response, which directly contradicted the existing industry paradigm of focusing on pattern-finding models, and using testing as a secondary method.

The experimental method permeates Capital One to an extent never before seen. The company tests everything: product offers, the color of the envelopes the product offers are mailed in, procedural changes, employee selection, and so on. Testing is integrated with normal business operations in an automated or semi-automated way. Fairbank attributes Capital One's success to its "ability to turn a business into a scientific laboratory where every decision about product design, marketing, channels of communication, credit lines, customer selection, collection policies and cross-selling decisions could be subjected to systematic testing using thousands of experiments." That's not just rhetoric: by 2000, Capital One was reportedly running more than 60,000 tests per year; by 2011, it had gone in a period of twenty-five years from an idea in a conference room to a Fortune 500 company worth about $50 billion. Through competitive pressure and professional osmosis, Capital One has transformed not only the credit card industry, but also most financial services marketed through direct channels, to the point that sophisticated randomized experimentation is now standard for the direct marketing of everything from credit cards to checking accounts to insurance policies.

And nonfinancial companies have begun to exploit these ideas too. Gary Loveman, a former Harvard Business School academic, became CEO of Harrah's Entertainment and revolutionized the company by carefully analyzing data collected from millions of customers through Harrah's frequent flyer–like Total Rewards customer loyalty program, and testing various resulting hypotheses on how to better market to customers. For example, Harrah's might identify a large number of people

who live in Southern California and usually visit Las Vegas on week-
ends; mail a randomly selected group of them an attractive hotel offer
for a Tuesday night; then compare the response of that group (the test
group) with the response of the rest of the sample (the control group).
In 2003, Loveman described, in a manner that sounds more like Las
Vegas than Harvard, the centrality of the controlled experimental
method to decision-making at Harrah's: "It's like you don't harass
women, you don't steal and you've got to have a control group. This is
one of the things that you can lose your job for at Harrah's—not running a control group."

Internet commerce brings conducting and exploiting randomized
experiments to a whole new level beyond the original direct-mail and
telemarketing channels Capital One used. Executing a randomized experiment—say, to determine whether a pop-up ad should appear in the
upper-left or upper-right corner of a web page—is extremely efficient
on a modern e-commerce platform. The leaders in this sector, such as
Google, Amazon, and eBay, are inveterate experimenters. Google claims
to have run approximately 12,000 randomized experiments in 2009,
with about 10 percent of these leading to business changes. These days
experimentation is something one assumes from a successful online
commerce company or division.

From Capital One to Google, large groups of tens of thousands or
more customers can be economically tested, and the gleaned insights
applied to millions of customers. Of course, much of consumer-focused
economic activity takes place in environments where this is not practical. For example, even the large convenience store chain in the Qwik-
Mart/FastMart example had thousands of stores, and might run a
realistic experiment in a few dozen of them. The same holds true for a
network of bank branches, a hotel or restaurant chain, a consumer pack-
aged-goods company selling through retail chains, or a pharmaceutical,
chemical, or professional services company selling to corporate accounts
through a distribution channel of a few thousand salespeople.

I left consulting after about ten years, never having given up on the
dream of pattern finding as a way of unlocking value in consumer busi-

nesses. So, in 1999 I started a software company called Applied Predictive Technologies (APT). We flailed around for our first year or so, until an early client pulled us into analyzing some primitive experiments they had already executed. These initial results seemed promising, and other senior team members at APT could see the power of this technique, but I still wasn't sure. Within a couple of months, when we were running low on cash, a much larger prospective client invited us in to try to apply our still-nascent software tools to help design and evaluate various experiments.

We wrestled with some of the analytical problems the small sample size of these experiments created, and without realizing it reinvented some early techniques of stratification and related methods. This several-month period of experimental analysis was a conversion experience for me. We had simply cut the Gordian Knot of complexity inherent in pattern-finding analyses, and *knew* the effect of these business programs when tested. Generalizing these results to make decisions remained tricky, but—finally—I saw how to put some solid ground under my feet analytically for this kind of a problem.

We focused the bulk of our investment and efforts into this concept, and began to grow rapidly. We started to discover informal experimentation everywhere. Company after company was struggling with how to do experimentation correctly in such a complex environment, and we continued to develop ever more sophisticated methods for using tests to measure the causal relationship between business programs and financial outcomes. Over the next decade, other new and established organizations targeting this idea started to come out of the woodwork.

By 2011 Applied Predictive Technologies had become a fairly large software company providing the technology used to automate design and measurement of experiments for dozens of the world's largest corporations. For example, on the order of 30 to 40 percent of the largest retailers, hotel chains, restaurant chains, and retail banks in America are executing repeated standardized tests on this platform. Companies implementing this technology have consistently measured very large increases in profitability as compared to the profit created through alternative methods of making relevant decisions, and the capability is therefore now rapidly diffusing to new industries and geographies.

Modern experimentation in business has started to emerge roughly simultaneously from many sources—strategists, operational business-people formalizing what they have always done, technical analytical specialists evolving toward this approach, business school academics, etc.—because need and technological capability have aligned. Though individual companies will surely come and go, the experimental revolution is likely to become a permanent feature of the business landscape. This is just the newest patch of ground in the race to apply the randomized testing Fisher described to ever more interventions in complex systems. And this in itself is only one part of the experimental revolution that Francis Bacon began four centuries ago.

Once Applied Predictive Technologies began to focus on software for experiments, I started to read and research the issues involved in experimental analysis of interventions, at first frantically, and then systematically over about ten years. I iterated between our practical experiences trying to implement the approach and the rediscovery of historical academic and industrial research that had addressed what were really the same analytical issues. Very roughly speaking, I worked my way backward through the topics in Part I of this book: from detailed study of the technical methods of clinical trials, back through Fisher, Donald Campbell, and other social scientists, ultimately to the pure philosophy of science. Again and again I confronted the reality that in an environment I came to call causally dense, experiments were necessary but not sufficient for rapid progress.

The Need for Iterative Experimentation

The job of experimentation in business is to put rounds on target. Abstract discussion of causality is a means to the end of using prior experimental results to more accurately predict the shareholder value impacts of various alternative potential courses of action. But as we shade from physics to biology to behavior, ever higher causal densities make the use of experimentation for this purpose more complex. Moving from physics to therapeutic interventions entails randomized assignment to exert adequate experimental control in a way that is far less relevant to most physics experiments. Moving from biological interventions to behavioral interventions entails rigorous methods to generalize results of RFTs, which is typically a far less important problem for biological interventions.

The famous "jam experiment"—reported in an academic paper in 2000 by a team of researchers led by Columbia University professor Sheena Iyengar—illustrates the hazards of over-generalization. Roughly speaking, the experiment showed that presenting a smaller selection of jams to a set of consumers in a supermarket could stimulate more total sales of jam than showing them a larger selection. It has become part of American business lore as proof of the very general proposition that consumers are overwhelmed by too many choices. I've heard it described in many business meetings, and presented by speakers at several conferences. Iyengar has described frequently having people explain it to her without realizing she is the author, including the head of Fidelity Research, a McKinsey & Company executive, and random strangers on airplanes. Barry Schwartz, a professor of social theory at Swarthmore College, wrote the best-selling book *The Paradox of Choice* (2004), which explicitly argues that this experiment, plus another classroom experiment reported in the same paper, "provide the evidence" to disprove the claim that "added options can only make us better off as a society."

Detailed examination of the experiment shows that it is extremely dangerous to make such general claims based on what happened in one store with sales of jam. Here is how the researchers described the actual experiment:

Two research assistants, dressed as store employees, invited passing customers to "come try our Wilkin and Sons jams." Shoppers encountered one of two displays. On the table were either 6 (limited-choice condition) or 24 (extensive-choice condition) different jams. On each of two Saturdays, the displays were rotated hourly; the hours of the displays were counterbalanced across days to minimize any day or time-of-day effects.

Consumers were allowed to taste as many jams as they wished. All consumers who approached the table received a coupon for a $1 discount off the purchase of any Wilkin & Sons jam. Afterwards, any shoppers who wished to purchase the jam needed to go to the relevant jam shelf, select the jam of their choice, and then purchase the item at the store's main cash registers.

Across the ten-hour experimental period, 145 people stopped at the extensive assortment booth, and of these four bought jam with the coupon (a 3 percent response rate). Of the 104 people who stopped at the limited assortment booth, thirty-one bought jam with the coupon (a 30 percent response rate).

First, note that all of the inference is built on the purchase of a grand total of thirty-five jars of jam. Second, note that if the results of the jam experiment were valid and applicable with the kind of generality required to be relevant as the basis for economic or social policy, it would imply that many stores could eliminate 75 percent of their products and cause sales to increase by 900 percent. That would be a fairly astounding result—and indicates that there may be a problem with the measurement.

Measurement problems could easily arise because the experiment was done for a total of ten hours in only one store, and shoppers were grouped in hourly chunks. There could be all kinds of reasons that those people who happened to show up during the five hours of limited assortment could have systematically different propensity to respond to $1 off a specific line of jams than those who arrived in the other five-hour period: a soccer game finished at some specific time, and several of the parents who share similar propensities versus the average shopper came in nearly together; a bad traffic jam in one part of town with non-average propensity to respond to the coupon dissuaded several people from going to the store at one time versus another; etc. This is one reason retail experiments for such in-store promotional tactics are typically executed for twenty or thirty randomly assigned stores for a period of weeks.

But the result is at least interesting, and the best way to figure out whether it is valid and generalizable is replication. Over the past ten years, a number of such experiments have been done by academics to evaluate the asserted paradox of choice for product categories ranging from MP3 players to mutual funds. A meta-analysis of fifty such randomized experiments was published in 2010 by a team led by University of Basel research scientist Benjamin Scheibehenne. Across all of these experiments, the average effect of increasing choice on consumption or satisfaction was "virtually zero." Further, this meta-analysis showed that experiments that tested the effect of increasing choices on consumption quantity, rather than some measure of satisfaction, as the outcome showed that a greater selection tended to increase consumption. That is, reducing the selection of products in a store generally causes sales to go down, not up, by a factor of ten. This is consistent with the substantial majority of relevant commercial randomized experiments on this topic that I have observed.

This example highlights a couple of important methodological points about conducting and interpreting randomized tests in causally dense environments that will be relevant to a discussion of RFTs in social science.

First, individual experiments need to encompass as much variation in background conditions as is feasible. It is almost impossible to run an experiment in one store that can produce valid conclusions. Social science RFTs that are executed across several school districts, court systems, welfare offices, or whatever are a much more reliable guide to action than single-site experiments. Experiments also need to run long enough to encompass changing background conditions over time. The combination of more sites and more time creates many more observations, and therefore reliability.

Second, the ultimate test of the validity of causal conclusions derived from an experiment is the ability to predict the results of future tests. We need to build the kind of distribution of multiple experiments that were summarized for the impact of breadth of choice on sales and satisfaction in Scheibehenne's meta-analysis. Such a distribution allows us to measure the scope (if any) of reliable prediction based on some sequence of experiments. In the case of the jam experiment, the researchers in the original experiment themselves were careful about their explicit claims of generalizability, and significant effort has been devoted to the exact question of finding conditions under which choice overload occurs consistently, but popularizers telescoped the conclusions derived from one coupon-plus-display promotion in one store on two Saturdays, up through assertions about the impact of product selection for jam for this store, to the impact of product selection for jam for all grocery stores in America, to claims about the impact of product selection for all retail products of any kind in every store, ultimately to fairly grandiose claims about the benefits of choice to society. But as we saw, testing this kind of claim in fifty experiments in different situations throws a lot of cold water on the assertion. In retail experimentation that I have seen up close, small variations in the offer—for example, $1 off versus three-for-two; an offer valid for grape jam versus grape juice, etc.—can have an enormous influence on the causal effects of the program. This problem frequently arises when social scientists make claims for predictive rules for a broad range of situations based on even properly randomized experiments. Harvard psychology professor Steven Pinker put this memorably, if somewhat cheekily, when he wrote in 2008, "When psychologists say 'most people' they usually mean 'most of the two dozen sophomores who filled out a questionnaire for beer money.'"

As a practical business example, even a simplification of the causal mechanism that comprises a useful forward prediction rule is unlikely to be much like "Renaming QwikMart stores to FastMart will cause sales to rise," but will instead tend to be more like "Renaming QwikMart stores to FastMart in high-income neighborhoods on high-traffic roads will cause sales to rise, as long as the store is closed for painting for no more than two days." It is extremely unlikely that we would know all of the possible hidden conditionals before beginning testing, and be able to design and execute one test that discovers such a condition-laden rule. Instead we might run a simple first test that would estimate the average effect of rebranding the stores, and would also allow us to create further hypotheses for conditionals to this rule. A second round of tests can then be designed and executed to confirm or refute the expected average effect, test the hypotheses for conditionals developed in the first test, and develop yet more refined hypotheses. A third round of tests can then be designed and executed to test and refine knowledge developed in the first two rounds of tests, and develop more refined hypotheses for continued iterative testing. Purveyors of analytical prediction methods often claim that they will "shed light" on a situation, but learning through experiments in environments of such high causal density recognizes that the best we can do is to find our way through a dark room by bumping our shins on the furniture.

Further, these causal relationships themselves can frequently change. For example, we discover that a specific sales promotion drives a net gain in profit versus no promotion in a test, but next year when a huge number of changes occurs—our competitors have innovated with new promotions, the overall economy has deteriorated, consumer traffic has shifted somewhat from malls to strip centers, and so on—this rule no longer holds true. To extend the prior metaphor, we are finding our way through our dark room by bumping our shins into furniture, while unobserved gremlins keep moving the furniture around on us.

For these reasons, it is not enough to run an experiment, find a causal relationship, and assume that it is widely applicable. We must run tests and then measure the actual predictiveness of the rules developed from these tests in actual implementation.

In practice, this is often done crudely. A company may find that testing alternative prices within six months or less of rolling out the price change usually leads to good enough accuracy to correctly identify the winner, and implement this as a testing rule; it may determine that the most effective promotional tactics (e.g., 10 percent off versus $1 off) tend to be stable for years, and therefore it only needs to conduct intermittent testing to confirm that this has not changed. It may also determine that response to advertising copy is so fluid that building formal validity distributions through iterative tests and rollouts is essential.

We can use similar analysis to measure the relative accuracy of various experimental and nonexperimental methods for predicting the results of future structured tests of the effects of various business interventions. Such exercises consistently establish a hierarchy of reliability of methodologies for predictive business rules: straight pattern-finding for some outcome is the least reliable, pooled regression and other analogous pattern-finding analysis on changes in some outcome is the next worst, quasi-experiments are the next worst, and true randomized experiments are the most reliable. The performance of experts obviously varies widely, based on degree of expertise and topic, but a good rule of thumb is that competent experts are better than straight pattern-finding models, but not as good as randomized experiments. The randomized experiment is the scientific gold standard of certainty of predictive accuracy in business, just as it is in therapeutic medicine. If a program is practically testable and an experiment is cost-justified (i.e., if the expected value of the incremental information is worth the cost of the test), experimentation dominates all other methods of evaluation and prediction.

But of course, even if we accept that RFTs, when we can practically apply them, are an important part of how we learn about the success or failure of business programs, significant roles remain for other analytical methods.

Integrating Experimental and Nonexperimental Methods

Just as with therapeutics, one role for nonexperimental methods is as an alternative to RFTs when they are not practical. Some decisions seem as though testing would be applicable—large shareholder value is at stake through many repeatable decisions with profitability that depends upon consumer reaction—but lack some element required for testing.

Consider the problem of a retailer selecting new store locations. A key issue is predicting sales, and therefore returns to investment, at each proposed spot where we might build a new store. The problem with applying experimental methods here is that no real company would build a bunch of new stores in randomly selected locations. We are left with cross-sectional pattern-finding (or making strong a priori assumptions) to estimate this through what are called site selection models. Many retailers build site selection models that take an approach similar to the regression method described in the QwikMart/FastMart example: build an equation that purports to relate the various factors that describe each existing site to the total sales for that store, then apply this equation to each new potential new store location to estimate sales there.

As you might imagine, real estate professionals within the company often have their own opinions about the likelihood of success at various potential store locations. We can evaluate the relative accuracy of various approaches, including the approach of expert judgment. Across a large number of new stores, we can compare the predictions various methods make for store sales prior to constructing the stores to what the actual sales were for each store over the next several years. Such tests consistently show that carefully constructed site selection models can more reliably predict new store sales than a new real estate employee, but that such models very rarely are superior to an expert real estate representative working a familiar retail concept in a familiar market. The model's findings are obvious to such an expert (even if he does not always articulate them well), and his decision-making incorporates these as well as other factors that are not included in any such model for the reasons indicated earlier in the QwikMart/FastMart example.

This illustrates the weakness of nonexperimental methods. A retailer would rationally overrule a new employee with a regression model, but overrule a regression model with an expert. In domains for which we can do experiments, however, our higher degree of certainty leads us to overrule any expert with an experimental result—dropping balls off a tower allows us to overrule Aristotle.

It would be theoretically possible for a large retailer to devote almost all of its resources to ensuring that it has only the best available real estate experts in every market, to choose never to enter new markets, and to never change its retail offer substantially; it would therefore never have rational use for site selection analyses. But this would not typically be the way to make the most money, and in the more realistic situation in which such expertise is extremely imperfect for some markets at some times, a retailer would rationally rely on such models in some situations.

This example also motivates the definition of "nonobviousness" as I use it in this book. A predictive rule is nonobvious if it is not a belief held by the best relevant expert whose knowledge can be applied to the prediction at viable cost by the institution or paradigm within which that expert sits. Other institutions may have different definitions of expertise, which is to say, opinions about the world. Expertise is only defined within some institution or paradigm. How do we decide who is the true expert, if the rules of the game in one institution point to one expert and the rules of the game in another organization point to a different expert? Ultimately, this can only be resolved through paradigm competition.

A second role for nonexperimental methods is for preliminary program evaluation. A new product idea, for example, often will go through a series of gated tests of increasing severity and cost that proceed from traditional research to a full-scale RFT: first, informal discussion with peers; second, lab experiments that can range in realism from exposing the idea to consumers in a focus-group setting to giving consumers real money and presenting them with the proposed new product plus alternatives in a research setting, to performing a targeted trial launch of the product on a website; third, a very small-scale launch in a few stores to test for operational problems with product provisioning, display, and so on; and fourth, a full-blown randomized experiment in a large enough sample of stores to draw valid conclusions about the product's economic impact. Further, even after the RFT has been completed and the product is rolled out to the chain, a group of stores often is held out to create a valid counterfactual to correctly measure the product's impacts. In effect, we move from what we call an experiment in which, say, 5 percent of all stores are in the test group that gets the product and the balance provide a pool of control stores, to a randomized experiment in which

95 percent of stores have the product and the 5 percent "holdout" stores provide a control pool.

We can think of this sequence as roughly a funnel that winnows out unpromising ideas at minimum expense before deploying the expensive tool of an RFT as the definitive arbiter of effectiveness, followed by structured measurement of success in actual implementation (though it is rarely a pure linear progression, and there often are many iterations and back-and-forth between steps as ideas percolate and are evaluated). This was not developed based on the model of therapeutic trials but obviously is directly analogous to the phases of a modern clinical drug trial. Of course, there is always some possibility that an innovation that failed to pass an early gate would have turned out to be successful if it got as far as an RFT. Over time, choosing some "losing" innovations from earlier stages of the process and testing them in RFTs (like mutation in the factory genetic algorithm) can provide insight into how to best structure such a staged evaluation process for different kinds of business decisions.

A third role for nonexperimental methods is to develop hypotheses that can subsequently be rigorously tested. This is analogous to the inhalation-exhalation model of theory and experiment in science. This theory-building, in turn, occurs at three levels. First is analysis that develops new program ideas, though this role is more limited in practice than most model builders would like to believe. Within some tightly defined contexts—say, estimating how to allocate media spending across multiple geographies and media types (e.g., "How much of our ad budget should be spent on radio in Chicago and how much on TV in Los Angeles?")—pattern-finding analyses can build useful theories. In most contexts, however, coming up with new program ideas worth testing is predominantly a creative and experienced-based process. Second is what we could call predictive generalization, or generalization from specific experimental results to reliable forward prediction rules. This enables us to answer the question "What will happen if I execute the following program?" Iterative experimentation interspersed with theory-building that relies on nonexperimental methods is the best way to address this problem. Third is what we could call strategic generalization, or integrating a set of forward prediction rules with many other types of knowledge, analysis, and judgments to answer what is ultimately the only question that matters: "What should I do?"

Based on this discussion, we can state some general principles for integrating business experiments and nonexperimental methods. First, RFTs should be used to evaluate the effect of business programs whenever feasible. Second, we should expect to execute sequences of RFTs to partially specify the variety of circumstances in which a given program is likely to be more or less successful. Third, in cases for which randomized experiments are not feasible, other analytical methods should be used as long as (1) they have been reasonably validated for this purpose, and (2) they are superior not only to other available analytical approaches or to "no information," but also to the best practical expert whose knowledge can be applied to the problem at viable cost. Fourth, we should expect extensive back-and-forth between experiments and nonexperimental analysis.

As described in the next section, moving from predictive generalization to strategic generalization—answering "What should I do?"—can be supported by experimentation, but will always require not just integrating nonexperimental analysis, but also making judgments.

Experiments and Strategy

I was once in a meeting with a true business genius, a self-made billionaire who had a deep, intuitive understanding of the power of experiments. His company spent significant resources trying to create great store window displays that would attract consumers and increase sales, as conventional wisdom said they should. Experts carefully tested design after design, and in individual test review sessions over a period of years kept showing no significant causal effect of each new display design on sales. Senior marketing and merchandising executives met with the CEO to review these historical test results in toto. After presenting all of the experimental data, they concluded that the conventional wisdom was wrong—that window displays don't drive sales. Their recommended action was to reduce costs and effort in this area. This dramatically demonstrated the ability of experimentation to overturn conventional wisdom. The CEO's response was simple: "My conclusion is that your designers aren't very good." His solution was to increase effort in store display design, and to get new people to do it.

Just as with the test of free medical care in Ghana—where the directly analogous question of generalization arose as to whether the test proved that incremental medical care *in general* does not do much good, or that the medical care provided in *those specific clinics* did not do much good—the same test result can be used rationally to justify opposite actions. We must, at some level, embed the individual test result into some kind of a theory if we are to use it to guide action. In science, theory precedes experiment; in business, strategy precedes tactics.

Consider that when we ran the hypothetical experiment in which we changed the names of a random selection of QwikMart stores to FastMart, and then evaluated the change in these stores' performance versus that of a control group, we assumed implicitly that the change in performance in the rebranded stores did not affect other stores in the chain (as we often assume in a therapeutic trial that improvement or lack of it in patient X will not have any causal effect on patient Y). But surely some of the sales gain in the test stores represents sales to customers who otherwise would have shopped in other of our stores, and have simply moved their purchases to the newly rebranded stores. For a 1 percent sales lift in a convenience store chain, this effect very likely would be immaterially small, but for programs that have a large enough sales effect on a chain that has high enough market share, this can be a material issue. Or what if the program to be tested is a television ad, so that there is no way to isolate test and control stores within a single city?

A corporation is, to some degree, an environment of holistic integration, and a relevant question for any proposed experiment is whether we can divide the business into units of analysis (e.g., stores, customers, regions, etc.) that will allow a large enough count of elements to provide sufficient numbers of test and control units to permit statistically valid

conclusions, but still have reasonably causally impermeable barriers between each pair of elements. For example, when repainting convenience
stores, we can treat individual stores as our elements of analysis, but if we
are testing a TV ad, we need to treat the groups of stores within the various metropolitan-area markets as our elements of analysis. In the extreme, some "bet the company" decisions are so fundamental and
long-term that they cannot be tested because the program can be executed only on the business as a whole.

Further, even for experiments in which we can identify enough
causally isolated elements of analysis to allow for valid test design, it is
not practical to try arbitrarily chosen test after arbitrarily chosen test to
figure out what to do; testing opportunities are a finite resource, and a
company needs coherence to decide what to test, and to interpret the results of tests once they are completed. Tiffany's, for example, is very unlikely ever to test the idea of selling the *National Enquirer* at checkout,
as so many grocers do. In theory, they could run a long-term experiment to prove that this would destroy shareholder value, but this would
be a ridiculous use of funds.

We can't entirely plan the company's future, but if we can get an edge
by doing some planning for some decisions, we ought to take it. And
there will always be some kinds of decisions for which we cannot apply
experiments to evaluate the value of planning, because a corporation
represents an environment that is somewhat holistically integrated, in
addition to being causally dense. So, even if Henderson's and Porter's
vision of strategy development is unrealistic, the need to set general direction remains.

We may be aided by frameworks, supporting analysis, and experience in forming strategic judgments, but strategic thinking remains an
intuitive process, and therefore retains an element of mystery. As with
the 2009 stimulus package, even evaluating after the fact what strategic
decisions were successful is difficult. Business magazines lionize executives at successful companies and demonize those at failures, but there
is usually no reliable way to answer the counterfactual of what would
have happened had alternative strategic decisions been taken. Of course,

it is in some cases obvious that a strategy was either correct or mis-taken—as with Pasteur's anthrax vaccine, or with jumping out of an air-plane without a parachute—but these are the exception. In general, sorting out which strategic decisions are correct or incorrect is an evo-lutionary process of corporate survival versus failure. As always, one major difference between evolution and experimentation is that in an evolutionary process we don't know what causes survival or failure—the corporate entities that maintain failure-inducing approaches simply tend to die out over time.

Corporate strategies play roughly the role for business experiments that paradigms do for scientific experiments. At the highest level, a styl-ized overall strategy might be: "We will be the grocer with the best mer-chandise and service." This might lead, as in our upside-down tree of scientific knowledge, to a set of department-level strategies that are sup-porting tactics at the corporate level, such as "We will have a greater fraction of organic produce than Walmart" and "We will invest more in employee training than any other company in our industry." This should, in theory, lead down through a set of partially interlocking branches to purely tactical leaves, such as "Place the following sign in the window of this store today."

Within this context, experiments do three things.

First, in a perfectly aligned organization, experiments allow better precision around tactical implementation of the strategy. This is the most obvious use of experiments and typically adds very large incre-mental profits.

Second, experiments provide feedback on the strategy's actual per-formance at various levels. Much like a paradigm, the strategy morphs and responds to evidence—even to sustained apparent experimental dis-confirmation. A strategy is abandoned only in response to a truly dev-astating series of experiments, and in the presence of a better alternative. Like a paradigm shift, this change in viewpoint is usually stimulated by an insurmountable practical crisis, and effected by a change in executive leadership. Whenever possible, the paradigm shift–like change in strat-egy is contained at the lowest possible level of the strategic hierarchy (e.g., "You need to hire different designers" as opposed to "Displays don't matter"). That said, just as in science, serious engagement with the feedback loop of experimental evidence drives much more rapid strategic advance than any other systematic alternative.

The third use of experiments arises because no corporation ever has perfect alignment. It is a category error to anthropomorphize a corporation; it is an alliance of individuals, and there are always competing theories, power centers, and knowledge silos within any firm. Various organizational entities and individuals within them are jockeying for control and advocating competing strategies. In such an environment, experiments down in the organization often provide surprising insights that never would have been discovered had all experiments been driven rigorously from a preexisting strategic framework. These often are the most valuable experimental results to an organization that is open to learning. At a higher level of abstraction, the firm as a whole is competing with other firms with different strategic beliefs in an evolutionary environment. Rational leaders recognize that this should imply constant doubt about their whole strategy, and the best organizations draw the implication that even the highest-level strategic bets should be hedged by encouraging (openly or tacitly) some amount of off-strategy experimentation.

The experimental revolution when applied to business creates a different and more limited paradigm for developing and using strategy than the Henderson/Porter concept of strategic planning, without going all the way to strategic nihilism. The cartoon version of a Henderson/Porter process is an annual strategic plan of Victorian-novel length, which is then executed and revised at some long interval. These thinkers weren't born stupid, and they rejected this kind of a caricature even at the time. The real version of the Henderson/Porter idea of strategy, however, does aim to comprehend an environment rationally and comprehensively to determine a longer-term course of action that anticipates and exploits multiple steps of a projected competitive process. In contrast to this vision, a strategy paradigm that proceeds from premises of epistemic humility calls for relatively lightweight theorizing and outright guesses about localized and fragmentary parts of the environment, but subjects them to rigorous measurement and feedback. The goal is to make the learning loop faster and more effective than that of competitors, so as to achieve Henderson's goal of time compression, but to do this mostly by going through more or less the same evolutionary stages as competitors faster and cheaper, because it is done in a "live laboratory." Only in cases where big decisions cannot be broken into smaller testable steps should, reluctantly, something like the Henderson/Porter process be applied. Further, these big bets that require irrevocably committing a significant fraction of the firm's resources should be hedged as much as is practicable. But perceiving and seizing those rare moments when daring should overcome caution remains at present an art, not a science.

A Culture of Useful Experimentation

I have observed the results of thousands of business experiments. The two most important substantive observations across them are stark. First, innovative ideas rarely work. Second, those that do work typically create improvements that are small compared to the size of the strategic issues they are intended to address, or as compared to the size of the dreams of those who invent them.

When a new business program is proposed, it typically fails to increase shareholder value versus the previous best alternative—the new "buy two get one free" promotion does not generate more profit than the incumbent "buy one get one free" promotion; the new sales associate training program does not create enough incremental sales gain versus the existing one to justify the incremental costs; the new shelf layout does not cause gross margin to rise.

The professionals who devise these programs believe strongly in them, and often various analyses will "prove" the programs will generate large profit improvements. Through a process of developing and analyzing the proposals, organizations become de facto committed to them (the most reliable motivator of human behavior in an organizational setting is avoiding embarrassment). But if every company in America had achieved a tiny fraction of the financial benefits such analyses "proved" would be created, the average Fortune 500 company would be worth a trillion dollars.

This is very similar to the results achieved in clinical drug trials. Only about one-fourth of the drugs that enter clinical trials—each of which is the product of extensive preparatory work, and many of which are simple extensions of previously proven molecular entities—are approved for use. And of the successful drugs, only a tiny number are so-called blockbusters.

This sobering news often frustrates many organizations, at least at first. In retrospect, it should be somewhat intuitive. Current business practices are the product of a poorly understood evolutionary process, which makes it hard to reason out how to improve current practices and tends to shroud in mystery any approach to coming up with new ideas. The lack of a feedback loop makes improvement in this process extremely difficult. Only by becoming serious about measuring success and failure can more rapid progress be made. I have consistently observed several process commonalities among organizations that can do this.

First, the sine qua non is executive commitment. The person or small group with ultimate operational responsibility for shareholder-value creation, typically the CEO or president, must legitimately desire reliable analytical knowledge of the business. This implies several crucial recognitions: that intuition and experience are not sufficient to make all decisions in a way that maximizes shareholder value; that nonexperimental methods are not up to determining causality with sufficient reliability to guide many actions; and that experiments can be applied in practice to enough business issues to justify the costs of the capability.

Second, the foxes have to be kept out of the henhouse. Debates about business programs can affect careers, prestige, and personal wealth. They become pretty rough-and-tumble, and most analysis is deployed within these debates as rhetoric. A distinct organizational entity, normally quite small, must be created to design experiments, and then provide their canonical interpretation. It must have analytical depth, a professional culture built around experimental learning, and an appropriate scope of interest that cuts across the various departments that will have programs subject to testing. It should have no incentives other than scorekeeping; therefore, it should never develop program ideas or ever be a decision-making body. The balance that must be struck, however, is that it should remain closely enough connected to the operational business that it does not become academic. This requires, at least at first, an articulate, politically savvy and analytically inclined leader of the testing function the senior executive team sponsors.

Third, a repeatable process must be put in place to institutionalize experimentation as a part of how the business makes decisions. This lowers the internal transaction costs per test, ensures that learning is retained, and maximizes the chances of the experimental regime outlasting individual sponsors and team leaders. The reason for the low per-test cost is that most new programs don't work, and as we've seen, once a competent experimental capability is developed, generalization is the central problem of converting experimental results to useful forward predictions, and therefore confirming or refining the applicability of test results usually is required. The orientation should not be toward big, onetime "moon shot" tests, but instead toward many fast, cheap tests in rapid succession whenever feasible. This almost always means integration with operational systems so that the company both exploits data that are being collected anyway and executes tests through existing human and information technology systems. This creates two important ancillary benefits: (1) it makes blinding participants in experiments easier, and (2) it improves fidelity between the test and implementation environments, therefore minimizing the problem of inflated impact estimates from tests that end up not being realized because implementation doesn't include specialized, enthusiastic staff and other resources present in the test. It also typically requires automation of the analytical tasks of test design and measurement.

All three of these essential conditions—senior political sponsorship, creation of an independent testing function led by an evangelical leadership, and routinization of the testing process—describe the rise of the therapeutic RFT. In a later chapter, we will see that these also describe the situations in which RFTs have been most effective in improving social policy.

This template sounds simple but is hard to implement. Like physicians, business professionals often resist constraints on their autonomy, and no matter what they say, often also resist being held accountable for results. Corporate staff members constantly make arguments that are perfectly analogous to those from physicians for why RFTs do not apply to them, do not apply right now, or do not apply in this case. This is a product of human nature, and therefore the tension is eternal. Tactical testing processes and technology are crucial in making sure the resulting constant probing to find weaknesses in experiments does not find problems with internal validity, so the debate becomes about external validity—that is, about generalization and strategy.

Credibility is built by a track record of useful nonobvious predictions generalized in an intuitive manner from discrete experiments to specific decisions that then measurably make money. Organizations end the debates about the utility of experimentation not by theoretical discussion, but by repeatedly doing such things as testing three alternative back-to-school promotions in May, finding a nonintuitive winner of this horse race, and then driving several million dollars of measurable incremental profit in August and September versus what they would have done without the test result. That is, experiments are justified not by discourse, but by works.

Over time executives and line managers begin to accept that this is not more "analysis as rhetoric," but really can help with such tactical decisions. Demand for experiments rises to the point that part of the management process becomes allocating available test slots. Imperceptibly, incorporating experimental results into strategic thinking simply becomes assumed and seems natural. True institutionalization is achieved when, like arithmetic, the experimental method is no longer seen as innovative or interesting, but simply as part of the firm's mental environment.

The parallels between randomized experimentation for business and therapeutics, especially therapies operating in causally dense environments, are obvious. In both cases, randomized experiments represent the best possible evidence of causality. In both cases, RFTs must be integrated with nonexperimental methods that include replication, non-experimental analysis, and intuitive judgment for various purposes including up-front theory-building, predictive generalization, and strategic generalization. In both cases they face resistance based on a similar combination of parochial interests and intellectually valid concerns around generalization. And finally, in both cases a similar set of organizational, process, and cultural tools is useful for addressing this resistance, including: separation of theory-builders and theory-testers; semiautomation of tests; integration with operational systems to allow rapid replication and near-replication of important experiments; and habituating power-holding decision-makers to demanding experimental evidence whenever appropriate.

In formal social science, we see exactly these dynamics repeated. Certain areas of social science and related areas of social policy have made partial progress in embracing the experimental revolution. They have had the same essential arguments and put in place the same kinds of mechanisms for managing and exploiting experiments.

CHAPTER 12

Experimental Social Science

The Development of Experimental Social Science

Almost as soon as I saw the power of experiments in business, I realized that the path from a test result to a business decision would not be a straight line. And as I tried to understand the topic, I kept uncovering academic studies that had carefully considered these issues decades ago. I became a student of experimental social science to make more money, and ended up being amazed and inspired by what the discipline had accomplished.

There was a flowering of large-scale randomized social experiments in the English-speaking world, and especially in the United States, from the late 1960s through the early 1980s. These RFTs typically attempted to evaluate entirely new programs or large-scale changes to existing government programs, and considered such topics as income maintenance (aka the "negative income tax"), employment programs, interventions to support prison inmates, housing allowances, and health insurance changes. Wide-ranging formal analysis of nonexperimental alternatives to social experiments has demonstrated the same result we observed in both business and therapeutic trials: as compared with experimental measurement of effects, nonexperimental methods introduce unpredictable bias that often is as significant as the effect itself. And any such analyses are a snapshot that grossly understates the real difference:

without the feedback loop of experiments, understanding tends to stagnate, while experimentation tends to drive at least some progressive learning. Therefore, in general, other means of testing theories cannot replace experiments.

In at least some limited fashion, then, controlled experiments can be applied in social science and can produce better tests of theories than nonexperimental methods. So, why did these large-scale social experiments fall out of favor a quarter century ago? First, just as with therapeutics or business program tests, most new ideas fail to show improvement when they are measured rigorously, and when they do, the improvement tends to be small. This is not a method designed to win favor with many political sponsors. Second, when the Reagan administration came to power, social-program budget cuts disproportionately affected research budgets. Combined with the (not wholly unfounded) belief by Reagan-era policy makers that social science practitioners were part of "the other side," these cuts reduced the federal government's interest in funding experiments. Third, it became obvious to sophisticated experimentalists that the idea that we could settle huge policy debates "once and for all" with a sufficiently robust experiment was naive.

In the long term, this third effect was the most important. Though social scientists sometimes look upon the era of large-scale social experimentation from the late 1960s to the early 1980s as a golden age, this is pure nostalgia. What really happened was that unrealistic expectations about our ability to develop unconditional evaluations of programs were dashed. It has become clear that the problem is more complex. We need to find an array of causal rules for the effect of programs that are localized in many ways—for particular implementations, in particular social contexts, for particular kinds of recipients, at particular times, and so forth. It is more the estimation through many iterative experiments of an always-evolving set of conditional rules for program success than it is the social-program analog of testing a polio vaccine.

The academic methodology debates that emerged during this period were highly instructive. Robert J. LaLonde's extremely influential

1986 journal article, "Evaluating the Econometric Evaluations of Training Programs with Experimental Data," generated econometric estimates (i.e., estimates developed using regression and other pattern-finding methods) for the effects of job training programs that had been the subject of RFTs. The econometric estimates varied widely and unpredictably from the experimental estimates. Similar comparisons of experimental and econometric and estimates for various policy interventions, both at that time and since, have also found this same basic result.

So far, so good. But these arguments stimulated a brilliant set of rejoinders from James Heckman, a Nobel Prize–winning economist at the University of Chicago. Heckman had been deeply involved in the econometric evaluation of social programs. In the course of this work he had invented the "Heckman correction," a nonexperimental mathematical technique to ameliorate exactly the kind of selection bias problems that motivate the use of randomization in the first place.

Heckman responded to these arguments in favor of experiments in two ways. First, he and his coauthors reanalyzed the data LaLonde and other critics had used, and argued that better econometric analysis would have eliminated the bulk of the variation in the estimates and would therefore have produced very similar estimates to the experimental results. Second, in 1991 Heckman produced "Randomization and Social Policy Evaluation," an article that after twenty years remains unsurpassed in its clarity and rigor in describing the limitations of the naive use of RFTs to measure—and more important, predict—program effects.

His reanalysis demonstrates that it is possible to define a logically defensible set of analytical procedures that approximately reproduce the impact estimates derived from prior experiments. This line of analysis has continued sporadically since, by both Heckman and others. But even accepting the result that it is possible to reanalyze data in a way that would replicate experimental results, this leaves unresolved whether a defined set of econometric procedures can be specified *before* a series of experiments, and subsequently produce the same effect estimates as *future* RFTs (or at least RFTs for which no information on results was available when the procedure was specified).

The scientific method, as Popper emphasized decades ago, segregates individual theories from individual experiments. At some point we must lock down a definitive mechanism (ranging from a complex set of procedures executed by a community of experts to an automated software algorithm) that we claim has some predictive capability, then subject it to a test. If our mechanism fails some test, we may use that information to change it to some new mechanism that can subsequently be tested. But claiming that this fixed mechanism "would have passed this test if only the following changes had been done" does not count as verification—we have to show that this new mechanism actually passes future tests.

The more rigorous the tests, the more weight we place on them. In science, these tests ideally are controlled experiments. Randomization, as covered in great detail in earlier chapters, is simply the means of achieving control in a causally dense environment. We should be open to the possibility that we can specify such non-RFT procedures that are useful for some cases—such is certainly the case in business program evaluation. This likely would represent a very fruitful research program in the more formal social sciences.

In his 1991 article, Heckman raises a number of objections to RFTs. One major theme is that all they can tell us is the average effect of the tested program on some measured outcome for one test group versus one control group. Heckman argues that in the absence of either econometric analysis or a priori theory, an RFT cannot explain why the program works better for some kinds of individuals or other experimental units than others, decompose the effectiveness of various stages or components of the program, or allow us to know how the program will perform for any population other than the one already tested. A second major theme is what Heckman calls randomization bias, or the point that those people, government agencies, or other participants who agree to enter into a randomized experiment may differ systematically, and in unknowable ways, from those who refuse.

All of the critiques are accurate, and are examples of the overall problem of generalization. Further, these problems are not purely philosophical—they are of limited practical significance for classical therapeutic trials but are of great practical significance for attempts to modify behavior. They can never be entirely eliminated, only ameliorated somewhat. I've reviewed some of the strategies to deal with these limitations in the chapters on experimentation in both business and more behaviorally oriented therapeutic contexts, and many of these same ideas will reappear later in this chapter in discussing social science and government policy.

Seen in light of these methodological debates, the period since the early 1980s has actually been one of slow, steady progress in experimental social science. Literature reviews indicate that the annual rate of randomized experiments in criminology, education, and social welfare continued to build from the 1970s through 2000, and appears to have accelerated rapidly over the past decade. Further, experiments for participants within laboratory settings, typically university students in campus facilities, became more common and influential within economics and other social sciences beginning in the 1990s.

What has changed is the nature of the experiments. Without a conscious strategy, the market for ideas has pushed experimenters to grapple with the problem of very high causal density, by increasingly testing many variations and modifications to programs, and by encouraging tests in a variety of localities to feel their way into a more conditional view of where policy improvements might work better or worse.

As experimentally inclined social scientists have recognized the centrality of replication and context sensitivity, they increasingly have emphasized integrating multiple RFTs on related topics to develop policy guidance. This requires both the collation of various experimental results with somewhat standardized design, execution, and reporting, and some framework for analyzing them. The term of art for analysis that integrates multiple RFTs (sometimes adding other quasi-experimental information) is a "systematic review." The leading program to do this is the Campbell Collaboration, named in honor of

Donald Campbell and directly inspired by the Cochrane Collaboration for therapeutic RFTs. It was founded in 2000 to conduct systematic reviews on various policy questions in the three social science areas of sustained experimentation: criminology, education, and social welfare. In addition, the US Department of Education built and maintains what is probably the most comprehensive collection of education RFTs in its What Works Clearinghouse. Other university-based and nonprofit organizations are also springing up to do this on a smaller scale for specific policy areas.

All of this represents real progress, but some perspective is in order. As noted earlier, researchers have executed something like 350,000 cumulative randomized trials for therapeutics. They are central to the progress of medicine, and significant new therapies rarely are introduced without one. Though the results, and even the existence, of specific business experiments tend to be confidential, within just the past few years businesses have performed thousands of structured experiments in the kinds of physical distribution channels, such as retail stores and bank branches, that are directly analogous to schools, police forces, or welfare offices. Businesses have also conducted, very conservatively, hundreds of thousands (and more likely, millions) of randomized tests through such direct channels as telemarketing, e-mail, and websites, where costs per test are very low. Once a large company adopts an experimental capability, this becomes the default method for program evaluation.

In comparison, only 100 to 150 cumulative relevant criminology RFTs appear to have been executed through 2004. The *Digest of Social Experiments* (2003) identified 240 cumulative randomized experiments across social welfare topics including job training, food stamps, substance abuse, and other related areas. Very few seem to have been performed in education until recently, though the number has increased in the past five to ten years. Perhaps a few hundred have been reported in political science and economics. A reasonable estimate is that in the history of global social science, through about 2005, no more than a few thousand such well-structured, relevant RFTs of reasonable size were reported in these areas (though many more randomized laboratory experiments were conducted by researchers in economics, psychology, and other disciplines that typically use university students as subjects). A single company, Capital One, reportedly does thousands of randomized field experiments every month.

When you lack a compact theory that provides a body of useful predictive rules in some scientific area, running lots of experiments that establish numerous micro-theories might not be very elegant but sometimes can get the job done. For example, think of Thomas Edison, who, without much theory about what substance would make a long-burning filament for lightbulbs, tried thousands of organic substances—according to the memoirs of one of his researchers "almost everything from the vegetable kingdom," and much from the animal world as well. Preliminary microscopic evaluation eliminated some materials from consideration, but the rest were put into lightbulbs to see how they performed. Or consider the contemporary example of high-throughput screening in the pharmaceutical industry. Machines methodically test thousands to millions of chemicals in "libraries" to see if any create a desired reaction with some target substance. We could try to build up some theory to predict this—and as with Edison's evaluation of filaments, might actually use simple theories to prioritize what we test—but if we can make each experiment cheap and fast enough, why not just do the test?

RFTs in social science have not operated at anything like this scale. And as we've seen, social science should require, all else equal, even more intensive experimentation than physical and therapeutic sciences, because the prediction rules it discovers will be so much more conditional. Unlike testing polio vaccine, "Does social policy X work?" is usually the wrong question to ask, because the real answer always starts with "It depends on . . ." This has certainly been the experience in business.

However, the limited number of RFTs that have been run to date has already generated a few significant findings that could be acted upon now. Although no review of a topic this broad could be comprehensive, I will try to highlight some of the most important lines of research supported by sequences of replicated social science RFTs.

Crime

The development of experimental knowledge in numerous social policy areas has followed a similar arc: a scholarly tradition of social experimentation proceeds in obscurity among a small group of researchers for a long period relative to theory-building social science; then an objective crisis is reached in practical affairs, and existing social science cannot provide useful guidance; desperation leads political actors to be open to experiments; and these in turn provide limited but valuable insights that help to drive reform. For criminology, the crisis was the explosion in violent crime between the early 1960s and the early 1990s.

Like any human social behavior, crime has complex causes and is therefore difficult to predict reliably. Regression methods have been applied many times and can't be made even to demonstrate good correlation with historical data, never mind to produce prediction rules that are demonstrably reliable in the face of rigorous testing. A detailed review of every regression model published between 1968 and 2005 in *Criminology,* a leading peer-reviewed journal, demonstrated that these models consistently failed to explain 80 to 90 percent of the variation in crime (again, using "explain" here in the narrow, statistical sense of "is correlated with in historical data," rather than the far more severe and practically important meaning of "can reliably predict the impact of changes in causal drivers on crime rates"). Even worse, no progress was demonstrated: regression models built thirty years ago were about as good as models built in the past few years.

Despite all of the sophisticated theory-building and empirical analysis, more than a century of formal criminological research has led to a very limited theory-based understanding of what causes crime. But randomized experiments have been increasingly used in criminology since the early 1980s. Several factors appear to have contributed. First, the soil is fertile: the quasi-military ethos and organization of police forces and other criminal justice organizations can make test execution simpler than in other areas, and can also increase the fidelity between program-as-tested and program-as-implemented. Second, in 1981 James Stewart, an effective supporter of randomized trials, became director of the National Institute of Justice and began to fund them. Third, and surely most important, was the post-sixties crime explosion. This wasn't just numbers on paper; anyone who lived through that period understands the air of menace that had descended upon most American cities (and many non-urban areas as well). The criminal justice system seemed powerless to stop it. Though police departments themselves were often resistant to change, desperation opened minds in the broader society to trying new approaches.

In 1970, the Ford Foundation established the Police Foundation, which sponsored a few early, key RFTs designed to evaluate policing techniques. One of the most important showed that a basic tool of modern American policing—increasing preventive patrols—seemed not to have much effect on crime at all when subjected to a controlled experiment.

In 1981–1982, Lawrence Sherman, a respected criminology professor at the University of Cambridge, led an extremely influential experiment that randomly assigned one of three responses to Minneapolis cops responding to misdemeanor domestic-violence incidents: they were required either to arrest the assailant, to provide advice to both parties, or to send the assailant away for eight hours. The experiment showed a statistically significant lower rate of repeat calls for domestic violence for the mandatory-arrest group. The media and many politicians seized upon what seemed like a triumph for scientific knowledge, and mandatory arrest for domestic violence rapidly became a widespread practice in many large jurisdictions in the United States.

But sophisticated experimentalists understood that because of the issue's high causal density, there would be hidden conditionals to the simple rule "mandatory-arrest policies reduce domestic violence." The only way to unearth these conditionals was to replicate the original experiment under a variety of conditions. Sherman's own analysis of the Minneapolis study called for such replications. So researchers replicated the RFT six times in cities across the country. In three of those studies, the test groups exposed to the mandatory-arrest policy again experienced a lower rate of re-arrest than the control groups did. But in the other three, the test groups had a higher re-arrest rate.

The danger of drawing conclusions based on a single RFT on a social policy topic is obvious in this example. Suppose Sherman had happened to run the original experiment in Memphis (one of the cities where the replication failed). Would we then have been justified in concluding that mandatory arrest doesn't work? Based on this set of replications, whether it works in any given city is roughly equivalent to a coin flip. Doing any one replication of the experiment is a draw from a prior distribution of possible outcomes, regardless of whether we have done enough trials to see this distribution empirically. It is important to keep this in mind when presented with the "scientific gold-standard evidence" of any one well-designed RFT.

The obvious question is whether anything about the situations in which mandatory arrest worked distinguishes them from situations where it did not. If we knew this, we could apply the program only where it is effective.

In 1992 Sherman surveyed the replications and concluded that in stable communities with high rates of employment, arrest shamed the perpetrators, who then became less likely to reoffend, while in less stable communities with low rates of employment, arrest tended to anger the perpetrators, who would therefore be likely to become more violent. The problem with this kind of conclusion, though, is that because it is not itself the outcome of an experiment, it is subject to the same uncertainty as any other pattern-finding exercise. How do we know whether it is right? We do so by running an experiment to test it—that is, by conducting still more RFTs in both kinds of communities and seeing whether they bear out this conclusion. Only if they do can we stop this seemingly endless cycle of tests begetting more tests.

And even then, the very high causal densities that characterize human society guarantee that no matter how refined our predictive rules become, conditionals will always be lurking undiscovered. As we saw with business experimentation, the relevant question then becomes whether the rules as they now exist can improve practices, and whether further refinements can be achieved at a cost less than the benefits they would create.

Sometimes we do stumble upon a policy innovation that appears to work consistently (or, much more often, not work). For example, various forms of intensive probation—in which an offender is closely monitored but not incarcerated—were tested via RFT at least a dozen times through 2004, and failed every test.

Criminologists at the University of Cambridge have done the yeoman's work of cataloging all 122 known criminology RFTs between 1957 and 2004 with at least one hundred test subjects. By my count, about 20 percent of these demonstrated positive results—that is, a statistically significant reduction in crime for the test group versus the control group. That may sound reasonably encouraging at first. But independent research groups formally replicated only four of the programs that showed encouraging results in the initial RFT, and all failed to show consistent positive results.

Twelve of the programs were tested in "multisite" RFTs: experiments in several cities, prisons, or court systems. Although not true replication, this is a better way to uncover context sensitivity than a single-site trial. But there, too, eleven of the twelve failed to produce positive results, and the small gains produced by the one successful program (which cost an immense $16,000 per participant) faded away within a few years. In short, no program within this universe of tests has ever demonstrated, in replicated or multisite randomized experiments, that it creates benefits in excess of costs. That ought to be pretty humbling.

But, to emphasize, the right conclusion is not that none of these programs can create improvement in certain kinds of situations, but rather that we haven't yet discovered the conditions under which any will work reliably. It might be that some will not work under any condition, and positive versus negative results in the first few trials for a program surely should influence how we allocate resources for future trials. But if we can lower the cost per test enough, we can continue to search for situations in which program ideas that seem reasonable can work. It does mean, however, that none of these trials have uncovered the analog of Pasteur's anthrax vaccine: an idea that is so powerful that we can see its positive causal results on crime rates under almost any conditions.

The same basic conclusion holds if you forget about formal replications and merely examine similar programs that have been tested at different times, despite material differences at the level of detail and execution. From those 122 criminology experiments, I extracted the 103 conducted in the United States and grouped them into forty "program concepts": mandatory arrest for domestic violence, intensive probation, and so on. Of these forty concepts, twenty-two had more than one trial. Of those twenty-two, only one worked each time it was tested: nuisance abatement, in which the owners of blighted properties were encouraged to clean them up. And even nuisance abatement underwent only two trials.

So what do we know, based on this series of experiments, about reducing crime? The fundamental finding is that the vast preponderance of promising ideas have not been shown to work reliably. Second, that nuisance abatement—which is at the core of what is often called broken-windows policing—appears promising and should be subjected to a structured program of replication trials. And in fact, subsequent to this universe of experiments, a research team led by Harvard professor Anthony Braga reported in 2008 on a complex series of randomized experiments in Lowell, Massachusetts, that provided further replication of this finding. In each experimental neighborhood where police applied these broken-windows-type nuisance abatement techniques, crime dropped more sharply than in the control areas. Further, it did not simply move to adjacent neighborhoods.

This, of course, does not exhaust society's collective knowledge for how to reduce crime, merely our most reliable scientific knowledge. Practical experts have enormous knowledge on the subject. Think of the experience of the New York City Police Department over the past couple of decades. Operational leaders often use social science data and analysis in an inherently judgmental decisions process. But crucially, beyond those policies that have been demonstrated in replicated experiments, advocates can claim that "studies show" whatever all they want, but operational expertise is the proper decision-making method. We should question (though not necessarily overrule) a practical expert who argues *for* juvenile boot camps (or any other of a defined list of programs shown to fail), or one who argues *against* broken-windows policing. Beyond this, the practical expert should decide what is best.

Randomized experimentation has proven no uniform answers for crime prevention. But in contrast, a series of experiments in the design of welfare programs in the 1990s yielded one of the greatest uniform insights into social policy in modern American history.

Welfare

What is usually referred to around the kitchen table as "welfare" originated as a Depression-era program to provide basic necessities to widows with children. It was explicitly designed to avoid the need for them to work outside the home. It evolved into its 1960s–1980s incarnation as Aid to Families with Dependent Children (AFDC), in which it increasingly provided assistance to divorced and never-married mothers with children. This program's political popularity declined dramatically as the social expectations for women to work outside the home grew, the absolute level of expenditure became much larger, and many voters saw the program as violating a basic norm of fairness by giving money to people who had children out of wedlock and then refused to support them. This program was deeply implicated in the tangle of social pathologies that emerged at the same time as the huge increase in crime. A crisis point was reached by the early 1980s in which social science and administrative practice seemed helpless in the face of relentlessly advancing welfare caseloads. During the late 1980s through the late 1990s, welfare was reorganized to focus aggressively on getting recipients to work and was renamed Temporary Aid to Needy Families (TANF).

Randomized experimentation in social welfare began with the famous series of negative income tax (NIT) experiments of the 1960s and

'70s. As a welfare recipient began to work and earn money, benefits would be reduced dollar-for-dollar as this outside income rose, creating, in effect, a 100 percent marginal tax rate. Academics, most prominently Milton Friedman, argued that this discouraged work and that this policy should be changed so that recipients would lose less than one dollar of benefits for each dollar they earned. The general term for such financial incentives for work on the part of welfare recipients is a "negative income tax."

These NIT experiments tested a wide array of combinations of program variants, largely focused on varying guaranteed levels of benefits and effective marginal tax rates on earnings. They generated two important findings. The less obvious of the two was that lowered tax rates had no material effect on how much recipients worked. The more obvious, but politically crucial, finding was that welfare benefits provided without work requirements reduced recipients' work effort compared with those of the control case, which required work effort to receive these benefits.

Experimentation continued to evaluate other ideas, consistent with the academic sociology of that era, intended to get welfare recipients into jobs. Two large-scale experiments tested major government programs designed to improve work and earnings for welfare recipients through training and support: the Supported Work Experiment and the AFDC Homemaker–Home Health Aide Demonstration. The first was an intensive program to develop work skills, and the second trained welfare recipients as home health care aids and placed them into jobs. Much as with the Job Corps, both programs could be shown to have some causal effect over some evaluation period (in this case, by causing earnings increases and welfare caseload reductions), but both were extremely expensive. Therefore, neither was pursued at scale.

In the 1980s, voter frustration over AFDC began to be converted to reform. Welfare in the United States is administered mostly through state governments, which have always had some discretion in program design and execution. Governors were elected, and reputations made, through attempting to reform welfare in several states. This created sufficient political incentive to encourage other governors to take risks in this area. The Reagan and George H. W. Bush administrations supported this movement, both on substantive and federalist grounds; eventually so did the combination of the Clinton administration and a Republican-led Congress.

To encourage innovation, the federal government began to grant waivers that permitted states to experiment more radically, even if this meant deviating from federal law. But the federal government made randomized experiments to evaluate these changes something like a de facto condition for granting the waivers. The federal and state governments often split the cost of the experiments, though the federal government maintained effective control over study design and analysis.

This confluence of events led to a series of distributed experiments. In general, they were much simpler than the NIT experiments. Since many states were trying overlapping ideas, and the federal government continued to play a coordinating role, there was extensive replication and near-replication of tests. The experimenters learned to take advantage of outcome data that administrative systems were already generating, and unlike the earlier NIT experiments, executed tests through the regular administrative apparatus of the welfare programs. This approach also drove down enormously the costs of testing. The first NIT experiments cost upward of $100 million; by the 1980s, this was reduced to about $1 million to $3 million per test.

The late-1980s to mid-1990s social welfare experimental environment, then, was characterized by numerous experiments executed by distributed entities with reasonably standardized methodologies; integration with operational information and administrative systems; lower costs per test; numerous replications of tests; tests of program ideas that were mostly incremental changes conceived by practitioners rather than by academics; and simple individual tests executed within unplanned series of many near-replications and variants as a method for exploring conditional rules for program impacts (as opposed to a smaller number of very complicated experiments designed to establish more formal models that define explicit equations that estimate program impact as a function of program components and environmental conditions—termed a response surface). This moved strongly in the direction of how one would design a testing regime to find useful innovations in social policy, though the number of experiments was still tiny compared with what a large business might execute. This period, not the period that preceded it, was the true golden age of social welfare experimentation. It came to an end with the 1996 welfare reform bill, which created TANF and allowed states extremely broad discretion in how they structured welfare programs. Because states were now free to do pretty much as they wished without needing waivers, the pressure for randomized experiments was lifted, and few major welfare experiments of this ilk have been undertaken since.

The RAND Corporation has collated the thirty-four major welfare experiments conducted in the early to mid-1990s as the welfare debate was at its most intense. They identified thirty-one qualified randomized experiments in the United States and produced standardized measures of effects on welfare caseloads, employment, earnings, and poverty across this group. By RAND's reckoning, thirteen of these thirty-one experimental programs focused on mandatory work requirements, four focused on financial incentives, four combined mandatory work requirements with financial incentives, four represented a TANF-like bundle of features (typically including mandatory work requirements, financial incentives, and other features), and six focused on other specific reforms, such as time limits for benefits. The insights developed through these welfare RFTs were clear and dramatic.

Mandatory work requirements get people off welfare, and nothing else has been demonstrated to do this. Twelve of the thirteen experiments focused on mandatory work requirements caused a statistically significant reduction in welfare caseloads. The effect of financial incentives on welfare use is more ambiguous but generally indicates that they are more likely to increase the welfare case burden than decrease it. The experimental programs that combine these two features appear to tend to cause a decrease in welfare caseloads when the mandatory work requirement predominates in the design of the experimental program, and do not when the financial incentives predominate.

But does a mandatory work requirement cause people to exit welfare and then starve? No, it does not. First, the recipients work more: nine of the mandatory work requirement experiments caused a statistically significant increase in employment, three a statistically insignificant increase in employment, and one a statistically insignificant decrease in employment. In effect, they tend to get off welfare and get jobs. Not surprisingly, this leads to an increase in earnings and income. Further, of the mandatory work experiments, those that emphasized just getting a job were three times as effective in creating this move to employment as were those that emphasized classroom-based skills-building and other training.

But did this trade of welfare for work, even if desirable from the perspective of taxpayers who would otherwise be footing the bill, end up making welfare recipients substantially worse off financially? Said differently, did the increase in work earnings only partially offset the reduction in benefits? No, it did not. By the end of the two-year measurement period, zero of the thirteen mandatory-work experimental programs showed a statistically significant effect on total income. Nine of the thirteen mandatory work experiments caused statistically significant declines in use of food stamps; the other four showed no significant effect. Only one of the mandatory work experiments tracked the effect on Medicaid use, and this one showed a statistically significant decline in use.

Welfare reform, as actually implemented in the TANF program, combined (1) mandatory work requirements; (2) financial incentives (which had the practical effect of sweetening the deal by creating a positive increase in net income for welfare recipients, rather than simply holding them harmless as mandatory work requirements alone would have done); and (3) other reforms unproved by experiment, including time limits and family caps, that likely created more pressure on recipients to get jobs. It was a practical political compromise that largely conformed to experimental knowledge for what should be done to humanely reduce the welfare population. This was one of the most successful reforms of a domestic federal government program in the United States in the past several decades, and is an imperfect but practical prototype for how an experimental regime can help to improve policy.

Even here, however, there is a need for ongoing retesting of work requirements. As we saw with business programs, as the environment changes, so may the effectiveness of a given program. There is a plausible argument that work requirements may have different effects in the current "long recession" than they did in the relatively more benign environment of the 1990s. We should maintain an ongoing series of experiments to probe for this.

Education

Purposeful randomized experimentation was historically less frequently applied to education than to criminology or social welfare. This is not because the methodology was unknown or inapplicable, but is much more likely due to the greater political power of teachers and parents than of indigents and criminals, combined with the ideology of educational institutions. This is a version of Heckman's randomization bias on a grand scale.

Leading Northwestern University education researcher and experimental expert Thomas D. Cook has identified only three randomized assignment experiments in education in the 1960s and '70s wave of social experiments: (1) the famous Perry Preschool experiment; (2) a school desegregation experiment with twelve students assigned to the test group; and (3) a test that provides some homes and not others with the TV program *Sesame Street.*

Though the use of randomized educational experiments did increase somewhat during the 1980s and '90s, they remained extremely limited. Probably the best-known randomized experiment in this period was the Tennessee STAR program, which tested the effect of smaller class sizes and is typically interpreted as showing some benefit from decreasing class sizes to about fifteen students in very early grades with experienced teachers. Like the original mandatory-arrest experiment, this program has been the purported basis for large expenditures in multiple states, but to my knowledge it has not been replicated in a large-scale RFT in the United States and has been subjected to alternative interpretations.

And though many RFTs have been performed inside school buildings for prevention programs for drug abuse, pregnancy, dropping out, criminality, and the like, the vast majority of high-profile academic interventions designed to increase academic performance still have had no replicated randomized testing. As recently as 2001, Professor Cook could assert that no randomized experiments had been completed for the effects of most of the key contemporary schooling interventions: standards-setting, "effective schools," movement to Catholic schools, Accelerated Schools, total quality management, charter schools, and smaller schools. He called out school vouchers, in which parents receive a voucher to pay for tuition at any private school, as a partial exception.

Vouchers are a form of school choice, and giving families a choice of school enables us to apply market pressures to drive improvement in school performance: schools that perform poorly in the eyes of parents will lose students. Broadly speaking, school choice also includes charter and magnet schools. Charter schools are publicly funded but not subject to many of the collective-bargaining and other political arrangements that govern normal public schools. Magnet schools also are publicly funded but typically operate under the normal collective-bargaining agreements and administrative control, though with greater flexibility in designing curriculum, student promotion, graduation, length of school day, and so on. School choice is the one educational intervention that has been subjected to large, repeatedly replicated randomized assignment in the United States. This has been the accident of history: because private-school vouchers and spots in charter or magnet schools typically are in such high demand, these schools often use lotteries to allocate them.

At least five large randomized voucher lotteries have taken place and been analyzed in America: New York; Washington, DC; Dayton, Ohio; Milwaukee, Wisconsin; and Charlotte, North Carolina. There are some deviations between lotteries and true RFTs. First, because these were in large part operational programs, record-keeping was sometimes very far from perfect, so we don't have educational attainment data on numerous students, and econometric modeling techniques typically are used to estimate this missing data. Second, the analysis published on these lotteries sometimes includes only estimates of the effect of winning the lottery *and* subsequently switching to a choice school, rather than applying the intent-to-treat principle and measuring the effect only of winning the lottery. Because those who actually switch schools will very plausibly be a highly biased subgroup of all lottery winners, accounting for this difference requires further econometric methods when comparing them to the overall control group. There are shades of gray from a crude natural experiment to an RFT, and imperfections in even the best RFTs. Although these analyses benefit enormously from randomization, each lacks the internal validity of a true RFT.

A comprehensive review of these randomized lotteries by Patrick J. Wolf, professor of law at Brigham Young University, in 2008 identified ten peer-reviewed analyses of the results across all lotteries. Wolf's summary of their conclusions is direct: "Of the ten separate analyses of data from 'gold-standard' experimental studies of voucher programs, nine conclude that some or all of the participants benefited academically from using a voucher to attend a private school. The evidence to date suggests that school voucher programs benefit many of the disadvantaged students and parents that they serve."

This is impressive, but the exact wording of this claim is important. First, these are conclusions about attending a school, rather than winning the lottery. This introduces the uncertainty of econometric adjustments. Second, the "some or all" qualifier is important. Even if these were strict RFTs, it would still be the case, as per Heckman's critique, that we cannot compare subgroups within the test and control populations with the same assumption that they are unbiased that we can apply to the test and control groups as a whole.

And beyond the need to confirm these results with well-structured RFTs, it is not time to declare that we have found the key to fixing America's schools. First, the effect as measured is fairly limited: according to Wolf's review, generally an increase in standardized test scores of a few percentiles. Second, these findings apply to a limited subset of the American school population: those living in fairly urbanized areas with available school alternatives within realistic commuting range; who are also in families motivated enough to apply for a lottery; and who are most likely African American or disadvantaged (the "some" students, in Wolf's summary, who benefit in some of the lotteries). Third, if such a program were to be scaled up, it likely would have unpredictable effects on overall supply and demand for schools and other educational resources in a city as a whole, which could radically increase or decrease the impact.

I don't want to undersell what the voucher lotteries have shown. Compared to econometric studies, these are very strong evidence. And as I've tried to emphasize, finding ideas that actually work is extremely hard. There is very encouraging evidence that school choice can create some improvement in educational performance for students in circumstances that encompass millions of people. A perspective that sees this as an avenue worth pursuing, but one that we should try incrementally because of our uncertainty, should inform how we pursue public policy in the area. I will try to describe some ideas for how to do this in the final chapter.

Researchers have also performed detailed analyses of lottery-based admissions to charter schools in New York, Chicago, and Boston, as well as comparable analyses of lottery-based admissions to magnet schools in Chicago and Boston. These studies consistently identify very roughly the same kind of achievement effect from attending a charter school as attending a private school with a voucher, and identify no discernible impact on achievement from attending a pilot or magnet school. (Of course, all of the same caveats that apply to analyses of vouchers also apply to these studies.) With those caveats, it appears to be the liberation from collective bargaining agreements and other workplace rigidities that is common to voucher and charter schools, but different in magnet schools, that accounts for the gains. What seems to matter more than whether my paycheck is issued by the City of Chicago or the Acme Schools corporation is the actual content of the work rules under which I operate. This will also directly influence the policy recommendations I will present in the final chapter.

Beyond just school choice, what is sorely lacking is a body of true RFTs to evaluate these and other educational ideas. Given that the United States spends about 4 percent of total GDP on K–12 education, it is amazing that we are flying this blind.

Fortunately, the use of RFTs in education has begun to accelerate substantially over the past few years, mostly because of changes in US law and administrative practice. Since 1998 Congress has funded a very large research program that explicitly privileges randomized trials. The National Research Council produced a major report in 2002 identifying the randomized trial as the scientific gold standard for evaluating educational programs, just as it is for other social science areas. That same year, Congress also established the Institute of Education Sciences (IES), with substantial funding authority and discretion, to bring more rigor to evaluating educational programs. Its very effective director through 2008, Grover J. Whitehurst, forcefully advocated using RFTs and established a group of regional educational laboratories and an ongoing set of research fellowships to train academics in the relevant techniques. This served to create incentives and infrastructure for a sustainable commitment to rigorous program evaluation anchored by randomized experimentation.

The early results have been impressive and—consistent with the introduction of randomized experiments to therapeutics, business, criminology, and social welfare—mostly negative. The IES *Director's Biennial Report to Congress* in November 2008 called out a handful of programs that have shown some success, in a sea of widely touted programs that have not demonstrated any improvement at all. For example, the IES sponsored a series of RFTs that tested fourteen well-known preschool curricula, and found only one curriculum that demonstrated some causal gains in performance that persisted through kindergarten (in one trial).

Even accepting that RFTs measure success in specific environments, we would expect a cohort of fourteen program ideas, each of which would show improvements in a material proportion of school environments, to lead to a higher average pass rate in this many trials. We likely need a lot of culling of these programs and should approach any new, hot idea of the moment with justified skepticism. Once again, though, succeeding or failing in a single trial doesn't usually constitute adequate evaluation of a program, and promising ideas likely need to be subjected to iterative randomized evaluation.

So this is not enough testing, but it is a start. It is the classical first phase of bringing experimentation to what has historically been a craft: going through the accumulated compendium of folklore and marketing to find a few interventions that actually do something, and more important, establishing the feedback loop that will enable forward progress.

Economics

Controlled experiments in economics date at least to the 1940s, when Edward Chamberlin ran simplified mock auctions in his classroom at Harvard to test the theory that supply and demand curves will combine to create a single market price. These experiments inspired one of his students, Vernon Smith, to lead the invention of the modern field of experimental economics. This intellectual tradition has used experiments in highly controlled situations—for a long time in classrooms; later in specially designed university laboratories. Experimental economics was a small niche through the 1970s and '80s, grew fairly rapidly over the next couple of decades, and is now a major growth area. About forty experimental economics papers were published in leading journals in 2009, as compared to five to ten in a typical year in the 1990s (though to put this in context, something like 95 percent of the papers in leading economics journals are nonexperimental). Smith shared the Nobel Prize in 2002 for his pioneering work on the topic.

The *Handbook of Experimental Economics Results* (2008) has 115 chapters, each of which summarizes multiple lab experiments concerning a discrete topic, but as a practical matter, this project has tended to focus on many variations on a short list of very important issues. Probably the most prominent of these has been the question of how markets, especially those resembling auctions, set prices. In part, this is likely because it is feasible to create a laboratory environment that is a reasonably close facsimile of a real stock exchange, auction house, or other similar institutional arrangement—which, after all, is designed precisely to manage exchange and price-setting according to formally defined and enforced rules.

At the highest level of abstraction, a key finding from this body of work is that many market designs that look reasonably like those in the real world will result in close to optimal prices (i.e., those that would be predicted by fully rational behavior on the part of each market participant), though the process of getting there tends to be messy. A second is that rational market outcomes are not a product of the interaction of individual actors each engaging in what Smith called a "cognitively intensive, calculating process of maximization in the self-interest." He went on to say that therefore we cannot test economic theory by testing "directly the economic rationality of individuals isolated from actual *experience* in social and economic institutions."

Experimental economics shows that the wide variety of market institutions in the real world reflects the unique challenges both of allocating various kinds of resources (e.g., telecom spectrum licenses, airport landing rights, natural resources, etc.) and of allocating resources in various cultural contexts, which can lead to very different results for the same experiment. As with field experiments in other social science disciplines, we don't discover a unitary and theoretically pure "market mechanism," but instead many evolving manifestations of the basic market concept that compose a never completely grasped set of conditional rules for success. Alternative market structures and norms interact and compete within an evolutionary framework, much as with the emergent social phenomena described in Chapter 4.

Despite the progress Professor Smith recognized experimental economics was making in incrementally improving markets, this recognition of the complexity and centrality of market institutions led him to a deeply Hayekian sense of epistemic humility:

> Like languages, economic institutions . . . are not the product of one mind or someone's logical experimental design, but are the product of thousands of minds over many generations of trial-and-error filtering, combined with a societal memory for those arrangements that are in some sense best, or good enough. . . . Can we consciously design new and better property-right exchange systems? There is good reason to be skeptical about whether any of us professionals knows or understands enough about the elements of institutional success to allow an affirmative answer to this question.

Or as Adam Ferguson, one of the leaders of the Scottish Enlightenment, put this same basic point in 1782, markets are "the result of human action, but not the execution of any human design."

On one hand, the laboratory setting allows experimenters to manipulate the environments in which their subjects are placed, but on the other hand, it always raises the question of fidelity—the match between the experimental environment and the actual environment about which we are theorizing. Because causal density in economics is so high as compared to that of physics or chemistry, even if we believe we are testing predictive rules of universal generality, it is rational to remain extremely skeptical about taking specific predictive rules discovered in a laboratory setting and applying them in the real world (or more precisely, to other parts of the real world). If we place actual stock traders in a lab setting that closely mimics an exchange, and have them use real money in amounts that matter to them in an experiment designed to understand behavior on the New York Stock Exchange, then fidelity is presumably quite high. Using a one-day laboratory experiment in a classroom to understand the behavior of technology entrepreneurs reacting to unstructured information about consumer preferences, competitive technology, scientific discoveries, tax rates and regulations, general economic trends, and so forth over a period of years is likely quite a bit less reliable.

We always need to test the predictions that arise from laboratory experiments in the field, and testing ideas well in the field, of course, implies RFTs. Experimental economists often describe trying out new institutional designs in the lab as being like a wind tunnel to evaluate new arrangements. The reason aeronautical engineers use wind tunnels is that they are much cheaper than building and testing numerous functional aircraft prototypes and trying to launch them. In fact, physical wind tunnel tests often go forward only after many design iterations on software programs that simulate the wind tunnel at much lower cost per "test" than even the physical wind tunnel. Eventually, though, real test flights with real aircraft are required before we declare a design safe and allow commercial passengers to board.

This is the same basic approach used by pharmaceutical researchers who proceed through a sequence of primitive, but cheap, tests to eliminate drug candidates, up through the early phases of a clinical trial, finally culminating in the Phase III randomized trial, to allocate the expensive resource of randomized field testing to highest-odds candidates. As noted earlier, this is also the same kind of sequence used by business researchers who proceed from market research to lab-oriented choice experiments to small-scale field trials to full randomized field trials for the same reason. In this way, we can see lab experiments in economics as a very successful method for rapid, iterative—but nondefinitive—testing of theories that ultimately must be tested in the field before we can claim that we have achieved true experimental validation of a predictive rule.

This process will not typically proceed in a linear fashion that winnows down a known list of initial theories through sequential testing to the "last man standing" at the end of the final RFT. Instead, there will be much iteration in the early, cheaper testing steps that involves nonexperimental theory-building, lab experimentation, theory modification, further rounds of lab testing, and so on. But ultimately the outcome of this entire process must be some predictive rule that can then be tested in the field. Note that lab experiments may predict the results of future RFTs better than current RFTs do. Much as was described for business experimentation, this question can be addressed experimentally by determining whether lab experiments, field experiments, or some nonexperimental methods predict future RFT results better for some intuitively relevant reference class of economic questions. Inevitably, though, laboratory experimental economics must lead to field experiments if it is to make even some parts of economics a Baconian science.

Over the past decade, this experimentation has moved into the field somewhat, as RFTs have increasingly become seen as a part of mainstream economics. Prominent examples include many of the research projects at the Poverty Action Lab at MIT, which under economics professors Abhijit Banerjee and Esther Duflo conducts RFTs of various poverty reduction, education, and similar campaigns in developing countries; many of the research projects at the Ed Labs at Harvard, which under economics professor Roland Fryer Jr. conducts RFTs of school interventions; and numerous experiments by University of Chicago economics professor John A. List on topics such as the nature of racial discrimination.

Lab experiments already are gaining share in academic economics, and in two out of the past ten years experimental researchers have won the Nobel Prize in economics. Randomized field experiments have more recently become prominent but clearly are recognized as part of the future of economics. Professors Duflo and Fryer were two of the eight young economists identified in a once-every-twenty-years survey by the *Economist* magazine in 2008 to identify the rising stars of the economics profession. Duflo received the John Bates Clark Medal in 2010, and List has been called out by Steven Levitt as the young economist most likely to win a Nobel Prize.

In 2009 Levitt and List produced a major review of the history, current practice, and projected future for field experiments in economics. What is so striking about such experiments to date is that, unlike economics lab experiments, they focus on the periphery of the core economic functions of production, logistics, and sales in the major sectors of the economy. Levitt and List say this is because the "great majority of existing field experiments has been done in partnership with government entities or non-profit entities like NGOs or charities." The authors call out two further strands of emerging research, in what we would normally think of as the core of the economy: (1) price and feature testing in the for-profit economy, especially direct mail solicitations for credit cards, and (2) employee compensation. They cite about ten experiments for the former, and two for the latter—a Swiss bike messenger service, and a fruit farm in the United Kingdom.

Based on this review, there is not yet a body of published academic findings based on randomized field experiments that would allow the kind of general observations that can be made for other topics, such as work requirements for welfare, or even those based on economics lab experiments. The real action in economics field experiments is within private companies—as we've seen, they run many thousands of RFTs every year—and I summarized findings from these in an earlier chapter.

Government and NGOs, however, are obviously more central to the related field of political science. And here, a string of recent RFTs have created some significant findings.

Political Science

Over the past twenty years laboratory experimentation has emerged as an accepted research tool. Political scientist Elinor Ostrom, who was awarded the 2009 Nobel Prize in economics, published seminal research on lab experiments that demonstrated means by which groups could manage shared resources through self-organized methods. Political science lab experiments have since been used to address other topics ranging from the nature of prejudice to how informational framing affects decisions.

In the past decade, the RFT technique has begun to be applied to questions ranging from election fraud, representation, and counterinsurgency to interpersonal communication. But by far the most widespread application of RFTs has been to test the effect of campaign tactics to get people to vote on election day.

There have been sporadic attempts at field experiments in political science focused on this topic that date back to political scientist Harold Gosnell's experiments that tested the effects on registration and voting of reminders mailed to prospective voters in Chicago prior to the 1924 presidential and 1925 municipal elections. Political scientist Samuel Eldersveld executed the first randomized field trial on this topic in the 1956 elections, and another attempt was made in the 1980 election. But this line of research was not taken up more broadly by political scientists. Zero field experiments were published in major political science journals in the 1990s on this or any other topic.

But starting around 2000, Donald P. Green and Alan S. Gerber, political scientists at Yale, began to conduct a series of randomized trials designed to measure the effectiveness of various get out the vote (GOTV) tactics, typically sponsored by various non-partisan groups like MTV's Rock the Vote. This work has resulted in empirical analyses showing that, once again, nonexperimental methods do not reliably get the same results as true experiments. This randomized experimental movement has snowballed to evaluate GOTV tactics including TV, phone banks, and door-to-door canvassing. It has recently been applied by partisan campaigns, prominently including Rick Perry's successful 2006 Texas gubernatorial election.

In 2008, Green and Gerber published the second edition of their book, *Get Out the Vote*, in conjunction with the Brookings Institution, that distilled the lessons from more than one hundred of these randomized GOTV experiments. Many of its conclusions are not surprising in light of the results from similar reviews of sequences of RFTs in business, education, and many other topics. First, they write that "one of the most important lessons" is that "campaigns seldom work miracles." Second, they summarize the theme of their observations about tactics that prove most effective in RFTs as "the decision to vote is strongly shaped by one's social environment."

In a prepublication excerpt of his book, *The Victory Lab,* former *Boston Globe* reporter Sasha Issenberg chronicles the dynamics of Green and Gerber's experimentation in support of Perry's 2006 campaign. The book profiles the executive sponsor of randomized testing in the campaign, Dave Carney, Perry's top political strategist. Carney forced experimentation on unwilling campaign practitioners, who often had financial stakes in the various campaign programs being evaluated. Issenberg also profiles Green, Gerber, and two other Republican-leaning academics (whom Carney collectively calls "the eggheads") who were the entrepreneurial leaders of the testing function, and extremely able communicators of results.

Issenberg reports Carney held an all-day meeting at the start of the campaign that was attended by Perry, his key campaign practitioners, and the eggheads. The eggheads gave a presentation on both the concept of RFTs and the empirical results that many campaign GOTV tactics had repeatedly failed to demonstrate effectiveness when tested in prior experiments. The practitioners reacted with the normal initial horror at the idea of using experiments to establish accountability and constrain their autonomy. In Carney's words, they were in "total denial." Carney's brutally pragmatic reaction was to say to the practitioners, "Either the eggheads are right or you're right. We're going to prove it out, and plan our campaign and allow these guys to develop experiments for everything we do."

Without his acceptance of the need for better knowledge, belief in the RFT methodology, and willingness to force the issue, nothing would have happened.

As the campaign progressed, the key serious intellectual objection to using the experiments to make decisions was, as always, the problem of generalization. One crucial experiment was run during the Perry campaign that showed that the effect of a tested TV ad rapidly declined in the weeks after it was aired. When it was argued that this therefore showed that the effect of TV campaign ads in general declines rapidly, one of the eggheads argued, "The real weakness of this study is it's a single ad, and you're extrapolating from that. You could make an argument that, OK, there's a diminution of effects, but that's just because it's not a very memorable ad."

Just so. And other obvious possible conditionals beyond the quality of the ad copy include when in the campaign it is being run; the level of competitiveness of the campaign; spending on other media at the same time; the size of the media market; and so on, ad infinitum. We likely would need many experiments to draw useful conclusions, and these likely would, in fact, be somewhat specific to each individual campaign.

Recognizing the power of iterative experimentation, Green and Gerber have now established a simple web-based tool that allows campaigns to automatically design and analyze simple GOTV randomized experiments.

So, we have an almost direct recapitulation in miniature and nascent form of what I have described in business, therapeutic medicine, and other social science areas where RFTs have been introduced. First, there's the substantive findings that there are no miracles, and that programs focused on changing environments are most effective. And second, we have the methodological observations of the pairing of an executive sponsor with an effective leader of the experimental analytical function to overcome practitioner resistance; the need for iterative experimentation to address the problem of generalization; and the use of information technology to partially automate experimentation to make this volume of testing feasible.

Summary of Experimental Results

Some themes naturally emerge from this review of experimental social science (defined broadly to include both business experimentation and behaviorally oriented therapeutic trials). Some of these themes relate to the methods that likely will be successful in using experimental knowledge to improve our understanding of policy, and others are substantive observations about policies that work or fail to work. All are pure pattern-finding, and therefore should be considered theories subject to verification, or more properly, are initial ideas that would need to be translated into more precise testable hypotheses. Nonetheless, I believe that their consideration is valuable, as I have not seen a review of this breadth elsewhere.

I will start with some observations concerning method.

First, controlled experiments are a necessary but not sufficient condition for scientific progress, and randomization, whenever available, is the best method to establish control in an experiment that can be embedded in a sequence of experiments and supported by theory to allow us to draw reliable causal conclusions about the effects of a specific social action. That is, in any field with sufficiently high causal density, RFTs comprise Bacon's "duly ordered" experiments that have always been essential to scientific progress. Biological sciences first operationalized this insight at scale with human therapeutic trials beginning in the mid-twentieth century. Randomized experimentation has demonstrated its superiority for program evaluation in business, and in the past twenty years commercial enterprises have rapidly scaled up this capability. Businesses now execute more RFTs than all other kinds of institutions combined. Over this same period, the RFT has confirmed its superiority, within the limits emphasized in this chapter, for this function in criminology, social welfare, and education. Even economics and political science, which have been laggards in this regard, have begun to deploy randomized field experiments for this purpose over the past decade or so. There are *no* relevant fields of high causal density for which the RFT has not proven to be the superior method for this task. Without substantial use of RFTs, social science cannot be scientific in the Baconian sense of the term.

Second, replicating experiments is required before drawing a conclusion. This is not as true for many biological agents tested in therapeutic RFTs, where the assumption of uniform biological response is often a tolerable engineering approximation, but should always be the refutable presumption for any program that relies on changing human behavior. At the simplest level, therefore, a single RFT should never lead us to conclude that a program works. We should demand, whenever practical, that independent research teams replicate a result prior to acting upon it. At a more comprehensive level, we should always think in terms of ever-evolving conditional rules for program success. In general, to develop practical knowledge we will need to do many more RFTs than we do today.

This also highlights that we do not face a choice between experimental and nonexperimental methods, but that in social science, theory and experiment are both needed, just as they are in natural science. The unique role of RFTs, however, is to test any predictive theory, but the theory may be developed through any combination of intuition, pattern-finding analysis, lab experiments, prior RFTs, or any other means.

Third, experimentation does not occur, and its results are not used, in a vacuum. If experimental results are to add value, they must change decisions, and this inevitably threatens some interests. The same dynamics of resistance occurred for therapeutic trials and within businesses that are now occurring in the social sciences and associated political entities. This resistance occurs at several levels. Analytical professionals resist using randomized experiments, because doing so renders previously valued skills less important. In the social sciences, for example, many of the exact features of RFTs that make them valuable—accuracy, simplicity, and repeatability—mean that they devalue the complex, high-IQ, and creative skills of mathematical modelers (at least for some purposes). In addition, politically powerful decision-makers resist the infringement on personal autonomy that program evaluation implies. The intellectually valid component of this resistance always ends up centering on the reasonability of generalizing results from experiments in an environment of high causal density.

Therapeutic medicine, business, and policy-making institutions that have overcome these challenges have evolved a very similar package of coping mechanisms. First, they have political sponsorship from ultimate decision-makers. Without this, the whole exercise is academic. Second, the political sponsor is paired with an agitator who directly leads the development of a testing infrastructure and community of experts with scientific values, ensures that this function delivers tangible value, and protects it from political interference. James Stewart at the National Institute of Justice and Grover Whitehurst at the IES, who both have been profiled in this book, are examples. Third, in areas other than therapeutics, where generalization means finding highly conditional rules to predict program impact, this infrastructure always embeds similar methods—integration with operational data systems, focus on multiple iterative simple tests, repeatable testing procedures, a combination of flexibility in choosing programs to test with consistent rigor in testing method, and others—that have the effects of lowering the cost per test, and making replication and near-replication far more practical and useful.

Now consider three substantive observations concerning those social policies that appear to work versus those that do not.

First, we should be very skeptical of claims of the effectiveness of new programs. Empirically, the vast majority of criminal justice, social welfare, and education programs fail replicated, independent, well-designed RFTs. Though almost any reasonable-sounding program will probably work under some conditions, most fail most of the time. The burden of proof should always be on those who claim that some new program is worth investment.

Second, within this universe of programs that are far more likely to fail than succeed, programs that attempt to improve human behavior by raising skills or consciousness are even more likely to fail than those that change incentives and environment. A litany of program ideas designed to push welfare recipients into the workforce failed to do so in cost-effective fashion when tested in a series of RFTs executed across America during the welfare reform debates of the late 1980s and early

1990s—only adding mandatory work requirements succeeded in moving people from welfare to work humanely. And within mandatory-work programs, those that emphasized just getting a job were more effective than those that emphasized building skills. The list of both "hard" and "soft" attempts to change people to make them less likely to commit crime that do not work is also almost endless—prisoner counseling, transitional aid to prisoners, multisystemic therapy, intensive probation, juvenile boot camps, Job Corps, etc.—but the only program demonstrated to reduce crime rates in replicated RFTs across 103 documented trials is broken-windows policing, which concentrates enforcement on targeted areas and changes the environment in which criminals operate. Similarly, it is extremely difficult to find any curricular, training, or related programs that drive sustained gain in academic performance in replicated RFTs, but creating choice for students in an environment in which schools are released from collective bargaining and other constraints appears to create improvement.

Therefore, we should generally seek to change incentives and environments, rather than try to change people. This is not to say that direct behavior improvement programs can never work—a program of nurse visitations to expectant and new mothers is a well-known example of a discrete program that has apparently succeeded in replicated independent RFTs—though, as with this example, those that succeed are often extensions of traditional public health measures.

Third, there is no magic. Nonexperimental methods frequently produce claims for fascinating, counterintuitive causes for social reality, such as the analyses that tried to show that rising American income inequality is really caused by electing Republican presidents, or that declining crime rates in the 1990s were caused by legalizing abortion in the 1970s. Such analyses often support idealistic and utopian claims, for example, that giving students choice is the panacea for poorly performing schools, or that counseling designed to raise the consciousness of hardened criminals will lead many of them to redemption. But real experiments almost always throw cold water on these theories, and those rare programs that do work usually lead to incremental improvements.

Further, the causal mechanism is usually something your mother could have told you: sending the local cop to talk to the owner of the store where the troublemakers hang out is probably a good idea; some people will get out of the house and look for work only when you stop feeding them; and teachers and school administrators (like all people) tend to stagnate if they face no competition or pressure to improve. The role of experiments, at least at this stage of development of social science, is really to sort through many plausible claims to find those that actually work in some specific circumstances, and to measure the relative effectiveness of alternatives.

It would be easy for me, at this point, to argue that we are just at the beginning of an experimental revolution in social science that will transform it over time into something that looks like physics or biology, and we are simply seeing the earliest stages wherein the insights seem tiny, but will ultimately lead to unimaginable discoveries. The future is unknowable, but I am extremely skeptical of such a vision. First, very high causal densities mean that rather than powerful, compact, and universal laws, we have extremely conditional, statistical statements. Second, many core questions in social science are so holistically integrated that experiments are, as a practical matter, impossible.

The experimental revolution is like a huge wave that has lost power as it moved uphill through topics of increasing complexity and holism. Physics was entirely transformed; therapeutic biology required statistical experimentation due to higher causal density but could often rely upon the assumption of uniform biological response to reliably generalize findings from randomized trials; the yet-higher causal densities in social sciences make generalization from even properly randomized experiments hazardous, and integrated complexity of certain topics in social science appears to be fully impervious to experimentation. One way or the other, it is certain we do not have anything remotely approaching a scientific understanding of human society now, and the methods of even experimental social science are not close to providing one within the foreseeable future.

The more plausible candidate for a methodology to create a scientific understanding of society would be reducing social science to biology—to use genomics and related disciplines to develop and validate predictive rules that explain human social behavior as a direct product of our physical makeup. But however promising current biological results are, no serious scientist believes that political economy can today be reduced to a reliable scientific model that starts with the published findings in biology and physics journals, and ends with the optimal design of political institutions. More typical is the frequently expressed viewpoint that we are approaching a scientific understanding of the functioning of the human mind, and that at least large aspects of social organization can be designed based on this understanding, without the messiness of endless trial-and-error. But predictions about what discoveries we expect science to make in the future cannot be the basis for action today. There is a long track record of scientists (and more typically, science popularizers) becoming overexcited about their purported knowledge of the future direction of scientific advances.

Our ignorance about humanity runs deep, and the complexities of mind and society continue to escape reduction to scientific explanation. Science may someday allow us to predict human behavior comprehensively and reliably; until then, however, we need to keep stumbling forward with trial-and-error learning and social evolution as best we can.

In a sense, if we were detached observers of the human comedy, there would not be much more to say. We would watch social evolution unfold, and some people, societies, and methods of government would emerge. In time we would learn which theories were effective. But in fact, we have commitments to specific people, societies, and methods of government. We want ourselves, our families, and our societies to thrive.

This requires us to harness the power of trial and error to the degree that it is feasible for one person or one society, but we also need guidelines for making decisions without knowing how the whole evolutionary process will turn out. And we do not just want ourselves, families, and societies to thrive by evolving in whatever direction leads to competitive advantage, but to do so while remaining what they are as much as possible. When we do science, we reject the Aristotelian idea of "essence," but when we think about what we love, essence is everything. So, we need to think strategically while remaining aware of our ignorance, and we need to exploit the power of trial and error while remaining aware of the essence of what we are trying to protect.

PART III

Political Action

The country demands bold, persistent experimentation.
It is common sense to take a method and try it. If it
fails, admit it frankly and try another.
—FRANKLIN DELANO ROOSEVELT

Where there is no vision, the people perish.
—PROVERBS 29:18

CHAPTER 13

Liberty as Means

The Paradox of Liberty

The most obvious application to politics of the first two parts of this book is to note that we usually have a very limited ability to predict the effects of alternative government policies. Then how can we decide rationally among alternatives? The simplest answer is to hedge bets whenever possible.

A starting point in making this aphorism more practical is to recognize that we are midstream in an evolutionary process we do not fully comprehend. Various social, economic, and political arrangements have competed for survival, and those that persist therefore embed information about what works (at least in the sense of survival), and what does not. This should lead us to see what is often termed "status quo bias" as, instead, a rational preference for the status quo. In colloquial terms, this would be roughly put as "If it ain't broke, don't fix it."

This is a basic libertarian-conservative insight, but is not as simple as saying that the fittest social arrangements have survived, and therefore we live in the best of all possible worlds. First, the environment around us is constantly changing, so to some extent, we should expect adaptive social arrangement to respond to this by changing as well. To relate this to the factory genetic algorithm example, there is no fixed "fitness function" for society, but rather a constantly changing fitness landscape. At a more practical level, though we may be unable to fully understand the implications of political actions within the society, we may have reliable knowledge of external threats that are moving quickly enough to compel the abrogation of such a trial-and-error process. Second, as we've seen, any evolutionary process tends to be glacial, statistical, and crude (in that it renders a verdict on packages of social arrangements as embedded in institutions and not on individual elements of these institutions). Therefore, constantly seeking improvement in how we organize society is rationally justified, even in the absence of external threats. In less academic language, over time people and societies that consistently follow the mantra of "If it ain't broke, don't fix it" usually will lose out to those who consistently seek opportunities for self-improvement.

There are at least two problems with seeking these societal improvements. First, it is hard to know what effects a given action will actually have. As we've seen, sometimes the solution to this problem is to run controlled experiments. Second, people disagree about what effects constitute improvement. Some people would prefer greater growth in average income at the expense of equality, and others the opposite; some people think that allowing same-sex couples to marry is a positive social development, and others think it is terrible. There is a partial solution to this problem as well. We can resolve some of these differences by referring to deeper goals—for example, we might gain support for same-sex marriage from some who oppose it if we could demonstrate that it tends to create less crime and greater social stability—but not all such disagreement can be resolved this way. For example, some people believe that same-sex marriage is a basic right, independent of its other consequences, while others believe it is immoral, independent of its other consequences.

When we can create scientific knowledge that demonstrates the causal effect of some proposed action, and we have broad agreement that this projected effect is desirable, then we are justified in taking action. This is the firmest basis for rational reform. Even in such cases, we ought to hedge, since we would have had to apply numerous methodological shortcuts in developing this knowledge (e.g., we can measure all causal effects in an experiment with a duration of a few years, etc.) that are always problematic in the context of social action. The problem of strategic generalization is eternal.

Of course, we often lack such evidence or alignment of values but still must take action. We cannot simply opt out of most decisions—we must operate schools (or choose not to), implement welfare programs, collect taxes, and so forth. How should we do this when we lack experimental evidence or agreement as to values? There is no algorithm, only some general principles.

First, for the reasons described above, in the absence of experimental evidence we should have a rational status quo preference, and therefore place the burden of proof on those who advocate change. Second, when we cannot conduct true randomized experiments but believe a reform is promising and needed, we should as a next fallback try new ideas on a small scale with reduced risk. Sometimes results will be so dramatic that, like surgeons observing that some procedure obviously improved a patient versus the counterfactual, we can declare tentative success, and once we have confirmed that it can be replicated and scaled, bring the reform to the broader society. When localized changes are not practical, and we have to make changes on a society-wide basis, we should have a strong bias to break the proposed change into pieces, and take these pieces one at a time—what Sir Karl Popper called piecemeal social engineering. Even if we determine that one of these small-scale or piecemeal reforms does not work, sometimes we will have introduced a new idea into the evolutionary process that will wend its way, through cross-pollination and diffusion, into later improvements in the society.

Sometimes, however, we will face an all-or-nothing reform decision, as in the case of the huge stimulus program the United States launched after the 2008 financial crisis. These types of decisions are dangerous and should be avoided whenever possible. Sensing those rare occasions when such an action is appropriate remains, like the decision to take a strategic action in a business, an art form. It is one of the essential characteristics of a great statesman, and it is not wise to have a system of government that relies on having such people routinely in office.

Third, to the extent practicable, we ought to accommodate differences in beliefs about what methods of social organization are best, rather than forcing compliance with some unitary vision. Our ignorance demands that we let social evolution operate as the least bad of the alternatives for determining what works. Subsocieties that behave differently on many dimensions are both the raw materials for an evolutionary process that sifts through and hybridizes alternative institutions, and also are analogous to the kind of evolutionary "reserves" of variation that may not be adaptive now but might be in some future changed environment. We want variation in human social arrangements for some of the same reasons that biodiversity can be useful in genetic evolution. This is the standard libertarian insight that the open society is well suited to developing knowledge in the face of a complex and changing environment. As per the first two parts of this book, it remains valid. But if we take our ignorance seriously, the implications of this insight significantly diverge from much of what the modern libertarian movement espouses.

I have argued that liberty is useful for progress in human social affairs, because it both provides space for creating the raw material of new ideas for approaches to economic, political, social, and other forms of organization or programmatic activity, and also provides a mechanism for testing, refining, and applying these new ideas. A separate argument for liberty is that it is a metaphysical good—that humans are in some ineffable sense better if free, or that they deserve morally to be free. In somewhat schematic terms, this second argument takes liberty to be a (or in extreme cases, *the*) fundamental human good in and of itself, though the argument I have made posits that liberty is a means to the end of discovery of methods of social organization that create material benefits. I'll call the more metaphysical argument liberty-as-goal, and the more prosaic argument I have made liberty-as-means. Obviously one can hold both of these beliefs simultaneously, and many people do. But these beliefs often conflict, raising what we could call the paradox of liberty, or more precisely, the paradox of liberty-as-means.

Consider an example practical question: Should prostitution be legal? The canonical Libertarian Party position is that prostitution is a consensual act between adults and therefore should not be prohibited by law. The liberty-as-means position is far more tentative. We don't know the overall effects of legalized prostitution. Some hold the theory that it will make people happier, provide income, and stabilize marriages. Others think it will contribute to personal degradation, female victimization, and societal collapse. It is very hard to know which theory is right, or whether there is only one right answer as opposed to different best answers for different social contexts, or whether the relative predictive accuracy of various theories will change over time as the environment changes. What the liberty-as-means libertarian calls for is the freedom to experiment: let different localities try different things, and learn from this experience. In some limited subset of cases this is literally consciousness learning from structured experiments; more typically, it is implicit knowledge, in that the localities with more adaptive sets of such rules tend to win out in evolutionary competition over time.

This leads then to a call for "states as laboratories of democracy" federalism in matters of social policy, or in a more formal sense, a call for subsidiarity—the principle that matters ought to be handled by the smallest competent authority. After all, the typical American lives in a state that is a huge political entity governing millions of people. As many decisions as possible ought to be made by counties, towns, neighborhoods, and families (in which parents have significant coercive rights over children). In this way, not only can different preferences be met, but we can learn from experience how various social arrangements perform.

The characteristic error of the contemporary Right and Left in this is enforcing too many social norms on a national basis. All that has varied has been which norms predominate. The characteristic error of liberty-as-goal libertarians has been more subtle but no less severe: the parallel failure to appreciate that a national rule of "no restrictions on non-coercive behavior" (which, admittedly, is something of a cartoon) contravenes a primary rationale for liberty. What if social conservatives are right and the wheels really will come off society in the long run if we don't legally restrict various sexual behaviors? What if some left-wing economists are right and it is better to have aggressive zoning laws that prohibit big-box retailers? I think both are mistaken, but I might be wrong. What if I'm right for some people at this moment in time but wrong for others, or what if I'm wrong for the same people ten years from now?

The freedom to experiment needs to include freedom to experiment with different governmental (i.e., coercive) rules. So here we have the paradox: a liberty-as-means libertarian ought to support, in many cases, local autonomy to restrict at least some personal freedoms.

Three Limits to Liberty

As with all political insights, this would lead to disaster if pushed to extremes. Determining what qualifies as extreme is, of course, the trick. I'll highlight three important categories of natural limitations to liberty-as-means.

The first flows directly from the paradox of liberty. Freedom of subsocieties to enforce (or not enforce) coercive rules on people who happen to live in some family, town, or state that limits behavior in some way these individuals find odious will by necessity confront them with a choice of either moving to some other location or being repressed or offended. This is also why, both morally and practically, the "right of exit" within a society is so important. The burden placed on individuals who feel oppressed or offended is much lower when they can more easily leave. Of greater practical importance, one of the primary mechanisms by which more successful methods of organization win out over others in evolutionary competition is through people voting with their feet. The broader society has a material interest in ensuring exit, so that it can adapt successfully.

So, one limit on the freedom to experiment is that subsocieties should not be allowed to trap adults. With extremely narrow exceptions, such as imprisoned felons, adults should be legally free to leave any neighborhood, city, or state within the society, and also be free to leave the society as a whole. This is so much a part of the constitutional fabric in the United States and most Western democracies that we hardly consider it, but such a right is fundamental to the functioning of the open society, and is not honored universally.

This does not imply a fully corresponding right of entry. At the level of political jurisdictions within the United States, a legal doctrine that extends back to the Magna Carta has created an effective though far from absolute right to travel. But nation-states have no ethical requirement to open their borders. Its existing citizens are justified in determining immigration policy based exclusively on their own interests.

A second limit can be created by external threats, of which one important type is foreign aggression, and another is rapid change in the physical environment. A paradigmatic example of the former would be a surprise military attack, and of the latter would be the discovery of a killer asteroid hurtling toward the earth. Each of these examples combines two aspects that can be used to justify abrogating internal freedoms. One is suddenness. The argument is that the evolutionary process is slow and cannot react to the threat quickly enough. The second is misalignment of public and private ends. The argument is that the invisible hand that somehow channels selfish desires to public ends under normal or historical conditions will not be sufficient to meet this new challenge.

In a healthy society, the characteristic of suddenness is often enough to galvanize immediate public support. At least in the short term, this means that reasonably spontaneous compliance with the need to centrally coordinate a response to the threat is very high. Either sustaining this in the face of a challenge that turns out to be longer term, or preparing for a less obvious longer-term threat, is the more typical basis for claims that the government must constrain and direct the free evolution of society.

Throughout most of human history, leaders have used the threat of future foreign aggression to justify state control, but in modern Western democracies, long-term threats to the physical environment are also used for this purpose. Characteristically, though not universally, the political Right cites threats of foreign military action, and the political Left cites threats to the physical environment. For example, in contemporary America Republicans usually argue that the potential for a large-scale radical Islamist terrorist action requires massive public expenditures and restrictions on specific liberties, and Democrats argue that the potential for damages from global climate change requires that we forgo significant economic growth and restrict specific economic activities through taxes, rationing, or regulation.

Both sorts of argument are plausible, hence their salience and durability. We cannot deal with them abstractly. A society must consider such threats seriously, but any such argument can be considered useful based only on the merits of the specific case. At root, this is another version of a knowledge problem. Key questions become how sure we are that the external threat is as we believe it to be, and how sure we are that the society will not adapt naturally to the range of threats we face more effectively than if we intervene.

The third limit on liberty is created by the evolutionary desirability of collective action. In a competitive environment, societies can create advantages through various means that require some amount of coordination across the bulk of the society. Two key examples are economies of scale, and social cohesion to improve efficiency. Innovation and variation in legal rules and cultural norms between various subsocieties can threaten each.

Variation directly threatens economies of scale. For example, if products must conform to fifty state-level specifications in the United States, or dozens of national specifications in the European Union, operating businesses at scale becomes more expensive across the entire geography. But this can also undermine certain kinds of technical innovation more subtly. As an example, the huge national consumer businesses in the United States could more easily afford to invest in the kind of software Applied Predictive Technologies created in its early, speculative phases. Social cohesion is "softer" than economies of scale but likely is at least as important.

The Nature and Importance of Social Cohesion

Suppose that US jurisdiction X, where you do not live and will never visit, decides to make orphanages mandatory for all children born out of wedlock. Suppose they then institute a system of corporal punishment for the children in them. Suppose they then institute the death penalty for eight-year-olds in them who are convicted of theft.

One argument for why you should stop them from executing eight-year-old orphans is consequentialist—for example, "Some of the children traumatized into serial criminality by growing up in such orphanages are likely to leave this place and move to where I live, and therefore increase my risks from crime." But even if we assumed that these effects were in practice minimal for some policy in a distant jurisdiction, we still have a basis for objection. At some point we recoil. We do not want to associate politically with those who would do such things.

This reaction is the product of nonrational attachment to a larger collective. The most narrowly defined rational actor should be indifferent to others' suffering. In a stylized evolutionary environment, the only rational person is a sociopath who is skilled at feigning empathy.

In such a world, the phenotypic organism we observe (hair, teeth, brain, and so on) is strictly speaking a mere organ of genes that seek only survival and reproduction. The very idea of a "self" is, in this framework, an illusion: "you" exist only as another on a list of organs. The genes—the beast within—will kill, maim, steal, and so on through the vehicle of the body. Genes-plus-body may manipulate others and pretend (even through chemical reactions that the "self" perceives as real feelings) to care for others, but these are all tactics.

And it is a mistake to interpret the language in the prior sentences, such as "seek," "pretend" and "kill," in a fashion that implies intentionality. Genes-plus-body no more "decides" to throw a child in front of a moving car than a tree "decides" in a windstorm to shed a branch that kills an ant walking beneath it. This language is simply a compact method of describing a very complex chain of biochemical reactions.

And there is nothing magic about the component of this machine called genes; they are in turn simply component machines built up from yet smaller subcomponents descending all the way down to subatomic particles. Genes-plus-body is really just body, and the body is just a collection of particles governed by rules for interaction. It may be that this overall machine has internal subsystems that create positive biochemical feedback for, by example, helping an old lady across the road, and that it is therefore prudential for most individuals to follow various social norms even if they are not subject to punishment or other external feedback. But in such a world, asking whether a given action is good or evil—or just or unjust, or fair or unfair—is like asking if it's Santa Claus or the Tooth Fairy who put the presents under the tree.

Further, even if we accepted the assumption of scientific materialism as a complete description of the universe, it is possible that feedback mechanisms for seemingly altruistic action could be the product of evolution, in any of three senses: an evolutionary advantage; an evolutionary spandrel that has arisen independently of adaptive advantage; or an evolutionary Frankenstein's monster—a by-product that is evolutionarily harmful to humans though potentially part of a trade-off for other linked evolutionary advantages. It could therefore be the case that we have evolved innate tendencies to attach to collectives, among other seemingly altruistic behaviors. And in such a world it might be that it would be impossible, barring physical manipulation of the genome, that we could escape such a physically bound consciousness to escape these feedback loops (at least for a very long time, until evolution might substantially change this element of human consciousness). That is, even if we rationally understood that such beliefs are nothing more than a product of biochemistry, we might still hold them and act on them for a foreseeable historical time.

Therefore, whether one considers humans' apparently widespread and durable need to belong to something larger than themselves as pure biochemistry, or as evidence of a transcendent human nature, simply ignoring it would be impractical. Even if we wanted to wish away this aspect of human psychology, attempting to implement a pure liberty-as-means regime would be another instance of the eternal radical's desire for the New Man who will conform to the specifications of some utopian scheme. Recognizing this aspect of human nature leads to messy complexity, but a humane political system conforms itself to the crooked timber of humanity, not the other way around.

Social evolution, regardless of whether it is enhanced by conscious efforts at reform, does not proceed in the abstract, but with real humans. For example, the idea of broken-windows policing is propagated via flesh-and-blood people who wear physical uniforms and carry real guns in real-world cities; it is not done just through talk. In this context, people organize themselves into families, kin networks, commercial enterprises, community associations, nation-states, and other entities with which they have both rational and emotional connections. Like science, which requires a community of scientists who share a specific morale, all real organizations that succeed over time are held together partially by common assent to ideals, and are not perceived by the participants as merely rational deals between entirely self-interested parties. Whether biochemical illusion or transcendent reality, this belief appears to be important to organizational success.

Any sustainably great collective—IBM, the Berlin Philharmonic Orchestra, the Pittsburgh Steelers, the US Marine Corps, the University of Cambridge, or the United States of America—appeals to the rational self-interest of its members but also creates a sense of irrational identification with the enterprise. Individuals within each will, to some extent and in some circumstances, sacrifice narrowly construed perceived self-interest for the good of the whole. When more of the participants do this more of the time than do those in competing collectives, it will tend, all else equal, to lead to competitive advantage, collective success, and greater success for the individuals within it.

There is an ongoing, decades-long debate in evolutionary biology about whether selection in genetic evolution through natural selection can occur at the group level, but for our purposes, this is not the issue at hand. What is crucial is that from the perspective of the self this behavior is not felt to be driven by conscious self-interest of participating in a collective that narrowly advantages the self. If everyone in the collective follows rules that benefit the whole only because of fear of punishment, it is very difficult to enforce these rules effectively and economically. What distinguishes successful organizations in this regard is that more members of the collective have internalized this desire to follow the rules—their sense of worth and self-satisfaction is enhanced by serving, to some extent, the greater good. I define social cohesion as the amalgamation of this subjective attitude (the combination of irrational loyalty to a collective and a belief of "we're all in it together"), the widespread expectation that this attitude is shared, and the behaviors that flow from it.

CHAPTER 14

Innovation and Cohesion

Social cohesion can be undercut by an economic system that makes people feel disenfranchised and less likely to achieve their material goals than under some alternative regime. The very processes of a regime of economic liberty that generate innovation and growth tend to create exactly this tension. Managing this tension is a core practical task of modern political economy, and a clear understanding of this trade-off between innovation and cohesion can help us in this task.

I've argued that human social systems, such as the economy, are always difficult to comprehend scientifically, but the innovative parts of the economy especially resist analysis because this is where the interposition of creative human mind and will is most central. William Baumol, a professor of economics at Princeton University and New York University, and a leading contemporary scholar on the mechanism by which a market creates continuing innovation, explains, "There is a good reason why entrepreneurship should elude the theorist, because by its very nature we cannot describe exactly what entrepreneurs do. . . . Anything done a second time is no longer an innovation."

Adam Smith famously used the example of a pin factory to explore the effects of the division of labor in the eighteenth century. Looking to this great thinker for inspiration, I will use the example of a software company to describe the process of innovation at the frontier of a twenty-first-century economy.

The Invention of Software as a Service

I described earlier how Applied Predictive Technologies (APT), the software company I helped to found, iterated its way into a focus on using experiments as a method to establish causality. In my experience, this inherently unplanned kind of process is how numerous innovations really occur. I'll describe in detail how this worked for a recent technical innovation that is causing enormous change in the software industry: software as a service.

Installing large-scale software for major corporations is complicated and expensive. Engineers come out to the customer's data center and load software onto computers. Large teams of people connect this software to the rest of the company's information systems, and many other people maintain it. The cost of installation and support is often many times greater than the cost of the software itself.

It seems quaint in a world of cloud computing, but in the early 1990s only visionaries believed software companies could operate their own data centers, and simply allow customers to access the software remotely via the Internet, much as consumers can access a website. This was a modern manifestation of the decades-old idea of timesharing. The innovative idea was to exploit the public Internet infrastructure to make it much cheaper. A series of well-funded start-ups were launched to attempt this in the 1990s, but they failed because they tried to force both software and business methods that had evolved in the heritage environment of on-premises software to fit into this new environment.

When we started APT in 1999, we used current software development languages and tools designed to allow access via the Internet. This was entirely incidental to us, since we assumed we would ultimately install our software in the traditional manner. When we delivered a prototype to an early customer, they didn't have IT people to install it, so we allowed our customer temporary access to our software via the Internet— that is, they could simply access it much as they would any website.

As they used it, two things became increasingly clear. First, this software made their company a lot of money. Second, despite this, the IT group had its own priorities, and it would be very difficult to get sufficient attention to install our software anytime soon. Our customer eventually floated the idea to us of continuing to use our software via the Internet, while paying us "rent" for it. We realized we could continue this rental arrangement indefinitely, but this would mean less up-front revenue than if we sold the software. This was the same period of crisis that led us to shift our focus from pattern-finding to experimentation: we were running low on money and had few options.

Our backs to the wall, we theorized that eliminating installation could radically reduce costs, if we designed our company around this business model differently than how traditional software companies were organized. Our engineering, customer support, and other costs could be much lower because we wouldn't have to support software that operated in many environments, just one. Sales and marketing could be done in a radically different, lower-cost way when selling a lower-commitment rental arrangement. We experimented with this approach with our first several customers. Eventually we made it work, and we committed to this approach. But this decision was highly contingent: the product of chance, necessity, and experimentation.

At about the same time, unbeknownst to us and others, a few dozen other disparate start-up companies were independently discovering that this model could work after all. The key was to design new software that was intended from the start for this environment, and to design the business processes of the software company—how the sales force was structured, how the product was priced, how customer support delivered, etc.—for this new environment as well. By about 2004, the delivery of software over the Internet, by then renamed software as a service (SaaS) by industry analysts, was clearly a feasible business model.

The SaaS model is now seizing large-scale market share from traditional software delivery. Industry analysts estimate SaaS is growing six times faster than traditional software, and that 85 percent of new software firms coming to market are built around SaaS.

Many things about APT turned out differently than we had expected. Settling on the SaaS delivery method was just one example and in fact was not even the most central; it is just a simple one to explain. The Hayekian knowledge problem is not a mere abstraction. Our innovations that have driven the greatest economic value uniformly arose from iterative collaboration between us and our customers to find new solutions to hard problems. Neither thinking through a chain of logic in a conference room, nor simply "listening to our customers," nor taking guidance from analysts distant from the actual problem ever did this. External analysis can be useful for rapidly coming up to speed on an unfamiliar topic, or for understanding a relatively static business environment. But at the creative frontier of the economy, and at the moment of innovation, insight is inseparable from action. Only later do analysts look back, observe what happened, and seek to collate this into categories, abstractions, and patterns.

More generally, innovation appears to be built upon the kind of trial-and-error learning mediated by markets. It requires that we allow people to do things that seem stupid to most informed observers—even though we know that most of these would-be innovators will in fact fail. This is premised on epistemic humility. We should not unduly restrain experimentation, because we are not sure we are right about very much. For such a system to avoid becoming completely undisciplined, however, we must not prop up failed experiments. And to induce people to take such risks, we must not restrict huge rewards for success, even as we recognize that luck plays a role in success and failure.

A loose tradition of heterodox economics uses exactly this lens of trial-and-error innovation to see the economy as a whole.

Evolutionary Economics

This tradition appears under numerous overlapping and imprecise labels—new institutional economics, experimental economics, the Austrian School, behavioral economics, and so on. Important examples of leading modern proponents include Frank Knight, Joseph Schumpeter, F. A. Hayek, Vernon Smith, Ronald Coase, and Douglass North. Though these traditions clearly are part of mainstream economic thought (four of these six men have won Nobel Prizes), the emphasis on uncertainty, experimentation, and evolution stands in contrast to the currently dominant paradigm within university economics departments of risk, quantification, and equilibrium.

Accepting that there are separate strands of this tradition, and that even the thinkers on this short list disagree about a lot, I believe that they can be unified by a focus on two factors: uncertainty and implicit knowledge. This tradition emphasizes uncertainty as a pervasive and critical reality in the human decision environment, and observes the need to conceive of any economic system, and the society in which it is embedded, as developing implicit knowledge as they unfold over time. I will use the term "evolutionary economics" to denote this broad perspective.

Evolutionary economics argues that firms and other collectives or organizations have an important role because of deep uncertainty—their formal and informal structures help to guide decision-making in an uncertain world, much as paradigms do for scientists. But we can never know that the assumptions embedded within these organizations are correct, so they compete for survival in an evolutionary environment. Hence this tradition emphasizes the value of trial-and-error and experimental methods for learning. By extension, therefore, this tradition is also very skeptical of governments that combine a monopoly on coercion with the assumption of reliable knowledge of society to foreclose options for behavior, or attempt to direct resources based on a plan, since this would restrict the long-term process of cumulative improvement and explicit knowledge discovery. Finally, this tradition recognizes that the political process tends to do exactly this, because change always threatens established interests.

The conclusion of Douglass North's Nobel lecture in 1993 directly summarizes this: "It is adaptive rather than allocative efficiency which is the key to long run growth. Successful political/economic systems have evolved flexible institutional structures that can survive the shocks and changes that are a part of successful evolution."

North described this in greater detail in *Institutions, Institutional Change and Economic Performance* (1990):

In a world of uncertainty, no one knows the correct answer to the problems we confront and no one therefore can, in effect, maximize profits. The society that permits maximum generation of trials will be the most likely to solve problems through time. . . . Adaptive efficiency, therefore, provides incentives to encourage the development of decentralized decision-making processes that will allow societies to maximize the efforts required to explore alternative ways of solving problems. . . . There is nothing simple about this process, because organizational errors may be not only probabilistic, but also systematic, due to ideologies that may give people preferences for the kinds of solutions that are not oriented to adaptive efficiency.

Uncertainty and change, and therefore the relevance of evolutionary economics, are most obvious in the innovative sectors of the economy. A traditional equilibrium analysis can provide a useful representation of the US aluminum market, much as the consulting analysis I described in an earlier chapter constructed a useful supply curve for a glass industry. But these methods are close to useless in describing the innovation of software as a service. This is not because different economic processes govern these two cases, but because in the case of the aluminum or glass markets, we can assume away (at least in the short term) many of the factors that dominate decision-making in the innovative parts of the economy. To see why all this is so, I'll incorporate both the innovative and mature sectors of the economy into a more general framework. This requires directly confronting the difficult and important issue of the nature of innovation.

The distinction between invention (e.g., constructing the first lightbulb) and innovation (e.g., figuring out how to embed lightbulbs in other products, modify them for specific uses, develop financing approaches that make them accessible, and so on) is widespread in the economics literature. As they progress in their careers, however, scholars of innovation from Schumpeter onward tend to emphasize a more useful distinction: between routine and nonroutine innovation/invention. Schumpeter's earlier work, for example, focused on the role of individual entrepreneurs, but later focused on the role of innovation by large firms. Baumol, in his later work, described the similar oligopolistic competition that occurs between large companies in the computer, pharmaceutical, and other technology-intensive industries as largely being based on innovation.

Baumol observes that these companies have routinized the development of innovations through large research facilities. Drug companies, for example, manage an explicit pipeline of therapeutic innovations according to a defined set of management protocols. Although such processes do not allow the companies to know in advance exactly which innovations will be created, they can, at a high level and to some extent, devote resources to specific topic areas (say, cancer drugs versus hypertension drugs) and can count on a roughly predictable rate of innovations. In my first job out of graduate school in AT&T's paradigmatic corporate research labs, I observed exactly such a process of funding research areas and then managing them to output targets.

Trade-offs are involved in any attempt to manage innovation rationally. On one hand, doing so can create competitive advantage as long as there are scale benefits to research, cumulative learning benefits analogous to the experience curve, or benefits derived from ongoing development of expertise in the research management function itself. On the other hand, efforts to create routine innovation tend to have blind spots that arise directly from attempting to direct it rationally.

Of course, AT&T's laboratories invented the transistor, the laser, and the C programming language; its researchers have won seven Nobel Prizes in physics. Xerox's comparatively tiny PARC lab developed the graphical user interface, Ethernet computer networking, and most of the other elements of the modern personal computer. IBM's Watson research centers invented the DRAM chip and the relational database; IBM employees have won five Nobel Prizes.

Routinized research centers clearly can produce groundbreaking insights. This is not their drawback. The problem comes later, when it's time for the parent company to exploit the insights when doing so would threaten its business model. Steve Jobs famously utilized the user interface, mouse, and other innovations developed at PARC to make Apple, not Xerox, a leading personal-computer company. What is less often remembered about that story, however, is that Xerox did manage to turn the laser printer invented at PARC into a multibillion-dollar business.

Nonroutine and routine innovation can be better thought of as just two shades of gray on a spectrum of innovativeness in business activities that run from the most speculative research to those that are so routine we don't think of them as potentially innovative. Ultimately this proceeds all the way to fully automated tasks; some jobs become so routine that we simply automate them out of existence. What differs along this spectrum of innovativeness is the level of abstraction at which the process can be rationally controlled. We can manage routine innovation in a corporate lab to some extent, but to do their jobs successfully researchers have to have more latitude than, say, insurance claims processors.

Innovation, however, occurs constantly in all these settings: successful researchers create technical breakthroughs, but successful claims processing supervisors develop new time-saving methods. Once a task goes all the way to automation, then the workers who develop or oversee the automated process develop innovations to improve it.

Much like earlier discussions of the inverted tree of scientific knowledge, or of the relationship of business strategy to tactics, both scientific paradigms and business structures serve to stimulate innovations within a defined scope but are threatened by innovations outside of this scope.

As with science or any other open system, this is a problem of both knowledge and incentives.

An insurance company can operate a claims processing group very tightly (i.e., focus on cost control and incremental process improvements), but only because we have a nested set of paradigm-like beliefs that descend down from beliefs about the overall structure of the economy, to the insurance industry as it exists today, down through the strategy and structure of the company in which the claims processing department exists. In fact, we must manage this function tightly to be competitive in claims processing. We "know" that we can and should assume away almost all of the uncertainty inherent in any human economic action. Departments for which innovation is a more central basis of competitive advantage—which is to say, departments for which we have more uncertainty about how to specify algorithmically the behaviors within that department that are vicariously adaptive for the firm as a whole—rationally allow greater scope for individual and subgroup initiative.

The claims processing supervisor who discovers a method for decreasing the time to process each claim by 10 percent with no reduction in quality will be rewarded. But if she discovers a method for entirely automating claims processing, thereby eliminating her boss's job, she will usually have a harder time getting her boss to accept this. If she discovers an alternative to traditional insurance that would make her company obsolete, it's unlikely that she'd be allowed to proceed by anyone at her company, except potentially a very farsighted chief executive.

In such a case, the market represents the "appeals court of last resort." And so either the entrepreneurial employee, realizing she is unlikely to capture the value she might create within the current organization, leaves and starts her own company, or some external entrepreneur sees the opportunity and tries to seize it. Echoing Bacon, they refuse "to abide by the sentence of a tribunal which is itself on trial." It is no accident (as Marxists of old were wont to say) that economist Frank Knight's distinction between risk and uncertainty, described in Chapter 6, was drawn in an attempt to explain the entrepreneur's role. Once an activity can be routinized, even if this routinization incorporates probabilistic risk, it no longer requires innovation of the kind that requires markets. At the level of the individual entrepreneur, this can be restated as the observation that it is very difficult to get rich doing something you can learn in school.

The key difference between discovering a new claims processing technique and inventing the transistor is not that one is a product invention and the other a process innovation. The most important difference is that we can operate successful organizations at a scale such that exploiting a new claims processing technique can take place within the organization, but we cannot operate rational structures capable of exploiting the transistor at anything approaching its potential. In direct analogy to Baconian science, a capitalist market is like the master paradigm within which we permit competition between alternative viewpoints.

Why can't we operate firms large enough to exploit all new innovations? Because innovations are surprising. Any firm that could exploit all new innovations would have to be as big as the entire economy. A very complicated set of dynamics establishes rational firm size, which includes the unique accidents of history for individual companies, industries, and societies. But if (following on Coase) the firm is an alternative, nonmarket mechanism for organizing production within its boundaries, then a company that could exploit all of the innovation it creates in effect would need to be an entire planned economy.

The entrepreneur's role is to upset the applecart—to challenge existing paradigms at anything from a small scale to the grand level. The market is a set of institutions for managing, at a very high level of abstraction, those innovations that the more directive institutions of individual firms cannot handle.

Contra Schumpeter's late career view that innovation was increasingly being rationalized within large organizations, external entrepreneurship if anything has grown in importance over the past thirty years or so. According to the National Venture Capital Association, about 10 percent of US GDP in 2008 was created by venture capital–funded firms. These companies account for about half of total industry revenue in many of the most productive and dynamic sectors of the economy, including electronics, semiconductors, telecommunications, biotechnology, and computers. They employ about 75 percent of all workers in the software, telecommunications, and semiconductor industries.

And this considers only the recent product of technically oriented individual entrepreneurship. Many of the major technology companies with which these venture-backed companies compete—think of HP and IBM—were created by individual entrepreneurs within living memory. Further, non-technical entrepreneurship that has appealed to the market to break up the cartel-like economy of mid-twentieth-century American industry has been important to US economic vitality. The leveraged buyout movement of the 1980s and 1990s, for example, broke the near-autonomy of corporate managements and boards by reconcentrating ownership of many large companies, forcing improved efficiency, and over time creating a true market for corporate control. This forced much of the painful restructuring of mature industries that has made them far more economically sustainable.

It appeared to Schumpeter, as well as many other evolutionary economists and corporate strategists from the early twentieth century up through at least about 1980, that the oligopolistic competition between large corporations had supplanted the so-called entrepreneur of legend and the classical conception of a market as comprising many small firms. But in fact the economic model characterized by large public companies with dispersed ownership and professional management, routinized innovation, and oligopolistic competition turns out to have been simply one localized phase in the development of capitalism. Even at this near-paradigmatic level, the system was subjected to challenge, and the market has staged a counterrevolution.

In summary, there is a tension *inherent* to the process of innovation. We must build institutions—corporations, craft guilds, definitions of professional skills, even entire industries—to help manage innovation in the face of uncertainty. To some extent, individuals must commit to these institutions. But all of these institutions must be destroyed, often with unpredictable timing.

It is deeply unnatural to knowingly assent to a system that requires us to commit to institutions, on one hand, and agree to their destruction, on the other. But unless we just give up on growth, which ultimately implies that we surrender control of our own destiny to societies that surpass us materially, there is no way out. The best we can do is to manage this tension more effectively.

The Fundamental Tension: Innovation Versus Cohesion

Consider that I told the story of APT as a happy tale from the innovator's perspective. But innovation isn't so pleasant for everybody. SaaS is a classic case of so-called disruptive innovation. It is very difficult for incumbent competitors to copy because this would require self-cannibalizing existing business arrangements that are extremely lucrative. This is why innovation can be the basis for sustainable competitive advantage for the innovators, and not just an idea that incumbents can easily co-opt.

Without SaaS plus the open-source movement—another disruptive business model, in which volunteers collaborate to create free software— the US software industry very likely would be a much more mature, slow-growth business. But almost all large incumbent software companies, and the ecosystem of consultants and others who make money installing traditional software, naturally fought this development tooth and nail. From their perspective, this was rational: they each would be better off if this innovation had never happened, since they could have harvested cash from a slow-growth industry for many years. This is why Schumpeter famously called this process "creative destruction."

This destruction doesn't happen just to abstract firms, but to real people. Consider, for example, the IT groups at our early client that had established a powerful position that enabled them simply to refuse to act. From their point of view, life was pretty good—they could work reasonable hours, make good money, and have significant control over their work. They now face increasing pressure to change and improve, or be replaced by machines. Further, SaaS effectively automates almost all of the IT consulting integration activity out of existence—and the people who did that work out of jobs, unless they can find other tasks to sell their clients at similar hourly rates. Such consultants become like manual ditch-diggers competing with a steam shovel.

I had a conscious, frequently expressed mantra for constructing our software tools at APT that summarized this process: discover, routinize, automate. This process eats jobs. But it also creates new ones, such as all of the employees at APT. The hope of a capitalist society is that the gains innovation brings outweigh the destruction it creates.

In general, and over the very long term, this appears to have been the case. Over the past 1,000 years, China, India, and the West have been the largest components of the world economy (from 1500 to 1800, each represented about one-quarter of global GDP). Starting with the Industrial Revolution in northern Europe, innovative capitalist societies have generated radically more per capita wealth than any available large-scale alternative:

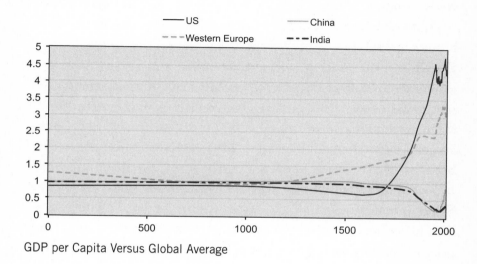

GDP per Capita Versus Global Average

One of the major points of this book is that econometric methods cannot usually establish reliable causal relationships between political actions and outcomes. Neither this empirical observation nor more complex analysis that would attempt to control for other factors could conceivably measure the attributable effect of capitalism on output per person. We can safely say, however, that the long-term track record of capitalist societies is one of higher and more rapidly rising general living standards than those found in societies with other methods of social organization.

Even if, however, one accepts that over time such innovation tends to grow the pie of the whole economy, that is cold comfort to the sales rep at a software company with now-antiquated competing technology who suddenly can't make quota, or the consultant who is laid off and finds that his skills are no longer so relevant on the job market. All of these people need to find modified niches or lose income. And none of this begins to address those who are alienated from the capitalist enterprise as a whole, and never had such attractive jobs to lose in the first place.

Many entrepreneurs hold the opinion that "I did it all on my own," which may be well adapted to leadership success in certain situations, but it is objectively myopic. The entrepreneur relies on an ecosystem of venture capitalists, risk-taking purchasers, and so on. This ecosystem itself rests on a deeper foundation of collective, government-led enterprise. The delivery of our software, for example, depended on the existence of the Internet, which is the product of a series of government-sponsored R&D efforts, in combination with subsequent massive private commercial development. Government funding has been essential to much of the university science that entrepreneurs have exploited. Honest courts and police are required for functioning capital markets and protection of assets; physical infrastructure is required for the roads and running water without which we would not spend much time thinking about artificial intelligence software. At the absolute foundation, national armed forces protect the whole system against external aggression. All of our exciting technical and economic innovations ultimately require men to stand watch all night looking through Starlight scopes mounted on assault rifles—and die if necessary—to protect our commercial, law-bound society. Would you do this to protect a billionaire hedge-fund manager who sees his country as nothing more than lines on a map?

The vessel of the broader society must survive if social evolution of any kind is to take place within it.

Innovation forces change, while humans generally resist change. The pain of the change tends to be visible, while the benefits are usually diffuse and invisible, and clearly involve luck when they are visible. It is therefore natural that people will attempt to organize to prevent the spread of innovation. The original Luddites were English cotton weavers who responded directly to their displacement by automated weaving technology: they smashed looms. This is easy to mock . . . as long as you're not the one who is going hungry. In the contemporary West, such people rarely assault property en masse; instead they form political coalitions to pass laws that restrict the use of the looms. Threats to cohesion are not met with violent overthrow of the government, but with use of the political process, broadly defined, to slow down disruptive innovation.

Thus the inherent tension built into the very structure of innovation manifests itself as the fundamental tension of democratic capitalism: winners in this scenario require shared resources produced by the losers. That is, the market economy requires broad social consent. Why should those who lose out in market competition give it?

This can sound abstract and bloodless, but its manifestations in the real world are not.

The structure of epochal change in political economy often is better seen at a distance. Consider America's transition from an agricultural to an industrial economy. In 1800 America was a nation of farmers. About three-quarters of the labor force worked in agriculture. This proportion has been in almost continuous decline since then. By the eve of the Civil War, it was a little over half; by 1900 it was about one-third. Today agriculture represents less than 3 percent of the workforce. This has been great for consumers. Farming has become incredibly efficient, and food is cheaper and more plentiful in real terms than ever before in human history—to the point that obesity is an enormous public health problem. American agriculture today is also a very successful industry. In 2007 the United States exported over $75 billion of agricultural products, and has maintained a positive trade surplus in food for decades. It's just not an industry that can provide employment for very many people anymore.

In 1800 agriculture dominated the national economy; by 1900 America had clearly become a manufacturing nation. This was a sweeping technological-economic change that produced enormous flux in social, political, and family relationships. Marx memorably described the capitalist industrialization of this period as "constant revolutionizing of production, uninterrupted disturbance of all social conditions, everlasting uncertainty and agitation." The search for permanence was emotionally understandable, and all but inevitably would seek political expression.

As farming's long-term decline in employment became undeniable, resisting these changes was a key basis of the populist movement in the late nineteenth and early twentieth centuries. William Jennings Bryan is often something of a laughingstock in contemporary culture because of his buffoonish treatment as the lawyer attacking the teaching of evolution in the 1960 movie *Inherit the Wind*, but he was an enormously influential political figure who won the Democratic Party nomination for US president in 1896, 1900, and 1908. He, more than any other person, incorporated the key themes of the populist movement into the two-party system.

Bryan was unabashedly attempting to stand athwart economic history shouting, "Stop!" In one of the most arresting passages in his famous "Cross of Gold" speech, he speaks bitterly: "I tell you that the great cities rest upon these broad and fertile prairies. Burn down your cities and leave our farms, and your cities will spring up again as if by magic. But destroy our farms and the grass will grow in the streets of every city in the country."

Bryan lost three presidential elections; but of course losing three times means he won the nomination three times, which is excellent evidence that he spoke for a good fraction of the American people of his era. In the end, though, accepting his broad program would have meant opting out of the modern world. Though sentimentally painful, rejecting Bryan was wise. The alternative would have been to attempt to prop up emotionally resonant family farms and retard the development of the industrial economy.

This same dynamic has been playing out for the industrial economy over the past sixty years. The United States has a huge and very productive manufacturing sector. Contrary to much current media hysteria, the United States remains a leading manufacturing nation. Though China will almost certainly become a larger manufacturer than America in the near future, the United States currently has about the same total manufacturing output as China, and substantially more than Japan. Like farming before it, manufacturing just doesn't employ much of the population anymore. At the end of World War II, manufacturing accounted for about one-third of the US workforce. Today it is about one-tenth. In terms of employment, we are no longer transitioning to a services economy; we are there.

As we have progressed from an agricultural to a manufacturing to a services economy, we haven't abandoned the maturing industries. We still need food and manufactured goods, and it would be foolish to become completely dependent on foreign supplies for either. In the event of a real shooting war, we couldn't protect ourselves from a determined adversary by booking conference rooms. But we are well able to feed ourselves, and we have an extremely robust manufacturing economy, with particular relative strength in defense-related sectors such as aircraft, capital goods, and precision equipment. In fact, had we tried to freeze in place either family farms or employee-intensive factories, we probably would have a far worse defense capability because we would have less domestic agricultural output and antiquated factories.

We can visualize the evolution of the economy as being like a huge conveyor belt in which sectors originate in entrepreneurial innovation, proceed through scale-up, and end with being compacted into low-employment/high-productivity automated sectors. It is "discover, routinize, automate" at the highest level. Looking today at entrepreneurial start-ups, then at high-growth technology sectors, then at more mature parts of the service economy, then at manufacturing, and then at agriculture is like burrowing down through layers of an archaeological dig. We see the various stages of this process in cross-section.

There appear to be some simple consistencies in how sectors change as they proceed down the conveyor belt. The new ideas that are the raw materials of this progress can originate via organizations and incentives that are embedded in the broadly defined market mechanism (e.g., large company laboratories, a venture capital–driven entrepreneurial ecosystem, or competitive university engineering departments), or the market can scavenge ideas from entirely external sources. As these ideas are vetted by the market, they begin to scale up. This is not only a simple process of building larger factories, but is the challenging process of generalizing the new idea in the face of a complex, unknown, and ever-changing environment.

In the current economy, key examples are large, growing technology companies, which provide most of the good jobs. The key is that these sectors have a lot of nonroutine work to be done that has large economic value. Eventually the tasks become so routine that they are mostly automated. That is, the growth sectors gradually ossify into the truly mature sectors that produce things we need, but don't provide many high-wage jobs.

Price and innovation are important dimensions of competition in all sectors, but the relative importance of innovation is highest at the frontier, and competition based on directly comparable prices for almost-identical products (and hence efficiency of the cost structure) is of greatest importance in the mature sectors. Just as classic corporate strategy frameworks apply more to the mature sectors, equilibrium economics is most applicable to these sectors as well. Because the dimensions of competition are known, the past is more relevant, and surprises are less important, these parts of the economy can be analyzed more usefully using quantitative techniques; they increasingly become environments of risk, not uncertainty—at least for extended periods of time.

Despite these limited consistencies, not much that is practically important about the overall development of the economy is predictable in the long term. Short-term forecasts of complex systems can sometimes be made on a combination of "momentum" and the assumption of a relatively simple set of causal mechanisms. Meteorologists can make five-day weather forecasts, for example, by using more complex versions of the observation that the weather in Ohio today highly correlates with the weather in Virginia some number of days later because of consistent wind patterns. In the same way, macroeconomic models can sometimes provide short-term forecasts for things like GDP growth over the next few quarters. Similarly, corporations can somewhat reliably predict at least portfolios of innovations over short periods by allocating capital to different areas based on guesses about technology and market momentum. In the long run, though, all bets are off because of surprising innovations. We have a very bad track record of predicting what new sectors will be the basis of growth, how firms should best be organized, or what skills will be most useful.

However, one thing has historically been consistent about the sequence of new sectors: each new economic growth sector, from agriculture to manufacturing to services, has tended to be more abstract than its predecessor. This often leads the sectors to be labeled as "not real work," and they seem to be a flimsy basis for an economy. As a comparison, I assume that the first farmers who started to scratch out little garden plots were mocked by the hunters on one side and the gatherers on the other who did the "real work" in their clan.

I've seen this dynamic in fast-forward in the software industry. From directly manipulating physical circuits to assembler code to early programming languages to modern object-oriented programming languages, software has been on a fifty-year journey of increasing abstraction from the physical movement of electrons. At each step, some experts in the prior art disparage practitioners of the new step as being not "real" engineers. What they fail to realize is that the skills the old guard mastered have become routinized, then automated, and no longer can provide high-wage employment. Software engineering is often seen in the public imagination as the epitome of secure knowledge work, but increasingly commodity software development is outsourced to India, Eastern Europe, and other low-wage, high-skill countries, just like manufacturing. And what was considered innovative work ten years ago is already commoditized. This is as bitter a reality for software engineers (or market research analysts, clinical trials administrators, quality assurance inspectors, and so on) today as it was for farmers in Bryan's day.

This is daunting, but our hypothetical software engineer is not doomed unless he refuses to respond to the changing world around him. He can thrive as long as he keeps upgrading his skills rapidly enough to continue to add value as yesterday's innovations become tomorrow's commodities.

I've tried to point out in this section that we can't ever go back to the economic world of 1955. Manufacturing can and should always be an important part of our economy, but it will not employ many people unless we force it to become unproductive. We must keep innovating to keep growing our employment base. One of the themes running throughout this book is that this growth demands innovation that will create powerful tensions, and we can't use planning to escape these tensions by achieving growth without unpredictable disruption. And we can't simply opt out of growth without eventually surrendering control of our own destiny to those external societies that surpass us materially. But there are some ways to manage this tension better. America, for all of its faults, has done this extremely well for a long time.

Societies are organic and cannot be fully comprehended, never mind controlled by governments. There are, however, three basic government methods in American history that help to manage the innovation-cohesion problem. The first is decentralization and experimentation. This allows us to try out more things, which seems to be more chaotic in the short run but reduces the costs and frictions in the long run, because the society can observe what works and does not without having to reorient the entire society. The most obvious and important example is the federalist structure of the US government. The second is to improve human capital faster than work is being routinized and automated out from under us. The classic example here is the introduction of universal public education in the United States far earlier than in most advanced economies. The third is to use a welfare state to redistribute economic value from winners to losers. This can be corrosive to trial-and-error progress. It can also be, in a sense, a measurement of the degree to which social cohesion plus the first two approaches have not worked to create assent and progress. But it appears to be a practical requirement for a real-world advanced capitalist democracy.

The next and final chapter puts forward some ideas for how to renovate and modernize government structures in the United States in each of these three areas—decentralization and experimentation, human capital, and the welfare state—to better manage the tension between innovation and cohesion.

CHAPTER 15

Sustainable Innovation

There is a bright line between this chapter and those that precede it. I'll present here not just description and analysis, but proposals for action. One thing I have learned the hard way, and tried to communicate in this book, is that correctly predicting the effect of proposed policy changes is very hard. But I believe that any responsible critic must always answer the basic question "If not this, then what?" In this spirit, my suggestions are meant as a starting point for discussion.

This chapter begins with the narrowest methodological recommendations that the analytical work in the book has most definitively supported, and telescopes outward to increasingly general proposals that combine this analysis with my views about America's contingent situation. None of them focus on changes that will, for example, decrease the unemployment rate next year; instead these recommendations are intended to help improve America's adaptive efficiency, which is the key to long-term success. Even considered all together, they do not compose anything as grandiose as an agenda for America, or even what under full consideration would be the most important priorities the nation faces, but are proposals that I believe satisfy two criteria for adding value: (1) they are informed by the book, and (2) they are either unusual or controversial in the context of mainstream American political economy.

Decentralize and Experiment

The foundation of social progress is the unconscious advance of trial and error through social evolution. Conscious reform efforts sit on top of this and attempt to improve on it for specific policy decisions. Ideally, these proposed reforms will be tested rigorously prior to implementation. Social evolution requires variation in institutions, plus a selection method that tends to retain more adaptive institutions. If we are to accelerate relevant learning, the first order of business is to encourage sufficient variation, cross-pollination of ideas, and selection pressure to encourage progress. Next we would establish a structure to use experiments to support rapid, reliable evaluation of proposed reforms. I'll take them in this order.

Institutionalize policy waivers. The federalist structure of American government has the positive effect of decentralizing power, and creating variation and selection pressure for competing institutions. The more we decentralize power, the more variation we are likely to get. People and resources moving between states will create inherent selection pressure. But as I've argued throughout the third part of this book, decentralization always involves trade-offs: we will lose some benefits of economies of scale, undermine social cohesion, and so on. And as much of the book has been dedicated to arguing, the technocratic idea that we can reconcile these conflicts through rationalized or planned innovation without the messiness of trial and error is a chimera.

I propose starting from our existing balance of federal versus state powers, and allowing deviations on a trial basis. This proposal can be made operational through aggressively using policy waivers. Within extremely broad limits, states should be permitted to change almost any aspect of federally mandated laws and policies on a trial basis—anything from school eligibility rules, to medical reimbursement schedules, to drug-use penalties—as long as they participate in the same kind of structured experimentation program that was operated during the welfare reform period of the 1990s. Doing this would create political incentives for governors to build political careers developing successful policies, and as in the welfare debate, successful policies would tend to spread. If broadly successful, they ultimately would be likely to change policy at the national level. This outcome sometimes would be more flexible for state-level variations in policy, but other times might end up with the demand for greater uniformity, depending on reliable evidence that emerged.

Waivers are similar to the perennial conservative idea of "block-granting" the major federal entitlement programs of Social Security, Medicare, and Medicaid. But the two proposals have two significant differences.

First, I believe that block-granting, even if achieved at one moment in time, is unlikely to be sustainable. If US taxpayers are required by law to transfer wealth between people living in different states, then they can attach whatever strings they want to the money. Social Security, Medicare, unemployment insurance, and similar programs exist in the first place because of some combination of intuitive feelings of fairness and rational self-interest. If voters nationally believe that some states are using these resources in a way with which the voters disagree deeply enough, then they will re-impose conditions. The real issue is how to discover what works in a practical sense (which will often be the realization that what works best in one jurisdiction does not work at all in another), and to provide these results in way that changes behavior so as to improve the fitness of the society. In some cases this will be explicit knowledge leading to conscious changes in policy, but in others it will be implicit knowledge reflected only in, for example, relative economic and population growth rates in some jurisdictions versus others.

This leads to the second difference. The federal government has certain specific roles under the waivers approach. It enforces whatever rules are in place at any given time. It guarantees consistent, reliable information: results of consistently executed RFTs when possible, and general statistical information when experiments are not feasible. These are closely analogous to the roles of a market regulator—the federal government would be metaphorically "making a market" in policy improvements.

Three themes in the "waivers versus block grants" discussion will arise several times in this chapter's further recommendations.

First and simplest is the principle of "start where we are, and try to improve iteratively." There is no scientific answer to strategic questions about balancing the need for innovation with the need for stability, and at a practical level, we will (hopefully) never get to work from the blank canvas of Year Zero of the revolution anyway. We should have some tentative view of where we think a process of change will end up, and this should influence where and how we start to apply trial and error, but we should recognize that any detailed vision of a desired end-state is almost certainly wrong, and want to be guided by real results as we proceed.

Second, libertarian-conservative ideas like "vouchering" public services, the negative income tax, and so forth are conceptually quite similar to block grants. In all these cases we imagine some government entity providing funds and voluntarily avoiding attaching conditions. But *some* conditions are attached to the money; otherwise it wouldn't be Social Security or Medicaid or any other specific program anymore, it would just be money sent to the state government. To imagine that we can freeze in place some minimal list of conditions today and then bind future electorates to them is to wish away human nature. Even if one were to achieve this in a moment of ideological victory, those who pay the piper will eventually insist on calling the tune.

Third, using the power of markets and competition to improve public services is another idea conservatives present frequently—and increasingly across the political spectrum on topics such as education reform. But the real underlying idea here is trial-and-error improvement, which can be achieved in different ways in different contexts. These will often be marketlike, though they will not necessarily look much like the New York Stock Exchange. As both historical observation and the laboratory economics experiments described earlier show, different kinds of market institutions work better or worse in different situations. And "giving consumers choice," as in the education debate, does not necessarily create trial-and-error improvement. Typically we also need to worry about the realistic availability of alternatives to the status quo (that is, the supply side of the market), incentives for market participants if the profit motive does not apply, market regulation to provide adequate information, and so on.

Institutionalize social experimentation. The federal government should put in place a strong experimental capability, building on successes already achieved in policy innovations such as welfare reform, and exploiting the lessons of how this has worked for clinical drug trials and business experimentation described in some detail in Chapters 7 through 12.

The federal government should establish an agency analogous to the Food and Drug Administration (FDA) to develop, promulgate, and enforce standards for designing and interpreting social-policy randomized experiments. This agency should also conduct and publish systematic reviews of multiple experimental and quasi-experimental analyses on specific policy issues. Unlike the FDA, this agency should not have the authority to forbid the deployment of any policies, but like the role of the Congressional Budget Office in scoring the projected budget effects of proposed legislation, policy proposals should be subject to standardized experimental evaluation and reporting to Congress whenever practical. In this function, the agency would be somewhat akin to the old Office of Technology Assessment, which performed an analogous task for technologies but had greater methodological flexibility that led to charges of liberal bias. Like the FDA, this agency likely would coordinate with other government agencies and private contractors carrying out actual experiments and analyses.

This agency would be similar in many ways to the Institute of Education Sciences within the Department of Education or the National Institute of Justice within the Department of Justice, which both were profiled earlier, but with a remit covering all domestic policy. Naturally, Congress, presidential administrations, and everyone else with power or money at stake would attempt to manipulate the findings this agency produced. This is why having one simple, transparent methodology plus organization independence is so important. The FDA, for example, is not above scandal or political influence, but has remained broadly capable of measuring therapeutic effectiveness in a reasonably objective manner.

As indicated in the prior section, the federal government should link the granting of policy waivers to participation in standardized structured experimentation, as was done in the case of welfare reform. This would be the primary impetus to push experimentation to the state level and below, where most domestic policy is executed. This agency should control the funds used to partially subsidize state-level experiments run in support of policy waivers.

We should invest in human and technology infrastructures to increase radically the annual volume of RFTs that can be conducted economically. The federal government's demand for this kind of evidence will naturally change incentives in academia and begin to reorient social science departments toward a more experimental view of these disciplines. This should be encouraged by National Science Foundation–style grants to support doctoral students, postdoctoral fellowships, and university research centers focused on randomized experimentation. Further, as operational procedures and information systems are naturally upgraded, we should build in the capacity to experiment much more simply. For example, as a given state welfare agency upgrades to a new operational software system, we should include in the specifications that this incorporate simple, menu-driven interfaces that randomly assign recipients to test and control groups, report standardized statistical results, and so on. Legal authority to conduct such experiments should be incorporated into enabling legislation, and administrative procedures should be established to become part of the "normal course of business."

To put a stake in the ground, I propose that we set a medium-term goal of conducting as many social policy RFTs in the United States each year as we do clinical trials: about 10,000. If this demonstrated value, and automating experimental design and analysis continued to progress, I could easily imagine that we could conduct a large multiple of this number of randomized social experiments in the United States every year. It could become part of the standard package of management tools used by school districts, county court systems, and state welfare offices.

Even in the most optimistic case, however, all of this effort will not bring us to the sunlit uplands of the scientific management of human affairs. At best, it will marginally improve the quality of the policies we implement (though that can be worth an enormous amount in absolute terms when applied across a nation of 300 million people with a $15 trillion economy). And it may not work at all. There is, however, good reason to be hopeful that it will provide some benefit, and we can course-correct as we go.

Build Human Capital

"Human capital" sounds like a term invented by a human resources consultant but was identified by thinkers as early as Adam Smith as one of the basic types of fixed capital available to a society. It is the stock of competencies, knowledge, and personality attributes that create the ability to perform labor so as to produce economic value. The long-term vector of growth through increasing abstraction places an ever-rising premium on its intellectual components, since new sectors generally have had greater cognitive demands.

The classic method for improving human capital is through improved education. When done successfully, this normally has the effects of both increasing the average level of competence and of reducing the kinds of disparities perceived as unfair. In this way, it can improve both innovation and cohesion. Harvard economists Claudia Goldin and Lawrence Katz have described the use of this strategy to ameliorate the problem of the automation of high-wage jobs as a "race between education and technology."

This is highly aligned with this book's perspective, but I believe it excessively privileges technology as a cause and formal schooling as a solution. In reality, all entities in a capitalist society are in an endless race between commoditization and profits; this applies to individuals as well as firms. But even at the high level of the economy as a whole, the exact process by which this commoditization occurs is unique to each society. Technology does appear to have been a leading factor in this process in the United States for more than a century, but it has not been the only factor. For example, the globalization enabled by overwhelming American military power has been another. Further, it is far from clear that more people spending more years in classrooms, at least as currently operated, will do much good. As described in Chapter 12, we have no convincing evidence that our current system of K–12 education can deploy more resources to generate economic improvement at scale. Nonetheless, it is hard to imagine efforts to improve our human capital that do not begin with our approach to schooling. I will present a view for how to encourage school improvements by exploiting the power of trial and error, and then supplement this with two additional proposals to further improve human capital through better immigration and science policies.

Deregulate schools. K–12 schools seem an obvious place to introduce trial-and-error improvement. Researchers are applying structured experiments to start identifying targeted reform opportunities, but as in most areas of social policy, we have very little scientific knowledge. School vouchers and charter lotteries provide good evidence that we probably can gain something by introducing choice, and in particular, allowing schools the freedom to operate outside of many existing collective bargaining agreements. Finally, the problem of provider capture by teachers' unions is obvious (and understandable, given that a union's goal is normally to represent the interests of its members, not those of their employers or customers).

All of this has led to sustained calls for introducing choice, competition, and markets into our education system. For several decades a stated goal of the libertarian Right has been to "voucherize" education. This is premised on the idea that a marketplace for K–12 schools will both increase productivity (i.e., improve the trade-off between cost and output, allowing us either to increase the measured productivity of education according to agreed-upon goals, such as standardized test scores, at any given level of expenditure, or to achieve a given level of performance at lower cost), and also provide a greater diversity of options to students to better meet their differing needs. One can imagine a wide array of specialized schools with arts or mathematics focus, further deconstraining the idea of school as a building that students in homogenous age groups go to each day, and so on. By this logic, students (or at least families) know their own needs and can meet them this way better than through a one-size-fits-all approach, and this should allow trial-and-error learning that improves the overall system over time.

This sounds fantastic, and is—in both senses of that term. This logic leads to the obvious question of why we should constrain this spending to a category that some government entity decides to call education. If individuals are the best judges of their own welfare, then why not let them decide how to spend this money? Taken to its logical conclusion, we should ask why we have such categories as school subsidies, health care subsidies, and all the rest. Instead, why don't we estimate the costs of a safety-net income plus the costs of buying catastrophic insurance, and provide this amount of money to everyone in the society?

This was the basic idea behind the negative income tax (NIT) experiments discussed earlier. Recall that one major finding in those experiments was that the guaranteed minimum income an NIT created reduced work effort. One reason we haven't implemented such a scheme is that we are afraid that many of the recipients will not work, and then blow the money on Cheetos, beer, and big-screen TVs. In more academic language, morally legitimizing the welfare system requires that the recipients earn and then use this money to support a lifestyle that comports in some rough sense with the idea of the good life held by taxpayers who provide the funds. Recall that the most politically salient finding of the 1990s welfare reform experiments was that people are much more likely to get a job when welfare programs have a work requirement. This same logic applies to all publicly funded schools.

The voucher movement's focus on immediate privatization through parent empowerment has been both too doctrinaire and too artificial. If school choice ever becomes more than Tinkertoy demonstration projects, taxpayers will appropriately demand that a range of controls and requirements be imposed on the schools they are ultimately funding.

Would we allow families to use vouchers to send children to "schools" that taught no reading or mathematics, but only bomb-making, or to schools that offered lavish "support payments" to parents that were, in effect, bribes? We would inevitably—and again, justifiably—have a fairly detailed set of regulations, along with inspection, adjudication, and enforcement mechanisms. At that point, what would be the difference between such private schools and public schools that were allowed greater flexibility in hiring, curriculum, and student acceptance, and had to compete for students to capture funding? Little beyond the label.

A publicly funded private school is a contradiction in terms, but the crucial requirements to provide greater flexibility to meet different needs and to improve general performance through trial and error would still be met in a public school system with parental choice, funding that follows students, and the freedom of schools to operate, if they desire, outside of collective bargaining agreements and other restrictions. That is, charter schools would be a great start, as long as we use the lever of funds to require states to comply with model legislation that makes it practical to start new charter schools without undue resistance, and insists that funding follows students. The most basic institutional requirements of a market would be present: consumer choice and widely distributed buying power on the demand side, and capacity and flexibility on the supply side. The analysis of randomized-choice natural experiments described earlier indicates that these, not privatization per se, drive whatever achievement gains limited market mechanisms have so far provided.

With such reforms under way, the next incremental role for the government beyond the standard regulatory functions of promulgating, adjudicating, and enforcing standards would be to provide the classic market support of increased information and truth in labeling. Suppose the federal government established a comprehensive national exam by grade level to be administered by all schools and universities that receive any federal money, and required each school to publish all results, along with other detailed data about school budgets, performance, and so forth, each year. Secondary, profit-driven information providers, anal-

ogous to credit-ratings agencies and equity analysts, would arise to inform decision-making. The federal role would be very much like that of
the Securities and Exchange Commission for equity markets: to ensure
that each school published accurate, timely, and detailed data.

If such a system proves out performance improvements to the satisfaction of families and taxpayers, the next logical extension would be to
allow schools to generate profits, to allow returns to investors. One reason the market scaled Starbucks from an idea to thousands of stores
within a couple of decades, while seemingly promising ideas for new
school constructs grew almost glacially, is that a fire hose of capital could
be directed to Starbucks once it demonstrated its profitability. Though
ongoing massive public expenditures in education can partially serve
this purpose now and in the future, the free flow of investment would
accelerate the replacement of the existing capital stock of school buildings and equipment more rapidly than the rate determined by normal
political and demographic processes. In this respect such schools would
become something like the publicly regulated utility companies that can
issue debt and equity instruments to raise capital in the public markets,
while still being required to meet defined regulatory objectives.

In the end, we would get to something like the vision of a partially
privatized school system, but would have to go through the hard work
of actually building market institutions, rather than trying to wave a
magic wand of just giving parents vouchers. Developing these institutions might be slow or surprisingly quick, or might never happen at all.
We need to learn this from experience. The trick is to be able to execute
a sequence of steps, each of which must both make progress toward this
goal and demonstrate practical improvement in and of itself. At a high
level, the sequence I have laid out is: (1) allow parents to choose among
public schools, with funding following students, and reform the char-
tering process to make it far easier to establish new schools that exist
outside of collective bargaining agreements; (2) institute consistent national annual testing for all schools that receive government funding,
and publish the results along with other performance information; and
(3) allow schools to operate at a profit to create incentive for private

investment. More precisely, this is the vision that would animate the first steps of this journey. We would surely modify our plan of action as we proceeded, and learned what worked and what did not.

This is not a panacea. In a nation in which about 40 percent of all births occur out of wedlock, many children will be left behind. But better schools will create material improvement. And this method is not theoretical: limited versions have already been implemented successfully in Sweden and the Netherlands, and a similar program is being implemented in Britain.

Treat immigration as recruiting. Assimilating immigrants is a demonstrated core capability of America's political economy. Immigration is a continuing source of vitality, and combined with birthrates around the replacement level, creates a sustainable rate of overall population growth and age-demographic balance. But unfortunately, the manner in which we have actually handled immigration since the 1970s has yielded large-scale legal and illegal immigration of a low-skilled population from Latin America. It is hard to imagine a more damaging way to expose the fault lines of America's political economy: We have chosen a strategy that provides low-wage gardeners and nannies for the elite, low-cost home improvement and fresh produce for the middle class, and fierce wage competition for the working class.

Instead we should think of immigration as an opportunity to improve our stock of human capital. Once we have reestablished control of our southern border, we should set up recruiting offices for the best possible talent everywhere: from Mexico City to Beijing to Helsinki to Calcutta. We should offer green cards to foreign students upon their completion of degrees in science and engineering subjects at approved universities. The H-1B visa program should be expanded and strengthened. On the other hand, we should deemphasize family reunification for immigrants already in the United States.

For many years Australia and Canada have demonstrated the practicality and utility of skills-based immigration policies. We should improve upon their example by using testing and other methods to apply a basic tenet of all human capital–intensive organizations that are managing for the long term: always pick talent over skill. It would be great for America as a whole to have, say, 500,000 smart, motivated people move here each year with the intention of becoming citizens.

There is a simple way to begin to test this concept. The United States currently runs lotteries for many types of visas. Why don't we randomly assign a subset of the visas awarded through each of these lotteries to individuals selected based on a test-based selection process, and then observe over several years the employment, crime, education and other social indicators for immigrants selected under this method compared to the current approach? This would be imperfect—for example, it would not consider very long-term, multigenerational impact—but it would produce a much more informed debate than we have now. If this demonstrates that selective immigration appears to work in practice, we could continue to use this approach to assign test groups to various alternative selection rules and improve our selection methods on an ongoing basis.

Prioritize science and technology. Every economically advanced society understands that technological innovation is a key to productivity growth. Trying to plan out the development of various technologies and sectors is a fool's errand, but the relevant responsibilities of government are to help ensure that conditions for innovation are present, and to invest in appropriate science, technology, and infrastructure projects that would not make sense for a private actor.

We should dramatically increase the budgets of our most successful government and government-backed university research and development (R&D) institutions: the National Institutes of Health, the Defense Advanced Research Projects Agency, Caltech, and so on. We should be consciously elitist about reinforcing demonstrated technical excellence, while constantly experimenting with new entities and concepts—such as ARPA-E, an analog to the Defense Advanced Research Projects Agency focused on new energy technologies, and prize-based competitions for achieving specified technical benchmarks open to all comers.

Our funding mechanisms should be ruthless about killing off the majority of new ideas that fail, and pointing a fire hose of money at those that succeed, as I argued in the case of education. We should have national technical projects at the scale of the moon landings or the war on cancer, and should spend past the point of apparent waste. These investments would be synergistic with better education and immigration policies. We would reinforce our position as a magnet for talent, improve our pipeline of domestic talent, and mobilize both more effectively.

The first two proposals hopefully would reduce costs, but this third proposal would increase them. The money has to come from somewhere. Most of the money is in the welfare state, which needs to be restructured, ideally making it more effective and lower cost, as I will describe in the next section. We should reprioritize spending for this purpose. As an illustrative example, take some money that would have been spent on providing a given drug to patients under Medicare, and invest it instead in research to develop a better drug. But in the end, each spending proposal needs to float on its own bottom by generating more value than it costs. If push comes to shove, and we need to raise taxes to fund these investments, we should do it.

Unbundle the Welfare State

Most government spending in an advanced economy is on the welfare state. In the United States, for example, excluding interest costs, the combined cost of pensions, health care, education, and welfare account for a majority of total public expenditures across federal, state, and local governments.

All wealthy and broadly capitalist nations have created and maintained a welfare system; such systems appear to be concomitant with the growth that capitalism creates. It is not obvious why this must be so, but is likely at least partially related to the reality that as the society becomes wealthier, the security and peace of mind it provides become more affordable. In any event, as far as can be seen from history, the idea of a capitalist society without a welfare system is misplaced nostalgia—

or more accurately, is an anachronism. It is like wishing for a commercial jet aircraft without stabilizers. Such a thing may be possible, but I'd want to see a few test flights before boarding one.

The primary requirement for a successful society is for innovation and growth, because the historical record indicates that in the long run this will make almost everyone in the society better off than in a less innovative society. But this creates the need for coping mechanisms, which almost certainly will include the welfare system. However, the welfare system must in turn be controlled and bounded, or in the long run it will undermine the process of growth and innovation it is actually meant to support. A correct understanding of liberty (in the sense of liberty-as-means), therefore, leads to a sustained defense of the welfare system. There should be no long-term libertarian goal of eliminating the welfare system, but rather of ensuring that it achieves its purpose with minimum negative side effects.

The negative side effects of the welfare state are several, and can be severe. One is moral hazard. If we soften a negative outcome—say, unemployment—over which the recipient has at least some control, this will, all else equal, make the outcome more likely. A second is that those administering a given program can become an important political force, and bend the program, consciously or not, to their own benefit. Think of the enormous political power of teachers' unions. And a third is the corrosion of initiative. The welfare system habituates a population to protection from uncertainty by a benevolent external power.

This third effect is the most subtle and difficult to confront analytically, but in the end is probably the most important. As usual, Alexis de Tocqueville saw this presciently more than 150 years ago when he prophesied the modern welfare state and its tightly linked regulatory apparatus:

> Above this race of men stands an immense and tutelary power, which takes upon itself alone to secure their gratifications and to watch over their fate. . . . It provides for their security, foresees and supplies their necessities, facilitates their pleasures, manages their principal concerns,

directs their industry, . . . covers the surface of society with a network of small complicated rules, minute and uniform, through which the most original minds and the most energetic characters cannot penetrate, to rise above the crowd. The will of man is not shattered, but softened, bent, and guided; men are seldom forced by it to act, but they are constantly restrained from acting. Such a power does not destroy, but it prevents existence; it does not tyrannize, but it compresses, enervates, extinguishes, and stupefies a people, till each nation is reduced to nothing better than a flock of timid and industrious animals, of which the government is the shepherd.

This passage is very widely quoted, but what is less often cited is Tocqueville's description of the Americans of whom he is speaking as characterized by "the mildness of their manners, the extent of their education, the purity of their religion, the gentleness of their morality, their regular and industrious habits, and the restraint which they almost all observe in their vices no less than in their virtues." Criticisms of the welfare system are often seen—sometimes correctly—as coded attacks on the undeserving poor. Tocqueville's prophecy here is not about the creation of an underclass, but rather the deterioration of initiative in the middle class: in modern language, the conversion of an entrepreneurial culture to a bureaucratic and managerial one.

This can seem pretty hyperbolic, not to mention pretentious, when applied to any individual proposed expansion of the welfare system. Extending unemployment insurance an extra four weeks will not usher in a regime of soft despotism. But a mountain can be built one pebble at a time.

We are approaching a financial rather than a philosophical crisis of the welfare state that is bringing these issues to a head. Widely discussed projections from many sources, including the Congressional Budget Office, emphasize the severity of our fiscal problem. It's easy to remember these long-term forecasts by using a lot of 80s: in 2080, government spending is projected to be a little less than 80 percent of GDP, and accumulated debt is projected to be over 800 percent of GDP.

The one thing I can state with some confidence about these specific forecasts is that they are wrong. In the real world, something—either more prudent management of our federal fiscal affairs, or else a painful and destabilizing crash—will intervene.

The long-term forecasts, however, illustrate the crucial point that we are sitting on the mother of all bubbles. Many, probably most, Americans anticipate a stream of consumption that will be provided for them into old age by the government (i.e., other taxpayers). Unfortunately, most American taxpayers apparently do not anticipate the kind of enormous increase in taxes required to pay for this stream of benefits. One or both of these expectations will not be met. Americans as a whole are simply less wealthy, in the most useful sense of rationally anticipatable future material consumption, than they think they are. And the size of this disconnect is vastly greater than, for example, the size of the subprime mortgage bubble that played a central role in initiating the current crisis.

The US government's borrowing capacity is vast, but it is not limitless. At some point that nobody can predict, we will not be able to borrow enough to continue spending consistent with current expectations without extremely large negative effects. Plans to deal with this problem by simply asserting that we will choose to control spending in the future by, for example, distributing vouchers for health care with declining aggregate value as a percentage of GDP as compared to current expectations (a conservative idea), or that we will have a government agency that will make health care availability decisions that will achieve the same aggregate spending path (a liberal idea), are mostly beside the point. These are proposals for ice cream sundaes for me today, and a strict diet for somebody else tomorrow.

We can't really control today what spending and taxation levels will be decades into the future, as each future Congress can change whatever it wants. These targets for spending cuts in the distant future are very much like proposed laws that would "guarantee" that carbon dioxide emissions will be 80 percent below today's level in 2050. They will, unless and until that future electorate decides they don't want to forgo the economic consumption that this would require, any more than we do today.

What we can do today is to change program *structures* so that we have the best set of options available to us in the future—incorporating considerations not only of efficiency and fiscal realism, but also minimization of negative side effects, and maximization of opportunities for trial-and-error improvement. Nothing is forever, and structures that can be changed today can be changed again in the future, but structures tend to be more enduring than spending or taxation levels.

There is a typical life cycle for the evolution of major process innovations in large businesses and across entire industries over decades. First comes innovation, then scale-up, then maturity, and optimization. Optimization almost always implies unbundling: examining the once-innovative process, breaking it into its component pieces, and parceling them out to exploit opportunities to improve both efficiency and effectiveness. The US welfare state is now many decades old, and I believe that looking at it through the lens of unbundling makes obvious large opportunities for structural reform.

As a result of its historical development, the welfare state is composed of multiple programs, each with a common structure that combines several functions. First, they often provide a true safety net: a fail-safe provision of consumption of important goods that represents some roughly agreed-upon minimum baseline of existence for any member of the society. Second, they incorporate some element of risk-pooling, as in the case of Social Security's protection against unforeseen setbacks that might prevent any one of us from having enough money or relatives for subsistence in old age. Third, they may redistribute wealth beyond what the first two goals require. Fourth, these programs also may require recipients to behave prudently: for example, the government requires that wage earners avoid some consumption today to provide funds for retirement. Fifth, the government may provide relevant goods directly, such as in the case of traditional public schools.

The first two of these functions—provision of a safety net and the exploitation risk pools—can enhance stability, but there is no reason to bundle them together beyond the political advantages this provides to welfare system providers and their political patrons. They should become separate programs. The requirement for prudential behavior can be linked more effectively to each of these separately.

For example, Social Security combines (1) a safety net for old people who have been extremely imprudent, unproductive, or unlucky, with (2) a mechanism that forces workers to save for their retirement, and then pools their savings. These should be separate programs. We should have a defined-contribution pension program, within which individuals must contribute a reasonable proportion of income (though some flexibility even in amount should be allowed) to an array of retirement investment vehicles to which they hold property rights. Separately, much as it does for people of all ages, the government should offer a safety net for those who end up penniless or nearly so in old age without either private savings, savings under this defined-contribution version of Social Security, or relatives who will offer support. Unlike such a safety net provided to those during working years, it should not have a work requirement. It should also not attempt to replicate the income of those who have prudently saved for retirement, but instead be a true minimum safety net.

Whether the government should engage in pure redistribution of wealth for reasons of equity, justice, or other moral concepts beyond the requirements of welfare system programs is an enormous philosophical question. In practice, the answer partially depends on the specific beliefs and attitudes of the people in any given society. Certainly in contemporary America support for such an idea is limited. But to the extent such redistribution is desired, it should be done explicitly, and outside the vehicle of either an old-age safety net or retirement savings program.

Finally, it is possible to separate the specification of welfare system goods from their provision; that is, a government that guarantees education and health care can still choose whether to run schools and hospitals directly, or to provide funds to nongovernmental organizations to do this directly. I've previously indicated that a long-standing goal of the libertarian Right has been to "voucherize" social programs so that government provides the cash equivalent of various services, but allows private firms to compete in markets to provide the services themselves. I've also described why at least immediately transforming public schools in this way is unrealistic, because society legitimately attaches controls to public money, and because market institutions can take time to build.

The same basic argument applies to each major welfare system program. The Right argues that we should privatize Social Security accounts. But like public schools, we surely would regulate what investment vehicles to allow—otherwise, I could simply "invest" in a retirement cache of Cheetos, beer, and big-screen TVs. And like schools, we would have to have a set of regulations, adjudication, and enforcement. How is this different than simply having a wide variety of independently operated retirement funds among which Social Security recipients can allocate their funds? If we want to replace Medicare with so-called health savings accounts, we would face the same dilemma.

The key question in separating specification from provision, then, is less whether the employees of the provider organizations that operate schools, hospitals, and other service groups have the name of some government agency printed on their paychecks than it is the breadth of specification. The extent to which the beneficiaries of some program can choose among a variety of providers, the degree to which these can permit providers to offer a variety of versions of the benefit, the extent to which new providers can enter or exit, and so forth is what matters. I propose that we seek to consistently test increasing flexibility on all of these dimensions in each entitlement program after unbundling, and generally have a bias toward flexibility when we must make a judgment call. Note that this is much more plausible when, for example, the program that is intended to help those with savings best use them to provide post-retirement income is not also the program keeping penniless elderly widows fed.

Obviously each of these programs will have unique challenges. For example, the degree of existing government entanglement varies widely. In the United States, the lack of an enormous existing government-operated physical delivery infrastructure for health and pensions (outside of specialized areas, such as the Veterans Administration hospital system) means that such a transition should be logistically simpler than it would be for education. On the other hand, the vast amounts of money at stake combined with the enormous political influence of doctors, insurance companies, pharmaceutical companies, and hospital groups will present a different set of challenges. But for each of the programs we would face the same need to create market institutions that produce the benefits of trial-and-error learning, while recognizing the limits created by the program's intention to coerce behavior, to some degree, in support of a social vision of the good life. Remembering that successful market institutions tend to be "the result of human action, but not the execution of any human design," the process of creating them in these cases is likely to require trial-and-error itself.

A Final Note

I developed the proposals in this chapter by applying what I had learned in writing the book to my understanding of the current situation of advanced democratic societies. Upon reviewing these suggestions, however, I made a retrospectively obvious observation: each is an attempt to embed a trial-and-error process within humane constraints. First, where possible, explicit knowledge is developed and used to compress the time evolutionary learning requires. Reliable knowledge overrules trial and error. And second, recognizing that this will be the exception, and that therefore trial and error will continue indefinitely, each process is contained within a policy vessel that tries to avoid it from becoming so disruptive that it excessively threatens social cohesion. Without these constraints, innovation will tend to become self-defeating. To repeat an earlier observation, the typical result of a threat to social cohesion in a contemporary representative democracy isn't overthrow of the government, but greater use of the political process to retard innovation.

My proposals aren't mostly about determining how to strike the right balance between innovation and cohesion, but instead are about engineering the structures of these contained trial-and-error processes so that we get the maximum practical benefit for a given amount of disruption. As an economist might say, they are about being at "the efficient frontier" in the trade-off between innovation and cohesion.

As to where on this trade-off a society should sit on a given policy issue—for what specific national regulations should we refuse to grant states waivers, or how generous exactly should the old-age provisions in Social Security be, and so forth—I doubt the answer is rationally knowable. Ultimately, democratic governance is required. This governance incorporates trial and error at a yet higher level of abstraction, but as I've emphasized, it must be more than that—it must include a view about the overall strategy and vision for the society. Each society, just as each individual, must find a way to compete in this world without losing its soul.

ACKNOWLEDGMENTS

A book like this is in many ways a collective enterprise that has one person's name on the cover, and I would like to thank a few of those involved. Of course, all errors remain my own.

Tim Bartlett, my editor at Basic Books, has helped to shape the book tremendously. The entire team at Basic, including Sarah Rosenthal and Michelle Welsh-Horst, has been instrumental in bringing this book to fruition. Lynn Chu, my agent, understood and supported what I was trying to accomplish before anyone in the book publishing world knew anything about it.

I have worked out preliminary versions of some of the ideas in the book in several online and print publications. Rich Lowry, managing editor of *National Review*, and Dusty Rhodes, former CEO of the magazine, have provided countless opportunities for me to publish articles and interact with experts and interested amateurs. Probably a majority of the editing staff at *National Review* have given me lessons in logic and grammar. Yuval Levin, managing editor of *National Interest*, has given me similar public exposure, guidance, and assistance. Andrew Sullivan and Megan McArdle of *The Atlantic* have done the same. Reihan Salam introduced me to blogging at *The American Scene* and has provided support in countless ways. Brian Anderson was instrumental in structuring the narrative of a *City Journal* article on social science that is closely related to the theme of the book.

A number of extremely talented writers, businesspeople, and academic experts on various historical, philosophical, and technical topics covered in the book have generously given me their time, attention, and feedback. Among them are Michael Knox Beran, David Brooks, Anthony Bruce, Ross Douthat, Richard Epstein, David Frum, Andrew Gelman, George Kelling, Arnold Kling, Yuval Levin, Walker Lewis, Donald Livingston, Larry Mead, Nigel Morris, Reihan Salam, Scott Setrakian, and Marcus Winters.

The Manhattan Institute has been supportive in many ways. Larry Mone, Howard Husock, and others have organized and participated in roundtable discussions of the ideas in the book that have sharpened my thinking and writing considerably. Bernadette Serton and Lindsay Craig Young have helped to find an audience for the book.

Finally and most importantly, Jane, Lincoln, and Cornelia have variously provided support, encouragement, and feedback. They have also had to put up with countless absences over a period of years. My gratitude to them is heartfelt.

NOTES

Introduction

x   **Paul Krugman:** "The Obama Gap," *New York Times,* January 9, 2009.

x   **Joseph Stiglitz:** "Nobel Prize Economist: Obama's Stimulus 'Not Enough,'" Media Research Center report, January 8, 2009. Accessed from www.mrc.org/bmi/articles/2009/Nobel_Prize_Economist_Obamas _Stimulus_Not_Enough.html on September 30, 2011.

x   **James Buchanan:** Online petition published by the Cato Institute. Accessed from www.cato.org/special/stimulus09/alternate_version.html on September 30, 2011.

xii   **"knowledge problem":** F. A. Hayek, "The Use of Knowledge in Society," *American Economic Review* 35, no. 4 (September 1945): 519–530.

xii   **"open society":** Sir Karl Popper, *The Open Society and Its Enemies, Vol. 1: The Spell of Plato* (Princeton, NJ: Princeton University Press, 1966).

xiii   *Road to Serfdom*: F. A. Hayek, *The Road to Serfdom* (Chicago: University of Chicago Press, 1944).

xiii   **"evolutionary epistemology":** Donald T. Campbell, "Evolutionary Epistemology," in *The Philosophy of Karl R. Popper,* ed. P. A. Schilpp (LaSalle, IL: Open Court, 1974), 412–463.

PART I: SCIENCE

Chapter 1: Induction and the Problem of Induction

4   **The Scholastics:** Andrea Falcon, "Aristotle on Causality," *Stanford Encyclopedia of Philosophy,* ed. Edward N. Zalta (Fall 2011). Accessed from http://plato.stanford.edu/archives/fall2011/entries/aristotle-causality on September 30, 2011.

4   **In *Physics*:** Aristotle, *Physics,* trans. Richard Hope (Lincoln: University of Nebraska Press, 1961), 36.

4   **Aristotle argued:** Falcon, "Aristotle on Causality."

5   **serving as:** Perez Zagorin, *Francis Bacon* (Princeton, NJ: Princeton University Press, 1998), 188.

5   **"The true and lawful goal":** Sir Francis Bacon, *The Works*, vol. 8, ed. James Spedding, Robert Leslie Ellis, and Douglas Denton Heath (Boston: Taggard and Thompson, 1863), 29. Accessed from http://intersci.ss.uci.edu /wiki/eBooks/BOOKS/Bacon/Novum%20Organum%20Bacon.pdf on November 19, 2011.

     In this quote Bacon clearly means "discoveries and powers" in a material sense. See, for example, an alternative translation of the quoted passage as: "But the real and legitimate goal of the sciences is the endowment of human life with new inventions and riches." Sir Francis Bacon, *Novum Organum*, ed. Joseph Devey, M.A. (New York: P.F. Collier, 1902), 87.

5   **"extend more widely":** Bacon, *The Works*, 8:47.

5   **"The sciences":** Ibid., 24–25.

6   **capacities . . . of individuals:** Ibid., 5.

6   **capacities . . . of groups:** Ibid., 7.

6   **"the human understanding":** Ibid., 11.

6   **"From a few":** Ibid., 52–53.

7   **"by a gradual":** Ibid., 6–7.

7   **"far greater evil":** Ibid., 20.

8   **"greatest obstacle":** Ibid., 37.

8   **"whatever deserves":** Ibid., 49.

8   **"true sons":** Ibid., 3.

8   **"labors and industries":** Ibid., 46.

8   **Salomon's House:** Sir Francis Bacon, *The New Atlantis* (Project Gutenberg, 2000), 23–24. Accessed from www.fcsh.unl.pt/docentes/rmonteiro /pdf/The_New_Atlantis.pdf on September 30, 2009.

8   **"experiments of Light":** Bacon, *The Works*, 8:40.

9   **"let no man":** Ibid., 29.

9   **"Both ways":** Ibid., 7.

9   **"nothing duly":** Ibid., 40.

9   **"shall proceed":** Ibid., 41.

10   **"simple enumeration":** Ibid., 42.

10   **Bacon warned:** Ibid., 19:

     "I foresee that if ever men are roused by my admonitions to betake themselves seriously to experiment and bid farewell to sophistical doctrines, then indeed through the premature hurry of the understanding to leap or fly to universals and principles of things, great danger may be apprehended from philosophies of this kind; against which evil we ought even now to prepare."

10   **"All reasonings":** David Hume, *An Enquiry Concerning Human Under-standing* (online edition scanned from Harvard Classics 37; P. F. Collier & Son, 1910), Section 4, Part 1. Accessed from http://18th.eserver.org /hume-enquiry.html#4 on September 30, 2011.

11   **"Our senses":** Ibid., Section 4, Part 2.

Chapter 2: Falsification and Paradigms

16   **Aristotle argued:** Aristotle, *On the Heavens,* trans. J. L. Stocks (online edition; University of Adelaide, 2010), Book 1, Part 6:

"A given weight moves a given distance in a given time; a weight which is as great and more moves the same distance in a less time, the times being in inverse proportion to the weights."

Accessed from http://ebooks.adelaide.edu.au/a/aristotle/heavens/book1 .html on October 1, 2011.

16   **Galileo supposedly:** Stillman Drake, *Galileo at Work: His Scientific Biography* (New York: Dover Phoenix, 2003), 19.

17   **Sir Karl Popper developed:** Sir Karl Popper, *The Logic of Scientific Discovery* (London: Routledge Classics, 2007), 3–26.

17   **Wolfgang Pauli once derided:** *The Encyclopedia of Physical Science,* vol. 1, ed. Joe Rosen and Lisa Quinn Gothard (New York: Infobase Publishing, 2010), 509.

18   **And Bacon:** Sir Francis Bacon, *The Works,* vol. 8, ed. James Spedding, Robert Leslie Ellis, and Douglas Denton Heath (Boston: Taggard and Thompson, 1863), 12. Accessed online from www.constitution.org/bacon /nov_org.htm on November 19, 2011.

20   **Popper refers:** Popper, *Logic of Scientific Discovery,* 24.

22   **under Stalin:** Ethan Pollock, *Stalin and the Soviet Science Wars* (Princeton, NJ: Princeton University Press, 2006), 41–71.

22   **Duhem/Quine Thesis:** A. F. Chalmers, *What Is This Thing Called Science? An Assessment of the Nature and Status of Science and Its Methods* (New York: Open University Press, 2004), 89.

22   **After the usage:** Imre Lakatos, *Criticism and the Growth of Knowledge* (New York: Cambridge University Press, 1970), 91–195; from Theodore Schick Jr., ed., *Readings in the Philosophy of Science* (Mountain View, CA: Mayfield Publishing Company, 2000), 20–23.

22   **Consider the textbook example:** Chalmers, *What Is This Thing,* 78.

23   **While studying at MIT:** The details of apparent superluminal motion are well beyond the scope of this book, but a review of the scientific issue as it was understood at the time I was doing this research is provided by K. I. Kellermann and I. I. K. Pauliny-Toth, *Compact Radio Sources,*

Annual Review of Astronomy and Astrophysics, vol. 19 (A82-11551 02-90) (Palo Alto, CA: Annual Reviews, 1981), 373–410.

24 **In 1962:** Thomas S. Kuhn, *The Structure of Scientific Revolutions* (Chicago and London: University of Chicago Press, 1996).

24 **idea of a paradigm:** Ibid., 10.

24 **A classic case:** Ibid., 68–69.

25 **he [Popper] claimed:** Sir Karl Popper, *Conjectures and Refutations: The Growth of Scientific Knowledge* (London: Routledge, 2002), 44–49.

25 **Bacon described:** Bacon, *The Works,* 8:8.

26 **paradigms come into direct competition:** Kuhn, *Structure of Scientific Revolutions,* 150–152.

28 **Popper grudgingly:** Popper, *Logic of Scientific Discovery,* 277–278.

Chapter 3: Implicit and Explicit Knowledge

32 **You can find:** R. Nowak, "Generalized Binary Search," in *Proceedings of the 46th Allerton Conference on Communications, Control and Computing,* 2008, 568–574; http://ieeexplore.ieee.org/xpl/freeabs_all.jsp?arnumber=4797609.

33 **Genetic algorithms:** Melanie Mitchell, *An Introduction to Genetic Algorithms* (Cambridge, MA: MIT Press, 1996).

33 **grains of sand on Earth:** Andrew Craig, "Astronomers Count the Stars," BBC News, July 22, 2003. Accessed from http://news.bbc.co.uk/2/hi /science/nature/3085885.stm on November 18, 2011.

37 **nested structure:** Donald T. Campbell, *Methodology and Epistemology for Social Science: Selected Papers* (Chicago: University of Chicago Press, 1988), 476.

40 **and Kuhn:** Thomas S. Kuhn, *The Road Since Structure, Philosophical Essays, 1970–1983* (Chicago: University of Chicago Press, 2000), 160.

40 **Bacon recognized:** Sir Francis Bacon, *The Works,* vol. 8, ed. James Spedding, Robert Leslie Ellis, and Douglas Denton Heath (Boston: Taggard and Thompson, 1863), 12. Accessed online from http://intersci.ss.uci .edu/wiki/eBooks/BOOKS/Bacon/Novum%20Organum%20Bacon.pdf on November 19, 2011.

42 **both Popper:** Sir Karl Popper, *Objective Knowledge: an Evolutionary Approach* (Chicago: Clarendon Press, 1972).

44 **reading the Bible:** A. Pereira, "When Did Modern Economic Growth Really Start? The Empirics of Malthus to Solow," University of British Columbia, 2003, note 25. Accessed from www.uoguelph.ca/~sday/cneh-rche /pdfs/pereira.pdf on October 7, 2011.

45 **quantum mechanics:** "What Is Quantum Mechanics Good For?" *Scientific American,* November 2, 2010.

45 **relativity theory:** D. Thibault et al., *General Relativity Today, in Gravitation and Experiment* (Basel: Birkhäuser Basel, 2007).

Chapter 4: Science as a Social Enterprise

48 **Practicing scientists:** S. G. Korenman, R. Berk, N. S. Wenger, and V. Lew, "Evaluation of the Research Norms of Scientists and Administrators Responsible for Academic Research Integrity," *Journal of the American Medical Association* 279, no. 1 (January 1998): 41–47.

48 **rarely question:** Pew Research Center, "Public Praises Science; Scientists Fault Public, Media," July 9, 2009. Accessed from www.people-press .org/2009/07/09/public-praises-science-scientists-fault-public-media on November 15, 2011.

48 **financial reasons:** Ibid.

48 **public to restricting:** Ibid.

50 **Bacon identified:** Sir Francis Bacon, *The Works,* vol. 8, ed. James Spedding, Robert Leslie Ellis, and Douglas Denton Heath (Boston: Taggard and Thompson, 1863), 37. Accessed online from http://intersci.ss.uci .edu/wiki/eBooks/BOOKS/Bacon/Novum%20Organum%20Bacon.pdf on November 19, 2011.

50 **The parallels:** M. Polanyi, "The Republic of Science: Its Political and Economic Theory," *Minerva* 1 (1962): 54–73.

52 **tacit knowledge:** Michael Polanyi, *The Tacit Dimension* (New York: Doubleday & Co., 1966).

53 **Popper called:** Sir Karl Popper, *The Open Society and Its Enemies, Vol. 1: The Spell of Plato* (Princeton, NJ: Princeton University Press, 1966).

Chapter 5: Science Without Experiments

56 **In 1980:** Lawrence Berkeley National Laboratory, "Alvarez Theory on Dinosaur Die-Out Upheld: Experts Find Asteroid Guilty of Killing Dinosaurs." Accessed from http://newscenter.lbl.gov/feature-stories/2010 /03/09/alvarez-theory-on-dinosaur on October 7, 2011.

56 **Many leading scientists:** Peter Schulte et al., "The Chicxulub Asteroid Impact and Mass Extinction at the Cretaceous-Paleogene Boundary," *Science,* March 5, 2010, 1214–1218.

57 **several hundred thousand years:** Gerta Keller, Thierry Adatte, Alfonso Pardo Juez, and Jose G. Lopez-Oliva, "New Evidence Concerning the Age and Biotic Effects of the Chicxulub Impact in NE Mexico," *Journal of the Geological Society* 166 (May 2009): 393–411.

Chapter 6: Some Observations Concerning Probability

62   **Nassim Taleb:** Nassim Nicholas Taleb, *The Black Swan: The Impact of the Highly Improbable* (New York: Random House, 2007), xvii–xx.

62   **Financial analysts:** R. Cont, "Model Uncertainty and Its Impact on the Pricing of Derivative Instruments," Finance Concepts Working Paper FC-04–02, June 2004.

62   **Frank Knight:** Frank H. Knight, *Risk, Uncertainty, and Profit* (New York: Houghton, Mifflin, 1921).

67   **A Roman general:** Mary Beard, *The Roman Triumph* (Cambridge, MA: Harvard University Press, 2009), 85.

Chapter 7: The Invention and Application of the Randomized Trial

69   **"more than 100,000":** Jason Lazarou, Bruce H. Pomeranz, and Paul N. Corey, "Incidence of Adverse Drug Reactions in Hospitalized Patients: A Meta-Analysis of Prospective Studies," *Journal of the American Medical Association* 279, no. 15 (April 1998):1200–1205.

70   **bloodletting:** Gerry Greenstone, MD, "The History of Bloodletting," *British Columbia Medical Journal,* 52, no. 1 (January–February 2010): 12–14.

70   **surgical procedure:** J. F. Nunn, "A Treatment That Has Stood the Test of Time for over Three and a Half Millennia," *JLL Bulletin: Commentaries on the History of Treatment Evaluation,* 2008. Accessed from www.james lindlibrary.org/illustrating/articles/a-treatment-that-has-stood-the-test -of-time-for-over-three-and-a on November 16, 2011

71   **book of Daniel:** Accessed from www.jameslindlibrary.org/illustrating /records/the-book-of-daniel-chapter-11–16/key_passages on October 4, 2011.

71   **Islamic scholars:** Dimitri Gutas, "Before and After Avicenna," *Proceedings of the First Conference of the Avicenna Study Group* (Leiden: Koninklijke Brill, 2003), 154–160.

71   **al-Razi:** Accessed from www.jameslindlibrary.org/illustrating/records /kitab-al-hawi-fi-al-tibb/key_passages on October 4, 2011.

71   **Ibn Hindu:** Accessed from www.jameslindlibrary.org/illustrating/records /miftah-al-tibb-wa-minhaj-al-tullab-the-key-to-the-science-of-me/title _pages on October 4, 2011.

71   **Avicenna:** Rabie E. Abdel-Halim, "Experimental Medicine 1000 Years Ago," *Urology Annals* 3, no. 2 (May–August 2011): 55–61.

71   **Ben Cao Tu Jing:** Accessed from www.jameslindlibrary.org/illustrating /records/atlas-of-materia-medica/key_passages on October 4, 2011.

71 **traditional remedies:** N. R. Farnsworth, O. Akerele, A. S. Bingel, D. D. Soejarto, Z. Guo, "Medicinal Plants in Therapy," *Bulletin of the World Health Organization* 63, no. 6 (1985): 965–981.

71 **dozens:** D. S. Fabricant and N. R. Farnsworth, "The Value of Plants Used in Traditional Medicine for Drug Discovery," Environmental Health Perspectives 109, Supplement 1 (March 2001): 69–75.

72 **In 1747:** Accessed from www.jameslindlibrary.org/illustrating/records /a-treatise-of-the-scurvy-in-three-parts-containing-an-inquiry/key _passages on October 4, 2011.

73 **The physiologists:** Harry M. Marks, *The Progress of Experiment: Science and Public Reform in the United States, 1900–1990* (Cambridge: Cambridge University Press, 2000), 21. *Progress of Experiment* provided the background for much of the discussion of nineteenth- and twentieth-century medical experimentation in this chapter.

73 **meant by "controlled":** Ibid., 30–31.

73 **anthrax vaccine experiment:** Accessed from www.scribd.com/mobile /documents/16319283/download?secret_password=2hqrvoyoyyk0zg neoe6w on October 5, 2011.

74 **pancreas:** D. Noble, "Claude Bernard, the First Systems Biologist, and the Future of Physiology," *Experimental Physiology* 93 (2008): 16–26.

74 **Nineteenth-century researchers:** Ted J. Kaptchuk, "Intentional Ignorance: A History of Blind Assessment and Placebo Controls in Medicine," *Bulletin of the History of Medicine* 72, no. 3 (Fall 1998): 389–433.

74 **first person:** Stephen M. Stigler, *Statistics on the Table: The History of Statistical Concepts and Methods* (Cambridge, MA: Harvard University Press, 2002), 192–196.

74 **blinded experiment:** Charles Sanders Peirce and Joseph Jastrow, "On Small Differences in Sensation," *Memoirs of the National Academy of Sciences* 3 (1885): 73–83. Accessed from http://psychclassics.yorku.ca/Peirce /small-diffs.htm October 4, 2011.

75 **Van Helmont:** L. Forsetlunda, I. Chalmers, and A. Bjørndala, "When Was Random Allocation First Used to Generate Comparison Groups in Experiments to Assess the Effects of Social Interventions?" *Economics of Innovation and New Technology* 16, no. 5 (2007): 371–384.

75 **sporadic attempts:** Ibid.

75 **Jerzy Neyman:** S. D. Levitt and J. A. List, "Field Experiments in Economics: The Past, the Present, and the Future," National Bureau of Economic Research Working Paper 14356, 2008.

75 **R. A. Fisher:** Ibid.

75 **design of experiments:** R. A. Fisher, *The Design of Experiments,* 9th ed. (New York: Hafner, 1971).

77   **Sir Austin Bradford Hill:** I. Chalmers, "Joseph Asbury Bell and the Birth of Randomized Trials," *Journal of the Royal Society of Medicine* 100, no. 6 (June 2007): 287–293.

77   **pertussis vaccine:** Ibid.

77   **Coronary Drug Project:** Michael P. LaValley, "Intent-to-Treat Analysis of Randomized Clinical Trials." Accessed from http://people.bu.edu /mlava/ITT%20Workshop.pdf on October 5, 2011.

77   **modern RFT:** Curtis L. Meinert, *Clinical Trials: Design, Conduct, and Analysis* (New York: Oxford University Press, 1986), 93.

78   **sequence of trial phases:** "Clinical Trial Phases," US National Library of Medicine, National Institutes of Health. Accessed from www.nlm.nih .gov/services/ctphases.html on October 5, 2011.

79   **more than 350,000:** H. Bloom, "The Core Analytics of Randomized Experiments for Social Research," MDRC Working Paper on Research Methodology, 2006. Accessed from www.mdrc.org/publications/437/full .pdf on November 18, 2011.

79   **about 10,000:** "The Clinical Trials Business," BCC Research, 2006. Accessed from www.pharmaceutical-market-research.com/publications/research_ development/clinical_trials/clinical_trials_business.html on October 7, 2011.

79   **about $30 billion:** Ibid.

79   **annual budget:** NASA Fiscal Year 2012 Budget Estimates. Accessed from www.nasa.gov/pdf/516674main_NASAFY12_Budget_Estimates -Overview-508.pdf on October 7, 2011.

79   **Large Hadron Collider:** CERN website. Accessed from http://askan expert.web.cern.ch/AskAnExpert/en/Accelerators/LHCgeneral-en .html#3 on October 7, 2011.

79   **by the early 1970s:** Marks, *The Progress of Experiment*, 129.

Chapter 8: Limitations of Randomized Trials

84   **In 1957:** Donald T. Campbell, *Methodology and Epistemology for Social Science: Selected Papers* (Chicago: University of Chicago Press, 1988), 151.

84   **Cochrane Collaboration:** Cochrane Collaboration website. Accessed from www.cochrane.org/about-us/history on October 7, 2011.

87   **free primary medical care:** E. K. Ansah, S. Narh-Bana, S. Asiamah, V. Dzordzordzi, K. Biantey, et al., "Effect of Removing Direct Payment for Health Care on Utilisation and Health Outcomes in Ghanaian Children: A Randomised Controlled Trial," *PLoS Medicine* 6, no. 1 (2009): e1000007.

87   **Some of these commentators:** Tyler Cowen, "The Marginal Value of Health Care in Ghana: Is It Zero?" *Marginal Revolution* (blog), January

2009. Accessed from http://marginalrevolution.com/marginalrevolution/2009/01/the-marginal-va.html on October 7, 2011.

90 **lung cancer:** National Cancer Institute website. Accessed from http://seer.cancer.gov/csr/1975_2007/browse_csr.php?section=1&page=sect_01_table.01.html on October 7, 2011.

90 **heart disease:** Centers for Disease Control and Prevention website. Accessed from www.cdc.gov/nchs/fastats/lcod.htm on October 7, 2011.

90 **extremely rare:** H. Witschi, "A Short History of Lung Cancer," Toxicological Sciences 64, no. 1 (2001): 4–6.

90 **increase in lung cancer incidence:** "Medicine: The Lung Cancer Epidemic," *Time*, July 11, 1955.

90 **several factors:** Witschi, "A Short History of Lung Cancer."

91 **successfully reduced:** Nicholas R. Anthonisen, Melissa A. Skeans, Robert A. Wise, Jure Manfreda, Richard E. Kanner, John E. Connett, and for the Lung Health Study Research Group, "The Effects of a Smoking Cessation Intervention on 14.5-Year Mortality: A Randomized Clinical Trial," *Annals of Internal Medicine* 142 (February 15, 2005): 233–239.

91 **2005 paper:** J. P. Ioannidis, "Contradicted and Initially Stronger Effects in Highly Cited Clinical Research," *Journal of the American Medical Association* 294, no. 2 (July 13, 2005): 218–228.

92 **one of the most cited:** A. B. Hill, "The Environment and Disease: Association or Causation?" *Proceedings of the Royal Society of Medicine* 58 (May 1965): 295–300.

92 **surgeon general's report:** "Smoking and Health," Report of the Advisory Committee to the Surgeon General of the Public Health Service, 1964.

92 **canons of induction:** John Stuart Mill, *System of Logic Ratiocinative and Inductive* (New York: Cosimo Classics, 2009), 185–296.

92 **decades of efforts:** J. S. Kaufman and C. Poole, "Looking Back on 'Causal Thinking in the Health Sciences,'" *Annual Review of Public Health* 21 (May 2000): 101–119. M. Hofler, "The Bradford Hill Considerations on Causality: A Counterfactual Perspective," *Emerging Themes in Epidemiology* 2 (2005): 11.

92 **algorithmic method:** D. L. Weed, "On the Use of Causal Criteria," International Journal of Epidemiology 26, no. 6 (1997): 1137–1141.

93 **more than common sense:** C. V. Phillips and K. J. Goodman, "Causal Criteria and Counterfactuals: Nothing More (or Less) than Scientific Common Sense," *Emerging Themes in Epidemiology* 3, no. 5 (May 26, 2006).

93 **"before we convict":** Hill, "The Environment and Disease."

93 **public health announcements:** Community intervention trial for smoking cessation (COMMIT): II, "Changes in Adult Cigarette Smoking Prevalence," American Journal of Public Health 85, no. 2 (February

1995):193–200. R. H. Secker-Walker, W. Gnich, S. Platt, and T. Lancaster, "Community Interventions for Reducing Smoking Among Adults," Cochrane Database Syst Rev. 3 (2002):CD001745. A. V. Peterson Jr., K. A. Kealey, S. L. Mann, P. M. Marek, and I. G. Sarason, "Hutchinson Smoking Prevention Project: Long-Term Randomized Trial in School-Based Tobacco Use Prevention—Results on Smoking," Journal of the National Cancer Institute 92, no. 24 (December 20, 2000): 1979–1991.

PART II: SOCIAL SCIENCE

Chapter 9: Nonexperimental Social Science

99   **fourteen findings:** N. Gregory Mankiw, *Essentials of Economics* (Cengage electronic edition, 2008), 35.

100   **James Buchanan:** Edmund Conway, "Barack Obama Accused of Making 'Depression' Mistake," *The Telegraph,* September 6, 2009.

100   **Joseph Stiglitz:** Joseph Stiglitz, "Farewell to the Dollar as the World's Currency of Choice," *Washington Post,* August 30, 2009.

100   **Gary Becker:** Gary Becker, "How to Increase Employment," *Becker-Posner Blog,* November 29, 2009. Accessed from www.becker-posner-blog.com/2009/11/how-to-increase-employment—becker.html on October 8, 2011.

100   **Paul Krugman:** Paul Krugman, "Would Cutting the Minimum Wage Raise Employment?" *Conscience of a Liberal* (blog), *New York Times*, December 16, 2009. Accessed from http://krugman.blogs.nytimes.com/2009/12/16/would-cutting-the-minimum-wage-raise-employment on October 8, 2011.

103   **French Enlightenment:** F. A. Hayek, *The Counter-Revolution of Science: Studies in the Abuse of Reason* (New York: Free Press, 1955).

103   **Comte argued:** Harriet Martineau, trans., *The Positive Philosophy of Auguste Comte* (London, 1853), vol. 1.

103   **popularized this positivist idea:** John Stuart Mill, *August Comte and Positivism* (Serenity Publishers electronic edition, 2008).

103   **Mill argued:** John Stuart Mill, *Essays on Some Unsettled Questions of Political Economy* (Batoche Books electronic edition, 2000), 100–108.

105   **2008 book:** Larry M. Bartels, *Unequal Democracy: The Political Economy of the New Gilded Age* (Princeton, NJ: Princeton University Press, 2008).

105   **served as president:** Larry M. Bartels, *curriculum vitae.* Accessed from www.princeton.edu/~bartels/vitae.pdf on October 8, 2011.

105   **2004 academic paper:** L. M. Bartels, "Partisan Politics and the US Income Distribution." Accessed from www.princeton.edu/~bartels/income.pdf on October 8, 2011.

108   **raw Census data:** Accessed from www.census.gov/hhes/www/income
/histinc/f01ar.html. Updated data location: www.census.gov/hhes/www
/income/data/historical/index.html

109   **One paper estimates:** O. Blanchard and R. Perotti, "An Empirical Char-
acterization of the Dynamic Effects of Changes in Government Spending and Taxes on Output," *Quarterly Journal of Economics* 117, no. 4
(2002): 1329–1368.

109   **The other paper:** Lawrence J. Christiano, Martin Eichenbaum, and
Charles L. Evans, "Monetary Policy Shocks: What Have We Learned
and to What End?" National Bureau of Economic Research Working
Paper Series, Vol. w6400, February 1998.

110   **2005 best seller:** Steven D. Levitt and Stephen J. Dubner, *Freakonomics:
A Rogue Economist Explores the Hidden Side of Everything* (New York:
HarperCollins, 2009).

111   **2001 academic paper:** John Donohue III and Steven D. Levitt, "The Impact of Legalized Abortion on Crime," *Quarterly Journal of Economics*
116, no. 2 (May 2001): 379–420.

112   **In response:** Theodore J. Joyce, *Abortion and Crime: A Review,* NBER
Working Paper No. 15098, June 2009.

112   **Other academics:** Leo Kahane, David Paton, and Rob Simmons, "The
Abortion-Crime Link: Evidence from England and Wales," *Economica*
75, no. 297 (2008):1–21.

113   **national crime reports:** FBI Uniform Crime Reports, prepared by the
National Archive of Criminal Justice Data. Accessed from www.ucrdata
tool.gov/Search/Crime/State/StatebyState.cfm on November 18, 2011.

116   **randomization for:** T. D. Cook and V. C. Wong, "Empirical Tests of the
Validity of the Regression Discontinuity Design," *Annales d'Economie et
de Statistique* (2008).

116   **"proverbial butterfly":** Levitt and Dubner, *Freakonomics.*

116   **Lorenz entered:** Peter Dizikes, "When the Butterfly Effect Took Flight,"
Technology Review, March/April 2011.

Chapter 10: Business Strategy as Applied Social Science

119   **manufacturing output:** Paul Kennedy, "The (Relative) Decline of America," *Atlantic Monthly,* September 1987.

120   **In 1963:** Walter Kiechel, *Lords of Strategy* (first eBook edition, 2010), 39.
Lords of Strategy provided the general background for much of the discussion of the early history of BCG in this chapter.

121   **Texas Instruments:** Ibid., 88–96.

122   **Henderson wrote:** Bruce Henderson, *The Logic of Business Strategy* (Pensacola, FL: Ballinger Publishing, 1984).

122   **natural competition:** Ibid., 1.

122   **strategic competition:** Ibid., 31–32.

122   **Henderson characterized:** Ibid., 19.

122   **Henderson was clear:** Ibid.

123   **the ability "to understand . . .":** Ibid., 32.

123   **promise of:** Ibid., 24.

127   **business best seller:** Thomas J. Peters and Robert H. Waterman, *In Search of Excellence: Lessons from America's Best-Run Companies* (New York: Harper & Row, 1982).

128   **massive tomes:** Michael E. Porter, *Competitive Strategy: Techniques for Analyzing Industries and Competitors* (New York: Free Press, 1980); Michael E. Porter, *Competitive Advantage: Creating and Sustaining Superior Performance* (New York: Free Press, 1985).

128   **graphical representation:** Accessed from http://en.wikipedia.org/wiki /File:Porters_five_forces.PNG on October 8, 2011.

135   **no way to know :** K. A. Clarke, "The Phantom Menace: Omitted Variable Bias in Econometric Research," *Conflict Management and Peace Science* 22, no. 4 (September 2005): 341–352.

Chapter 11: The Experimental Revolution in Business

144   **Fairbank was clear:** Charles Fishman, "This Is a Marketing Revolution," *Fast Company,* April 30, 1999.

145   **more than 60,000:** Cap Gemini Ernst & Young Center for Business Innovation, *Perspectives on Business Innovation* 8, 28. Accessed from www.leader -values.com/Downloads/CBI/Journal_Issue_8.pdf on October 8, 2011.

145   **about $50 billion:** Quote accessed from http://finance.yahoo.com/q/ks ?s=COF on October 8, 2011.

146   **decision-making at Harrah's:** J. Pfeffer and V. Chang, "Gary Loveman and Harrah's Entertainment," Stanford GSB Case Study OB45, 2003.

146   **approximately 12,000:** Hal Varian, "Federalism Offers Opportunities for Causal Experimentation," *The Economist,* April 25, 2011. Accessed from www.economist.com/node/21256696 on October 8, 2011.

149   **Iyengar has described:** Virginia Postrel, "Indecision-Making," *New York Times,* April 15, 2010.

149   **Barry Schwartz:** Barry Schwartz, *The Paradox of Choice: Why More Is Less* (HarperCollins e-books, Kindle Edition, 2008), 18.

149   **the actual experiment:** Sheena S. Iyengar and Mark R. Lepper, "When Choice Is Demotivating: Can One Desire Too Much of a Good Thing?"

Journal of Personality and Social Psychology 79, no. 6 (December 2000): 995–1006.

151 **A meta-analysis:** Benjamin Scheibehenne, Rainer Greifeneder, and Peter M. Todd, "Can There Ever Be Too Many Options? A Meta-Analytic Review of Choice Overload," *Journal of Consumer Research* 37, no. 3 (October 2010): 409–425.

152 **Steven Pinker:** Steven Pinker, "The Moral Instinct," *New York Times,* January 13, 2008.

164 **about one-fourth:** "About Clinical Trials," Chicago Research Center. Accessed from www.chicagoresearchcenter.com/Chicago-Research-Center /About-Clinical-Research on October 8, 2011.

Chapter 12: Experimental Social Science

169 **analysis of nonexperimental:** Steven Glazerman, Dan M. Levy, and David Myers, "Nonexperimental Replications of Social Experiments: A Systematic Review," *Mathematica Policy Research* (September 2002); MPR Reference No. 8813-300. D. Weisburd, C. Lum, and A. Petrosino, "Does Research Design Affect Study Outcomes in Criminal Justice?" *Annals of the American Academy of Political and Social Science* 578, no. 1 (November 2001): 50–70.

169 **therapeutic trials:** R. Kunz and A. D. Oxman, "The Unpredictability Paradox: Review of Empirical Comparisons of Randomised and Non-Randomised Clinical Trials," *British Medical Journal* 317 (October 31, 1998): 1185–1190.

170 **golden age:** A. Oakley, "Experimentation and Social Interventions: A Forgotten but Important History," *British Medical Journal* 317 (1988): 1239.

171 **1986 journal article:** R. J. LaLonde, "Evaluating the Econometric Evaluations of Training Programs with Experimental Data," *American Economic Review* 76, no. 4 (September 1986): 604–620.

171 **Similar comparisons:** T. Fraker and R. Maynard, "The Adequacy of Comparison Group Designs for Evaluations of Employment-Related Programs," *Journal of Human Resources* 22, no. 2 (Spring 1987): 194–227.

171 **"Heckman correction":** P. Puhani, "The Heckman Correction for Sample Selection and Its Critique," *Journal of Economic Surveys* 14, no. 1 (February 2000): 53–68.

171 **reanalyzed the data:** J. Heckman, V. J. Hotz, and M. Dabos, "Do We Need Experimental Data to Evaluate the Impact of Manpower Training on Earnings?" *Evaluation Review* 11, no. 4 (August 1987): 395–427; J. Heckman and V. J. Hotz, "Choosing Among Alternative Nonexperimental

Methods for Estimating the Impact of Social Programs: The Case of Manpower Training," *Journal of the American Statistical Association* 84, no. 408 (December 1989): 862–874.

171   **Heckman produced:** J. Heckman, "Randomization and Social Policy Evaluation," National Bureau of Economic Research Technical Working Paper 0107, 1991.

173   **Literature reviews:** Frederick Mosteller and Robert F. Boruch, eds., *Evidence Matters: Randomized Trials in Education Research* (Washington, DC: Brookings Institution Press, 2002), 50–79.

173   **increasingly testing:** D. Greenberg, D. Linksz, and M. Mandell, *Social Experimentation and Public Policymaking* (Washington, DC: Urban Institute Press, 2004), 24.

173   **Campbell Collaboration:** www.campbellcollaboration.org.

174   **What Works Clearinghouse:** http://ies.ed.gov/ncee/wwc.

174   **100–150:** D. P. Farrington and B. C. Welsh, "A Half Century of Randomized Experiments on Crime and Justice," *Crime and Justice—Chicago* 34 (2006): 55–132.

174   **240:** D. Greenberg and M. Shroder, eds., *The Digest of Social Experiments,* 3rd ed. (Washington, DC: Urban Institute Press, 2004).

175   **long-burning filament:** F. Jehl, *Menlo Park Reminiscences,* Part 2 (Whitefish, MT: Kessinger Publishing, 2002), 605.

176   **detailed review:** D. Weisburd and A. R. Piquero, "How Well Do Criminologists Explain Crime? Statistical Modeling in Published Studies," *Crime and Justice* 37, no. 1 (2008): 453–502.

176   **James Stewart:** D. F. Farrington, "A Short History of Randomized Experiments in Criminology: A Meager Feast," *Evaluation Review* 27 (June 2003): 218–227.

177   **preventive patrols:** G. L. Kelling et al., "The Kansas City Preventive Patrol Experiment: A Summary Report," 1974. Accessed from www.policefoundation.org/pdf/kcppe.pdf on October 8, 2011.

177   **randomly assigned:** L. W. Sherman and R. A. Berk, "The Minneapolis Domestic Violence Experiment," Police Foundation Reports, April 1984. Accessed from www.policefoundation.org/pdf/minneapolisdve.pdf on October 9, 2011.

178   **In 1992:** J. D. Schmidt and L. W. Sherman, "Does Arrest Deter Domestic Violence?" in *Do Arrests and Restraining Orders Work?* ed. E. S. Buzawa and C. G. Buzawa (Newbury Park, CA: Sage Publications, 1996), 43–53; L. W. Sherman and H. Strang, "Policing Domestic Violence: The Problem-Solving Paradigm," from Problem-Solving Policing as Crime Prevention conference, Stockholm, Sweden, 1996. Accessed from http://

citeseerx.ist.psu.edu/viewdoc/download?doi=10.1.1.122.743&rep=rep1& type=pdf on October 9, 2011.

179   **122 known:** Farrington and Welsh, "A Half Century of Randomized Experiments on Crime and Justice."

179   **faded away:** P. Z. Schochet, S. McConnell, and J. Burghardt, "National Job Corps Study: Findings Using Administrative Earnings Records Data," final report, Mathematica Policy Research, 2003; MPR Reference No. 8140-840. Accessed from www.mathematica-mpr.com/publications /pdfs/jobcorpsadmin.pdf on November 19, 2011.

180   **Anthony Braga:** Anthony A. Braga and Brenda J. Bond, "Policing Crime and Disorder Hot Spots: A Randomized Controlled Trial," *Criminology* 46, no. 3 (August 2008).

181   **Randomized experimentation in social welfare:** R. A. Moffitt, "The Role of Randomized Field Trials in Social Science Research: A Perspective from Evaluations of Reforms of Social Welfare Programs," National Bureau of Economic Research Technical Working Paper 0295, 2003. This article provided the general background and much of the detail for the discussion of the history and context of social welfare programs and experimentation in this chapter.

183   **experiments cost:** Ibid.

184   **RAND Corporation:** J. Grogger, L. A. Karoly, and J. A. Klerman, "Consequences of Welfare Reform: A Research Synthesis," prepared for the Administration for Children and Families, US Department of Health and Human Services, July 2002. Accessed from www.acf.hhs.gov/programs /opre/welfare_employ/res_systhesis/reports/consequences_of_wr/rand _report.pdf on November 19, 2011.

186   **Thomas D. Cook:** Thomas D. Cook, "Sciencephobia," *Educationnext,* Fall 2001.

187   **Tennessee STAR:** B. Nye, L. V. Hedges, and S. Konstantopoulos, "The Effects of Small Classes on Academic Achievement: The Results of the Tennessee Class Size Experiment," *American Educational Research Journal* 37 (March 20, 2000): 123–151; E. A. Hanushek, "Some Findings from an Independent Investigation of the Tennessee STAR Experiment and from Other Investigations of Class Size Effects," *Educational Evaluation and Policy Analysis* 21, no. 2 (Summer 1999): 143–163.

188   **Patrick J. Wolf:** P. J. Wolf, "School Voucher Programs: What the Research Says About Parental School Choice," *Brigham Young University Law Review* 2008, no. 2 (2008): 415–446.

189   **charter schools:** W. Dobbie and R. G. Fryer, "Are High-Quality Schools Enough to Close the Achievement Gap? Evidence from a Social

Experiment in Harlem," National Bureau of Economic Research Working Paper 15473, November 2009; C. M. Hoxby and M. Muraka, "Charter Schools in New York City: Who Enrolls and How They Affect Their Students' Achievement," National Bureau of Economic Research Working Paper 14852, April 2009; C. M. Hoxby and J. E. Rockoff, "The Impact of Charter Schools on Student Achievement," 2004, accessed from www .vanderbilt.edu/schoolchoice/downloads/papers/hoxby-rockoff2004.pdf on October 9, 2011; A. Abdulkadiroglu, J. Angrist, S. Dynarski, T. J. Kane, and P. Pathak, "Accountability and Flexibility in Public Schools: Evidence from Boston's Charters and Pilots," National Bureau of Economic Research Working Paper 15549, November 2009.

189   **magnet schools:** Ibid.; J. B. Cullen, B. A. Jacob, and S. Levitt, 2006, "The Effect of School Choice on Participants: Evidence from Randomized Lotteries," *Econometrica, Econometric Society* 74, no. 5, (2006): 1191–1230.

190   **4 percent:** Accessed from http://nces.ed.gov/edfin/tables/tab_gdp.asp on October 9, 2011.

190   **major report in 2002:** R. J. Shavelson and L. Towne, eds., *Scientific Research in Education,* Committee on Scientific Principles for Education Research, National Research Council (Washington, DC: National Academy Press, 2002), 109–110.

190   **Congress also established:** G. D. Borman, "The Use of Randomized Trials to Inform Education Policy," in *Handbook of Education Policy Research,* ed. G. Sykes, B. Schneider, and D. N. Plank (New York: Routledge, 2009), 129–138.

190   **November 2008:** Institute of Education Sciences, US Department of Education, *Relevance and Rigor Redux: Director's Biennial Report to Congress* (IES 2009-6010), Washington, DC, 2008.

191   **found only one:** Institute of Education Sciences, US Department of Education, *Effects of Preschool Curriculum Programs on School Readiness: Report from the Preschool Curriculum Evaluation Research Initiative* (NCER 20082009REV), Washington, DC, 2008.

191   **Edward Chamberlin:** E. H. Chamberlin, "An Experimental Imperfect Market," *Journal of Political Economy* 56, no. 2 (April 1948): 95–108.

191   **Vernon Smith:** T. Bergstrom, "Vernon Smith's Insomnia and the Dawn of Economics as Experimental Science," *Scandinavian Journal of Economics* 105, no. 2 (2003): 181–205.

192   **About forty:** From the presentation "Using Field Experiments in Economics: An Introduction by John List," University of Chicago and National Bureau of Economic Research. Accessed from www.streaming meeting.com/webmeeting/matrixvideo/nber/index.html on October 9, 2011.

192   **95 percent:** A. Falk and J. Heckman, "Lab Experiments Are a Major Source of Knowledge in the Social Sciences," *Science* 326, no. 5952 (October 23, 2009): 535–538.

192   *Handbook of Experimental Economics Results*: *Handbook of Experimental Economics Results,* vol. 1, ed. Charles R. Plott and Vernon L. Smith (New York: North-Holland, 2008).

192   **what Smith called:** Vernon Smith, *Bargaining and Market Behavior: Essays in Experimental Economics* (Cambridge: Cambridge University Press, 2000), 8–9.

192   **kinds of resources:** Ibid.

193   **"Like languages":** Bergstrom, "Vernon Smith's Insomnia and the Dawn of Economics as Experimental Science."

193   **epistemic humility:** Ibid.

193   **Adam Ferguson:** Adam Ferguson, *An Essay on the History of Civil Society,* 5th ed., Part 3, Section 2 (London: T. Cadell, 1782).

195   **survey:** "International Bright Young Things," *The Economist,* December 30, 2008.

196   **most likely:** "Experiments with Dough," *University of Chicago Magazine,* May–June 2009.

196   **major review:** Levitt and List, "Field Experiments in Economics."

196   **laboratory experimentation:** D. P. Green, J. H. Kuklinski, and A. Lupia, "Experimentation in Political Science," in *Cambridge Handbook of Experimental Political Science,* ed. James N. Druckman, Donald P. Green, James H. Kuklinski, and Arthur Lupia (New York: Cambridge University Press, 2011).

197   **Harold Gosnell:** R. A. Jackson, "Voter Mobilization: The Scientific Investigation of Getting the Electorate to the Polls," in *New Directions in Campaigns and Elections,* ed. Steven K. Medic (New York: Routledge, 2011), 108–110.

197   **the past decade:** Ibid.

197   **Zero:.** D. P. Green and A. S. Gerber, "The Underprovision of Experiments in Political and Social Science," *Annals of the American Academy of Political and Social Science* 589, no. 1 (2003): 94–112.

197   **as true experiments:** K. Arceneaux, A. S. Gerber, and D. P. Green, "A Cautionary Note on the Use of Matching to Estimate Causal Effects: An Empirical Example Comparing Matching Estimates to an Experimental Benchmark," *Sociological Methods and Research* 39 (2010): 256–282; D. P. Green, T. Y. Leong, H. L. Kern, A. S. Gerber, and C. W. Larimer, "Testing the Accuracy of Regression Discontinuity Analysis Using Experimental Benchmarks," *Political Analysis* 17, no. 4 (2009): 400–417.

197 **series of randomized trials:** Donald P. Green and Alan S. Gerber, *Get Out the Vote: How to Increase Turnout,* 2nd ed. (Kindle; Washington, DC: Brookings Institution Press, 2008).

198 *Get Out the Vote:* Ibid.

198 *The Victory Lab:* Sasha Issenberg, *Rick Perry and His Eggheads: Inside the Brainiest Political Operation in America* (eBook edition; New York: Crown Publishers, 2011).

198 **pragmatic reaction:** Ibid., 54.

199 **eggheads argued:** Ibid., 66.

199 **web-based tool:** Green and Gerber, *Get Out the Vote,* Box 10-3.

203 **nurse visitations:** Coalition for Evidence-Based Policy, *Evidence Summary for the Nurse-Family Partnership,* January 2011. Accessed from http://evidencebasedprograms.org/wordpress/wp-content/uploads//NFP-updated-summary-for-release-Jan2011.pdf on October 10, 2011.

PART III: POLITICAL ACTION

Chapter 13: Liberty as Means

211 **Popper called:** Sir Karl Popper, *The Open Society and Its Enemies, Vol. 1: The Spell of Plato* (Princeton, NJ: Princeton University Press, 1966), 158.

213 **Libertarian Party position:** Munroe Eagles and Larry Johnston, *Politics: An Introduction to Modern Democratic Government* (Peterborough, ON: Broadview Press, 2008), 110.

215 **right to travel:** L. B. Boudin, "The Constitutional Right to Travel," *Columbia Law Review* 56, no. 1 (January 1956): 47–75.

Chapter 14: Innovation and Cohesion

221 **elude the theorist:** William J. Baumol, *The Free-Market Innovation Machine: Analyzing the Growth Miracle of Capitalism* (Princeton, NJ: Princeton University Press, 2002), 58.

223 **Industry analysts:** International Data Corporation, *Worldwide Software as a Service 2010–2014 Forecast: Software Will Never Be the Same,* June 2010.

225 **"It is adaptive":** Douglass C. North, "Economic Performance Through Time," Nobel Prize Lecture, December 9, 1993. Accessed from www.nobelprize.org/nobel_prizes/economics/laureates/1993/north-lecture.html on October 12, 2011.

226 **"In a world of uncertainty":** Douglass C. North, *Institutions, Institutional Change, and Economic Performance* (Cambridge: Cambridge University Press, 1990), 81.

226 **Schumpeter's earlier work:** Josef Schumpeter, *Capitalism, Socialism, and Democracy* (New York: Harper, 1943), 106.

227 **Baumol observes:** William J. Baumol, "Education for Innovation: Entrepreneurial Breakthroughs vs. Corporate Incremental Improvements," National Bureau of Economic Research Working Paper Series, Vol. w10578, June 2004.

227 **won seven Nobel Prizes:** "Bell Labs' Latest Nobel Laureates, Creators of 4bn Images and Counting," *The Observer,* December 13, 2009.

227 **PARC lab:** Malcolm Gladwell, "Creation Myth: Xerox PARC, Apple, and the Truth About Innovation," *New Yorker,* May 16, 2011.

227 **won five Nobel Prizes:** Accessed from www.economicexpert.com/a/International:Business:Machines.htm on October 12, 2011.

227 **Steve Jobs famously:** Gladwell, "Creation Myth."

230 **following on Coase:** R. H. Coase, "The Nature of the Firm," *Economica* 4, no. 16 (1937): 386–405.

230 **National Venture Capital Association:** National Venture Capital Association, "Venture Impact: The Economic Importance of Venture Capital-Backed Companies to the U.S. Economy," 2009. Accessed from www.nvca.org/index.php?option=com_docman&task=doc_download&gid=482&Itemid=93 on October 12, 2011.

232 **Schumpeter famously called:** Schumpeter, *Capitalism, Socialism, and Democracy,* 82–85.

232 **the past 1,000 years:** Angus Maddison, "The World Economy: Historical Statistics," OECD Development Center, Paris, 2003. Accessed from www.ggdc.net/maddison/Historical_Statistics/horizontal-file_02–2010.xls on October 12, 2011.

233 **about three-quarters:** David R. Meyer, *The Roots of American Industrialization* (Baltimore, MD: Johns Hopkins University Press, 2003), 3.

235 **about one-third:** E. Nosal and M. Shenk, *Is Manufacturing Going the Way of Agriculture?* Federal Reserve Bank of Cleveland, February 15, 2007. Accessed from www.clevelandfed.org/research/trends/2007/0307/02ecoact.cfm on October 12, 2011.

235 **In 2007:** US Department of Agriculture, Economic Research Service Report ERR-46, "Global Growth, Macroeconomic Change, and US Agricultural Trade," Appendix A, September 2007.

236 **"Cross of Gold":** Accessed from http://historymatters.gmu.edu/d/5354 on October 12, 2011.

236 **remains:** *Economic Survey of China 2010: Achievements, Prospects and Further Challenges,* Organisation of Economic Co-operation and Development, February 2, 2010. Accessed from www.oecd.org/document/0/0,3746,en_2649_34571_44478336_1_1_1_1,00.html on October 12, 2011.

237   **accounted for:** Nosal and Shenk, *Is Manufacturing Going the Way of Agriculture?*

Chapter 15: Sustainable Innovation

244   **described:** C. Goldin and L. F. Katz, *The Race Between Education and Technology* (Cambridge, MA: Harvard University Press, 2008).

252   **40 percent:** "Changing Patterns of Nonmarital Childbearing in the United States," National Center for Health Statistics, May 2009. Accessed from www.cdc.gov/nchs/data/databriefs/db18.htm on November 11, 2011.

252   **Sweden and the Netherlands:** Mark Berends et al., eds., *Handbook of Research on School Choice* (New York: Routledge, 2009), 348–349.

254   **Most government spending:** OECD Economic Statistics, Table 11: Government Expenditure by Function for 2009 (TLYCG: Total Government Expenditures; GS13: General Government). Accessed from http://stats .oecd.org/Index.aspx?DataSetCode=SNA_TABLE11 on October 12, 2011.

255   **Tocqueville:** Alexis de Tocqueville, *Democracy in America* (London: Saunders and Otley, 1835), Book 1, Chapter 6. Accessed from http://xroads .virginia.edu/~HYPER/DETOC/ch4_06.htm on October 10, 2011.

256   **long-term forecasts:** US House of Representatives, Committee on the Budget, FY 2012 Budget Resolution, April 5, 2011. Accessed from http:// paulryan.house.gov/UploadedFiles/PathToProsperityFY2012.pdf on October 10, 2011.

INDEX